The Quest
for Fruition
Through Ngoma

The editors and contributors
gratefully acknowledge
the generous support of the
African Studies Centre, Leiden,
who have provided a grant which makes possible
the distribution of this collection in Africa

The Quest
for Fruition
Through Ngoma

Political Aspects
of Healing
in Southern Africa

Edited by
RIJK VAN DIJK
RIA REIS
MARJA SPIERENBURG

David Philip
Cape Town

Kachere
Zomba

Bookworld
Lusaka

Mambo Press
Gweru

James Currey
Oxford

Ohio University Press
Athens

James Currey Ltd
73 Botley Road
Oxford
OX2 0BS

Ohio University Press
Scott Quadrangle
Athens, Ohio 45701, USA

Kachere Press
PO Box 1037
Zomba, Malawi

Bookworld
Permanent House
Cairo Road
Lusaka, Zambia

Mambo Press
Senga Road
PO Box 779
Gweru, Zimbabwe

David Philip
Publishers (Pty) Ltd
PO Box 23408
Claremont 7735
Cape Town, South Africa

First published 2000

1 2 3 4 5 04 03 02 01 00 06

British Library Cataloguing in Publication Data
The quest for fruition through ngoma : the political
 aspects of healing in South Africa
 1. Traditional medicine – Political aspects – Africa,
 Southern 2. Medicine, Magic, mystic and spagiric – Africa,
 Southern 3. Altered states of consciousness – Therapeutic
 use – Africa, Southern
 I. Dijk, Rijk A. van, 1959- II.Reis, Ria III.Spierenburg,
 Marja
 306.4'61'0968

 ISBN 0-85255-263-7 Paper (James Currey)
 ISBN 0-85255-262-9 Cloth (James Currey)

Library of Congress Cataloging-in-Publication
The quest for fruition through ngoma : the political aspects of healing in South Africa /
edited by Rijk van Dijk, Ria Reis, and Marja Spierenburg.
     p. cm.
 Includes bibliographical references.
 ISBN 0-8214-1303-1 (cl.: alk. paper) – ISBN 0-8214-1304-x (pa.: alk. paper)
 1. Traditional medicine–Africa, Southern. 2. Africa, Southern–Social conditions. 3.
 Rites and ceremonies–Africa, Southern. 4. Africa, Southern–Politics and government. I.
 Dijk, Rijk van, 1959-II. Reis, Ria. III. Spierenburg, Marja.

 GR358 .Q47 1999
 398'.353'0968–dc21

Front cover piece by R.W.J. Baas
Typeset in 9.5/11 Palatino by Saxon Graphics Ltd, Derby
Printed in Great Britain by Villiers Publications, London N3

Contents

Preface

This study has arisen out of a fascination with the vibrant nature of African societies, their vitality and particularly the way in which they seem to be able time and again to overcome tribulation and turmoil. The contributions included in the volume intend to transmit a genuine admiration for the social capability of African societies to turn misfortune, affliction and repression into a valued experience of growth and fulfilment; the patient is transformed into a healer, the ruler into a servant, rituals for the ailing and the deprived become public celebrations of personal and social fruition. In the southern-African region, *ngoma*, an indigenous ritual of healing, dance, rhythm and rhyme, is at the heart of the social effort of turning the tables for individuals and communities so that their well-being is restored. This volume investigates ngoma in its many, culturally diverse, manifestations. It seeks to explore how these manifestations are perceived, how they function in relation to the needs and requirements of individuals and communities and how they maintain their key functions in the face of modern developments and institutions. It is the conviction of the authors that no encroaching western medical system and no political conflict resolution model will ever be capable of fully replacing what ngoma is offering to large sections of the population in this particular region of the world.

Contributors

Henny Blokland read theology and also studied anthropology and African linguistics at the University of Leiden. She conducted extensive fieldwork in Tabora, Tanzania, in the period 1988–1992 and returned to the field once more in 1996. She is currently preparing her PhD thesis on Ngoma in West Central Tanzania under the working title 'Recycling Death: the Role of Women in Ngoma'.

Annette Drews is professor of medical anthropology at the University of Applied Science in Zittau/Goerlitz (Germany). In 1995 she was awarded a PhD in social and political science by the University of Amsterdam. Her thesis was based on extended research (from 1989 until 1993) in the Eastern Province of Zambia on communication in pregnancy and birth. From this research she published *Words and Silence. Communication about Pregnancy and Birth among the Kunda of Zambia* (1995). Later she worked as an anthropologist on issues of gender, reproductive health and population policies. At present she is conducting research on the influence of Yoruba healing rituals on the psycho-social well-being of participants in Nigeria and in Brazil.

John M. Janzen is professor of anthropology at the University of Kansas and author of *Lemba, 1650–1930. A Drum of Affliction in Africa and the New World* (1982); *Ngoma. Discourses of Healing in Central and Southern Africa* (1992); and, with Wyatt MacGaffey, *Anthology of Kongo Religion: Primary Texts from Lower Zaire* (1974).

Cornelis Jonker, BA, MA, Dip Ed, MSc, studied anthropology at the University of Amsterdam and epidemiology at the Free University (Amsterdam). He has conducted research projects in Zambia on the interface of indigenous and cosmopolitan health care systems, and taught medical anthropology at the Medical Anthropological Unit of the University of Amsterdam. Presently, he is preparing his PhD dissertation on spirit churches in Zambia and is involved in research on health concepts among primary school children and on parasuicide among youngsters in England. He is Lecturer of Research Methods at the School of Health of the Liverpool John Moores University.

Ria Reis is an anthropologist and senior staff member of the Medical Anthropology Unit (University of Amsterdam) and programme manager of the Master's in Medical Anthropology at the same university.

Matthew Schoffeleers read theology in the Netherlands and anthropology in Kinshasa and Oxford (St Catherine's College), where his D Phil was on the Mang'anja religion of Malawi (1968). He was a senior lecturer in Anthropology at the

University of Malawi's Chancellor College until 1975 and afterwards professor of religious anthropology at the Free University of Amsterdam and the University of Utrecht in The Netherlands until the mid-1990s. He has published extensively on African religions and Malawian precolonial history. A recent publication is *River of Blood* (1992) which explores the religious response to a period of severe political repression in southern Malawi around AD 1600. His most recent book, *Religion and the Dramatisation of Life* (1997), deals with spirit beliefs and rituals in Southern and Central Malawi. At present he is engaged in a study of the role of the local churches in Malawi's democratisation movement.

Marja Spierenburg is an anthropologist and associate expert at the Department of Social and Human Sciences of the UNESCO Regional Office in Dakar, Senegal.

Rijk van Dijk is an anthropologist and researcher at the African Studies Centre, Leiden University, the Netherlands. He has researched extensively on pentecostalism in Malawi and Ghana, and his current research focuses on the relationships between Ghanaian pentecostals in Accra and those in the diaspora. He has published several articles on pentecostalism both in Malawi and Ghana, and a book entitled *Young Malawian Puritans* (Utrecht: ISOR press, 1993). He co-edited with Richard Fardon and Wim van Binsbergen *Modernity on a Shoestring* (London: SOAS, 1999) and with E. van Rouveroy van Nieuwaal *African Chieftaincy in a New Socio-Political Landscape* (Hamburg: Lit Verlag, 1999).

1

Introduction

Beyond the confinement of affliction: a discursive field of experience

Rijk van Dijk, Ria Reis
& Marja Spierenburg

Ever since the 1960s the study of ritual phenomena in which spirits announce their presence has been of central concern to the anthropology of religion in the Southern African region. The academic practice of anthropology led to the production of analytical distinctions between phenomena which in fact belonged to a varied and multifaceted spirit domain. In some cases such distinctions closely followed indigenous theory and perception of the various forms by which spirits manifest themselves, while in other cases academia invented them. Manifestations of spirits in varied forms prompted their classification and categorization in anthropology under such headings as 'trance', 'possession', 'divination', 'healing', 'masks' and so on.

These diverse types of spirit manifestation were further explored, from the 1970s onwards, on the basis of a cultural understanding of subjective involvement. That is, it was acknowledged that subjects were involved in distinguishable 'routes' of spirit manifestations not as if they were victims of natural forces from which no escape is possible or feasible, but as active participants in the creation of meaning. The acknowledgement of historicity, flexibility and mutability in forms of spirit possession, however, did not lead to a concomitant change in analytical instruments – within anthropology the myriad of spirit forms was analytically explored in two almost exclusive categories.

Spirit possession was studied mainly *within* two academic discourses, one on 'cults of affliction', the other on 'divination'. In both discourses the significance of personal healing, its symbolic and ritual repertoire and the central position of mediums, healers and leaders became emphasized.

In the development of the anthropological study of cults of affliction and mediumistic activity, several episodes can be distinguished on the basis of how diverse and localized possession phenomena were placed in overarching theoretical models. In the school of psychological anthropology that arose particularly through the work of Tart (1969), Bourguignon (1973), du Toit (1977) and Ward (1989) from the mid-1960s, phenomena of affliction and its responses in terms of therapies, trances, mediumship, etc., were regrouped and ordered under the different banners of altered states of consciousness (ASC). In this school the leading question was how a cross-cultural understanding of such psychological states could lead to the discovery of pan-humane universals of which disorders cause which type of altered state. On a comparative social level it also explored what sort of psychological states in terms of possession and trance are invoked and induced in individuals by specialists. As a result of this school of thought the knowledge of the relationship between shaman-istic techniques and certain psychological states of the mind and their expression in various trance forms was greatly enhanced since the inception of this line of enquiry through the work of M. Eliade.

In Southern Africa, however, where possession and trance states are predomi-nantly linked to spirit possession, this model that sought to explain states of consciousness in terms of the psychological received only modest attention (neither Zaretsky (1966) nor Beattie and Middleton (1969) refer to this field of knowledge). Rather, the search for universals received profound critique from a relativist position emphasizing the cultural understanding of the 'grammar' of behavioural models that are implied in forms of spirit manifestations (Crapanzano 1977, Lambek 1989, 1993). Writing about the perceived relationship between trance and possession as the school of ASC proposed, Lambek, for one, stated about possession in Mayotte among Malagassy-speakers:

> While trance, like sex, eating or vocalization, is 'natural' in the sense that, under the right stimuli, it is a condition or activity . . . of which the human species at large is capable, the form of manifes-tation of trance in any specific context is no more 'natural' (necessary, unmediated, given) than the model that guides it.
>
> Possession is secondary, an indigenous hypothesis or theory put forward to account for the facts of trance . . . subtle enough to situate the behaviour appropriately in its social context.
>
> (Lambek 1989, 38–9).

Hence the ASC studies constituted a groundlayer upon which in the early 1970s a form of theorizing developed that placed affliction and healing, as well as their social representation in cults and mediumistic leadership, in the perspective of broader socio-cultural dimensions. Possession and trance states were empirically correlated to the functioning of social groups in society. The salience of certain political and economic power relations became a further interpretative framework. Particularly in the early work of Lewis on the *sar* cults of the Horn (Lewis 1971) the characteristics of the possession states' local embeddedness were foregrounded in a singular theorem that highlighted the 'war of the sexes'; the region's character-istic inequality in power balances between the sexes and their genderized expression in women's spirit-affliction cults. The ground-breaking study on the marginality versus the centrality of possession cults *vis-à-vis* strongholds of power in society later reached greater sophistication (Lewis 1986), at which point also the Weberian notion of charisma was included in the explanation of the cultural signif-icance of these phenomena.

Similarly, Parkin (1972), also within a functionalist framework, identified power imbalances in age relations in the Kenyan context that were reflected in particular expressions and manifestations of possession and trance states. In order to stand a chance of opposing the oppressive claims of their elders, young men engaged in Islamic possession cults that prevented and even prohibited them from fulfilling their many (ritual) obligations to the elderly.

Again, in the early 1980s Van Binsbergen moved ahead by showing that local cults of affliction in the Zambian rural and partially urban context did not only arise out of intrinsically imbalanced power relations, but also resulted from the encroachment of new modes of production in African societies (Van Binsbergen 1981). He emphasized that the penetration of capitalist modes of production and consumption would usually lead to a reordering of the superstructural representations which materialize 'on the ground' in cults of affliction, anti-witchcraft movements, specific forms of mediumistic activity and the like. Possession and trance states, as they become manifest in cultic forms, are the reflection of the problematic nature of the articulation of the old within the new, of the domestic mode of production within the Western capitalist mode. Thus, as these processes of articulation and the concomitant occurrence of possession cults could be recorded in a wide variety of locations in Africa (see Van Binsbergen and Geschiere 1985) an overarching and interpretative model was created that placed the social above the psychological.

The study of the myriad of spirit manifestations and their ritualized presence in terms of divination and mediumistic activity formed a second aggregate domain. Following the distinctions made by Devisch (1985) and Peek (1991) in their reviews of scholarly approaches to the study of African divination systems, in addition to the (structural) functionalist analyses as have been discussed above, the symbolical and 'internal, semiotic and semantic' interpretations of possession forms provided overarching models as well. Starting with the ground-breaking studies of Turner on Ndembu cosmologies (1975) the symbolist interpretations of divination and revelation provided profound insights into processes of signification, attachment of meaning to human agency and ideation. The symbolic meaning of the mediating positions that divination, revelation and healing take between 'structure' (social ordering) and 'communitas' (social experience) were explored in great analytical depth. As, however, the shortcomings of Turner's approach became clear over time particularly in terms of power and the cultural 'invention' of ritual and symbolic practice, Devisch (1985, 1991) proposed a model for the interpretation of divination in which the praxis of creating meaning in the interaction that evolves between patient and healer is put at the heart of the analysis. Although the semiotics and semantics of the interaction are deeply rooted in local systems of meaning, symbolism and the overall process of signification (the way in which meaning is created) they lend themselves to wider, thus regional comparison. This line of enquiry has been strongly developed from the earlier work on symbolic meaning by Turner (1967) in studies by Werbner (1985) on healing churches, by Jacobson-Widding (1979) on colour, body and space symbolism, and recently by Taylor (1992) in his seminal study of Rwandan healing systems.

These studies seem to be strong where the structural-functionalist analyses appear to be weak – in the interpretation of idiosyncrasy, signification and the personal process. On the other hand, the symbolist studies remained unavoidably empty of reflection on political processes, more specifically on the politics of bodily experience which later interpretations that developed out of the critiques of Lewis-type arguments seemed to underscore. In the work of Lambek (1989, 1993), Boddy (1989) and Giles (1987) a more critical as well as hermeneutical interpretation of spirit manifestations followed, aiming to take into account the shortcomings of both analytical 'traditions'. The discursive practice – the 'grammar' of the spirit manifestation models in African societies – became a central concern. Adapting Foucault's archival method, the coming into existence of cultural models of bodily experience was questioned and examined. Exploring how societies turn certain models into 'natural' and taken-for-granted realities of bodily experience, and foreground them in language and emotion, is seen by these authors as a royal route for moving the study of spirit manifestation forward.

However, none of these interpretative maps has presented a perspective that enables the integration of the social and the personal in the delineation and explanation of systems – or, better, 'sets' of rituals – that foreground well-being, healing, crisis management *and* political transformation in one single framework. The structural-functionalist as well as the symbolic and semantic approaches, created confined fields of interpretation which would each highlight certain phenomena, to the exclusion of an analysis of the relationship between ritualism and political crisis.

In the work of Janzen (1992), however, to which the present volume intends to pay tribute, a new trajectory for the integration of a seemingly unbounded variety of such ritual practices has been presented. In his book, *Ngoma,* Janzen sheds new light on how a discourse of personal and social wellbeing can be delineated that extends beyond the realm of affliction and healing into other areas of human activity. Although focusing on therapeutic ritualism in particular, Janzen has been able to show, drawing from sources ranging from Cameroon to the Cape and from there to Nairobi, how a variety of healing practices, affliction cults and political rituals can be grouped, compared and analysed within one regional discourse: *ngoma.* Janzen propounds the view that these phenomena can comprise what he calls a calculus (Janzen 1992: 79; 1995: 159): a comprehensive body of healing practices, discursive forms, music, rhythm and rhyme which form an integrated whole. Here the dissection into analytical distinctions, as proposed by an anthropology that led to the bracketing of certain phenomena under specific headings, does not apply. Although 'it is difficult to formulate a strict calculus of the myriad range of transformations ngoma may undergo across the region where it has been reported' (Janzen 1992: 79), ngoma refers to a distinctive indigenous theory (Janzen 1992: 9). This theory or hypothesis primarily places the communicative relationship between the subject and the spirit (or spirits) within a specific discursive form which can be described by referring to: 1) its regional expansion and 2) its historic manifestation. In dealing with personal suffering and what he calls 'difficult experiences', as ngoma does, song and dance are of singular importance and here the communicative and the performative essential element of this indigenous theory are made profoundly clear:

> Ngoma brings together the disparate elements of an individual's life threads and weaves them into a meaningful fabric. It does this, particularly, through devices of mutual 'call and response' sharing of experiences, of self-presentation, of articulation of common affliction, and of consensus over the nature of the problem and the course of action to take. (110)

> Within the complex symbol 'ngoma' there are at least two levels of narrative and performative understanding. The first is the importance of song-dance in defining and coming to terms with the suffering; the second is the importance of moving the sufferer toward a formulation of his or her personal articulation of that condition. (118)

This specific formula of a song-dance manifestation in communicating and articulating difficult experiences, personal suffering and healing to the spirit world Janzen recognizes in a range of different religious forms, cults of affliction, churches and music groups throughout the various cultures of the Southern African region.

Irrespective of the fortunes or the constraints of socio-economic systems within these societies, the positions of specific groups therein such as women or the young, or their idiosyncratic production of meaning, ngoma – that is, healing through the use of drums and by working upon spirit relationships – has existed by accommodating itself to changing circumstances. The work of Janzen allows us now, for the first time, to draw together concepts, representations and practices revolving around the use of drums in an area covering an extensive part of the continent. Janzen has focused our attention on the possibility of (re-)constructing and exploring a regional discursive practice which as a groundform, a calculus in his terms, has been pervasive in the linking of personal, idiosyncratic experiences with culturally specific religious forms.

This new departure by Janzen whereby different healing cults are grouped together under one particular regional umbrella resembles and runs parallel to interpretations of political cults which in the Southern African region also embraced larger areas. In the 1970s these political cults have been analysed in numerous ethnographic studies for their regional significance. Fardon has noted in *Localizing Strategies* that ethnographies tend to emphasize and elaborate upon specific cultural issues that lend a specific 'regional' character to their production (Fardon 1990: 5). For quite a number of years, the issue of regional political cults dominated the Manchester School ethnography of the Southern African region. Within the religious anthropological ethnography of the Southern African region a growing number of studies show an increasing interest in the issue of the production of regionality in religious forms. In Schoffeleers's *Guardians of the Land* (1978) and Werbner's *Regional Cults* (1977) specific cultic forms for this area were investigated that cater to the fertility of the soil, the management of natural resources, droughts, rainmaking and the like. Ranger (1993) has emphasized again how important these types of traditional but regional cults were and still are in the engagement of local communities with wider networks and relations of exchange.

For healing and divination practices, however, 'regional' approaches such as these are relatively rare. One could point at Van Binsbergen (1995), who investigates the development and spread of a four-tablet divination system across local and national boundaries, while others have been tracing the spread throughout the region of independent churches that likewise include elements of healing and purification (see, among many others, Daneel 1971). Janzen's position, however, is rather unique as rituals are brought together on a regional basis that does not belong to any of the constructs of 'healing', 'divination' or 'fertility', but includes a set of features and ritual practices that refer to all of these sorts of categories under ngoma.

By comparing diverse healing practices that include drumming and thus are referred to as ngoma in local settings, Janzen distils a list of characteristics that to a large extent are shared by all of them. These core features are predominantly of an experiential nature and thus lead to a high level of shared recognition within the region. Ngoma, in other words, indicates a 'grammar' for personal experiences which in a Foucauldian sense operates as a discursive for the way they are embraced in local ritual practices, and hence may lend these practices an 'institutional' quality. Note here that similar to the development of the discipline of psychology in Western societies, the development of ngoma and its variety in diverse ritual forms is culturally specific and mediates specific models of bodily experience *vis-à-vis* the socially acceptable and the politically viable. In Janzen's view, there is a communicative link between personal 'difficult experience' and spirits in the sense that spirits are an a priori hypothesis in which the individual's coming to terms with such conditions is cast. The ritual practice is produced through language, rhythm and rhyme within ngoma. This discourse – its operation as well as the experiences which it includes and excludes – can and should be studied in its own right as an indigenous institution, produced within a regional cultural and historical setting.

The point of departure for this volume, however, is that the exact limits of the discourse Janzen intends to investigate are not defined by affliction and healing alone. Our quest to the 'edges' of the discourse which is indicated by the term ngoma starts with the question: what is its subject and its object?

The subject and object of ngoma and the production of its perimeters

Although Janzen criticizes classical approaches to ngoma for their concentration on divination, possession and trance, he too chooses the same analytical unit: ngoma as a therapeutic institution which transforms sufferers into healers. The seven formal properties or core features by which he defines ngoma all pertain to this process of transformation. This is particularly clear from what Janzen calls 'the core ritual', in which all other features come together and without which we cannot speak of ngoma: the therapeutic and initiatory ngoma song-dance in which the meaning of the individual lives and suffering of the ngoma practitioners is articulated and recreated (Janzen 1992: 86, 128, 174). In other words, Janzen's prime subject continues to be *cults of affliction*. In fact he limits the scope even further by focusing almost exclusively on the healers, and ignoring lay participants in the cults.

We differ from this approach by a wider delimitation of ngoma, which we believe does more justice to the use in many Bantu languages of the proto-Bantu construction *-goma (Meeussen 1980: L9), 'drum', as well as to the fact that as a discourse ngoma informs diverse activities, not only in the field of healing, but also in life-cycle rituals, seasonal rituals and royal rituals, to name only the most conspicuous ones.

In this reader, ngoma denominates a Southern African discourse whose subject is the coming to fruition of life and whose object is to ensure this fruition and to remove obstacles to it. We differ from Janzen's approach in that we do not attempt to define the doing of ngoma in one specific realm of action, nor in one specific discourse of healing. From our different research projects in culturally divergent localities in Southern Africa it has become clear that as a discourse ngoma may pertain to all spheres of life – the personal, the social, the political, the economic or the ecological.

All ngoma, such as healing, initiation rituals and kingship rites, share a common concern with the person in transition and the society in transition. The contours of ngoma discourse are made clear and tangible to the developing person and the social body through ritual, music, rhythm, rhyme and masks. The transforming or tran-sitory qualities of ngoma that may change an individual patient into a healer equally apply to processes in larger groups in society. In this capacity ngoma articulates and accompanies the transition which initiation rituals prescribe for the younger gener-ation, as well as the rituals of kingship creating the leadership of a society. All of these processes imply a notion of the liminal, the anti-structural, the wild and un-civilized in order to make the mode of transition and transformation really work.

In ngoma, healing power (the power to counteract illness and misfortune) and political power (the power to order and reorder social relations) are closely inter-woven. Both powers draw on claims to specific relations with the spirit world. Furthermore, the boundary between healing and the (re-)ordering of social relations is often difficult to draw. Communal problems can be reduced to personal afflictions, or personal afflictions can be explained by referring to communal issues. Healing through ngoma can constitute a manifest political act and a political mode of transition. In healing, personal motives, experiences and fantasies can be 'channelled' into social ones, thus turning healing into politics.

There are, however, limitations to the 'width' and 'depth' of what we propose to capture under the umbrella, ngoma. With regard to debates on histories in Indian temples, Appadurai (1981) points to the fact that these debates do not take place in unbounded variety, but in reality have their limitations, their perimeters that mark off what is acceptable within the discourse from what is no longer acceptable. Following his suggestion we propose that ngoma is defined by three perimeters, that is by three interconnected themes which each manifestation of ngoma has to address, if this discourse is to be recognized by its participants:

1 ngoma is a way of articulating and commenting on processes of transition or transformation;
2 it produces a certain type of power and authority which is based on claims to a specific association and communication with the spirit world;
3 this power is embodied, expressed and effected in rhythm (drumming, singing, dancing).

As Appadurai shows it cannot be taken for granted that members of society almost as if 'by nature' understand which manifestation – which 'version' – can be accepted and which cannot. Even more importantly, in society debates are continuously going on concerning the issue of where exactly the 'outskirts' of the possible, acceptable and negotiable are located. In a Foucauldian sense the (re-)production of the perimeters provokes a process of discipline and, as shown by some of the contributions in this volume, the conflicts over the acceptable and the unacceptable may run parallel to other sources of conflict, such as gender relations or age relations. The social production of perimeters that demarcate the modes of transformation or transition to which different manifestations of ngoma refer, is highlighted and referred to in all of the contributions to this volume.

In his description of various ngoma institutions, Janzen briefly refers to political processes and reaction to social problems. Yet, by focusing mainly on the 'doing' of ngoma, the aspects of (re-)ordering social relations and the ideological core of many ngoma institutions remain largely out of sight. With this volume we hope to contribute to a better understanding of ngoma by including articles that deal specifically with the issue of political power and the ordering and reordering of social relationships. All articles, some emanating from the field of religious anthropology and others deriving from the field of medical anthropology, investigate the character of the relationship between healing power and political power.

About the contributions

In Chapter 2, Henny Blokland concentrates on what is shared in rituals of transition in which drums are used. Janzen's proposal to establish ngoma as a term for a widespread African institution centres around one specific use of the drums – that connected with healing. Though advocating a definition of health as social reproduction, throughout his book he implicitly applies a much more restricted definition of health and healing, as therapeutics in the sense of 'fighting disease' and 'saving lives'. This form of healing serves in his book as a model for metaphorical types of healing as practised in political ngoma. Secular or performative ngoma seems to fall outside the category of ngoma altogether.

Blokland proposes to regard the way in which drums are used in weddings as the key to their use in healing cults and performance, as well as in politics. The wedding shows a movement from competitive drumming between the groups of bride and groom to the sacred drumming which is the intercourse between bride and groom, which resolves the distinction between the groups in the offspring uniting both groups.

This distinction between competitive and secular drumming on the one hand and unifying or sacred drumming on the other serves as a tool to analyze Nyamwezi society's ability to handle competition and violence, be it in the form of disease, war, famine or social tensions.

While Chapter 2 describes connections and interdependencies within the fabric of ngoma, Annette Drews contemplates the way in which its inherent contradictions are manipulated in gender relations. She maintains that the antagonism between political and therapeutic ngoma reflects, expresses and constitutes other contradictions found in many African societies like those between women and men, family matters versus regional and national politics and individual needs versus common interests. She argues that we should therefore expect to find a certain degree of reflection and representation of the power relations constituting society within the discourse of ngoma. In Chapter 3 Drews discusses how gender relations are expressed and constituted within ngoma among the Kunda of Eastern Zambia, and how gender identities are contested and defended through the ritual use of drums.

In Chapter 4, Ria Reis takes a closer look at therapeutic ngoma by analyzing healing as it is practised by Swazi healers. She distinguishes between the doing of ngoma – the transformation process by which wounded healers are created – and the work of ngoma aimed at identifying and expelling evil from lay patients. Contrary to Janzen, who concentrates on the first, she claims that the core function of therapeutic ngoma lies in the discourse on suffering and healing which is produced in the interaction with lay patients. With an example of a healing ritual she shows that Swazi healers employ powers constructed through and within the wounded healer complex to create new illness concepts which sustain and comment upon social changes. In this fashion Swazi healers are active on the interface of political and therapeutic ngoma.

Focusing on the relation between politics and healing in the *Mhondoro* territorial cult in Zimbabwe, Marja Spierenburg discusses the influence of the healers' clientele in this cult in Chapter 5. The healers mainly deal with collective problems of the wider community of adherents. However, contrary to Janzen who described this cult as *defining* primary values and social patterns, she maintains that the cult mainly functions as an arena where socio-economic and political developments are *discussed* by the clientele. The power of a medium to issue social or political commentaries and the range of problems which is presented to him (respected mediums also function as healers of individual problems), depends on his reputation. The influence of the clientele is reflected in the continuing process in which this reputation is alternately questioned and preserved.

In Chapter 6, Matthew Schoffeleers defines regional cults as a series of therapeutic ngomas which function in respect of the population as a whole. Rain cults are seen as a kind of collective and inclusivist therapeutic ngoma, in contrast to more limited types of ngoma. There is much literature on these cults, and they therefore form a well-studied and easily identifiable group, one which should have a place in the ngoma discussion.

Janzen distinguishes between therapeutic and political ngomas, but with regional cults such as the *Mbona* cult it is often impossible to make a sharp distinction between the two. In the context of regional cults rituals are performed which are therapeutic in themselves (rain and fertility), but these rituals are often performed in a highly charged political context, and they often have serious political consequences.

Janzen does not have much to say about political ngoma, but the principal observation he makes in that context is that in centralized state systems the therapeutic ngoma tends to become marginalized as the state itself takes responsibility for public health. In other words, he notes the existence of a negative correlation. The article in turn argues that it is more likely that there will be a kind of *dialectical relation*, the two ngomas opposing and 'needing' each other at one and the same time, as it were. The *Mbona* medium criticizes the chiefs and the chiefs criticize the medium, but one cannot do without the other.

Finally, Chapter 6 may add something to the discussion about the concept of the wounded healer by exploring its relationship to the concept of the scapegoat king. The scapegoat emerges as a wounded healer of a different type: not one who sustained some serious illness which predestined him to become a healer, but one whose supposed failure to function adequately in the social and political field transformed him into a provider of rain and fertility.

In Chapter 7 Cor Jonker stresses that political activities and political ideology are often the nucleus of therapeutic ngoma organizations. The case study of the Zionist churches in urban Zambia shows that ritual healing and political activities are indeed each other's prerequisite and may act as synergetic forces. In the case presented, the two ngoma modalities – political activities and therapeutics – are combined in one ngoma movement and therefore cannot be treated as separate entities. Even though gender differences provide the basis of a number of organizational differences in political activities per se, the healing activities have a political ideological context as well as a political intention. Therapeutic ngoma is an alternative for candid political activities for some, because individual healing cannot be separated from social healing according to the political ideal of the movement. It is the specific combination of healing and political modalities that places these churches in the ngoma tradition.

Contemporary developments in the movement show that the somewhat concealed political potency is surfacing. As a consequence it is now possible to get a much clearer view of the intra-dynamics of religious organization. These dynamics show that the various segments of a single organization may very well have different ritualistic and organizational characteristics but still may have economic motivational or ideological similarities. The case study will illustrate that if one studies the various organizational groupings and ritual aspects within a healing church separately, as well as their practical consequences, a more sophisticated perspective emerges on the relationship between politics and healing.

In Chapter 8, by Rijk van Dijk, the reflection by ngoma on a society's capacity of social reproduction is approached as a discourse with rather distinct and socially perceived perimeters. Other groups in the 'healing business' such as Born-Again fundamentalists in Malawian society debate or contest the discursive claims of ngoma *vis-à-vis* the social reproduction, stability and wellbeing of society. The Born-Again's contestation of the discursive claims of ngoma practices rests primarily on the formulation of a different spatio-temporal perception and model of how their society develops in a modern, present-day context. As the ngoma discourse on individual and social healing therefore loses its sheer hegemonic qualities, the article explores the ways in which this alternative, contesting perception represents and indicates further social conflict in Malawian society.

In the Afterword, John Janzen takes up critically the challenges to his own work presented by the contibutions in this book. By interpreting these studies as a 'doing of ngoma' in its own right, he specifically proposes to dissolve the distinctions the contributions put forth of the political and the therapeutic in ngoma. While acknowledging the 'revisionist shift' the book aims to establish in metaphors of power in African societies by introducing the term 'fruition', he simultaneously points to the wider implications this may have for understanding present day changes in healing rituals, exposed as they are to processes of globalization. This certainly provides an entirely new context for the exploration of ngoma: a transcultural milieu extending beyond the confines of the continent, whose contours have yet to emerge.

Literature

Appadurai, A. (1981) 'History as a Scarce Resource'. *Man* 16: 201–19.

Beattie, J. and Middleton, J. (1969) *Spirit Mediumship and Society in Africa*. London: Routledge & Kegan Paul.

Boddy, J. (1989) *Wombs and Alien Spirits: Women, Men, and the Zar Cult in Northern Sudan*. Madison: University of Wisconsin Press.

Bourguignon, E. (1973) *Religion, Altered States of Consciousness and Social Change*. Columbus: Ohio State University Press.

Crapanzano, V. (1977) 'Introduction.' In V. Crapanzano and V. Garrison (eds) *Case Studies in Spirit Possession*. NY: Wiley & Sons.

Daneel, M.L. (1971) *Old and New in Southern Shona Independent Churches*, vol. I. The Hague: Mouton.

Devisch, R. (1985) 'Perspectives on Divination in Contemporary Sub-Saharan Africa'. In W. van Binsbergen and M. Schoffeleers (eds) *Theoretical Explorations in African Religion*. London: Kegan Paul Int.

—— (1991) 'Mediumistic Divination among the Northern Yaka of Zaire; Etiology and Ways of Knowing'. In P.M. Peek (ed.) *African Divination Systems. Ways of Knowing*. Bloomington: Indiana University Press.

Fardon, R. (1990) 'Introduction: Localizing Strategies; The Regionalization of Ethnographic Accounts'. In R. Fardon (ed.) *Localizing Strategies. Regional Traditions of Ethnographic Writing*. Edinburgh: Scottish Academic Press.

Giles, L.L. (1987) 'Possession Cults on the Swahili Coast, A Re-examination of Theories of Marginality'. *Africa* 57(2): 239–58.

Jacobson-Widding, A. (1979) *Red-White-Black as a Mode of Thought. A Study of Triadic Classification by Colours in the Ritual Symbolism and Cognitive Thought of the People of the Lower Congo*. Stockholm: Almguist & Wiksell Int.

Janzen, J.M. (1992) *Ngoma; Discourses of Healing in Central and Southern Africa*. Berkeley: University of California Press.

—— (1995) 'Self-presentation and Common Cultural Structures in "Ngoma" rituals of Southern Africa'. *Journal of Religion in Africa* 25: 141–62.

Lambek, M. (1989) 'From Disease to Discourse: Remarks on the Conceptualization of Trance and Spirit Possession'. In Colleen A. Ward (ed.) *Altered States of Consciousness and Mental Health. A Cross-Cultural Perspective*. Newbury Park: Sage.

—— (1993) *Knowledge and Practice in Mayotte: Local Discourses of Islam, Sorcery, and Spirit Possession*. Toronto: University of Toronto Press.

Lewis, I.M. (1971) *Ecstatic Religion*. Harmondsworth: Penguin Books.

—— (1986) *Religion in Context; Cults and Charisma*. Cambridge: Cambridge University Press.

Meeussen, A.E. (1980) *Bantu Lexical Reconstructions*. Terruren: Musée Royale de l'Afrique Centrale.

Parkin, D.J. (1972) *Palms, Wines and Witnesses: Public Spirit and Private Gain in an African Farming Community*. London: Intertext.

'Peek, Ph.M. (1991) 'Introduction: The Study of Divination, Present and Past'. In P.M. Peek (ed.) *African Divination Systems. Ways of Knowing*. Bloomington: Indiana University Press.

Ranger, T.O. (1993) 'The Local and the Global in Southern African Religious History'. In R.W. Hefner (ed.) *Conversion to Christianity: Historical and Anthropological Perspectives on a Great Transformation*. Berkeley: University of California Press.

Schoffeleers, J.M. (ed.) (1978) *Guardians of the Land: Essays on Central African Territorial Cults*. Gwelo: Mambo Press.

Tart, C.T. (ed.) (1969) *Milk, Honey and Money. Changing Concepts in Rwandan Healing*. Washington: Smithsonian Institution Press.

Toit, B. du (1977) *Drugs, Ritual and Altered States of Consciousness*. Rotterdam: A.A. Balkema.

Turner, V. (1967) *The Forest of Symbols*. New York, Ithaca: Cornell University Press.

—— (1975) *Revelation and Divination in Ndembu Ritual*. Ithaca, New York: Cornell University Press.

Van Binsbergen, W.M.J. (1981) *Religious Change in Zambia; Exploratory Studies*. London: Kegan Paul Int.

—— (1995) 'Four-tablet Divination as Trans-regional Medical Technology in Southern Africa'. *Journal of Religion in Africa* 25(2): 114–40.

Van Binsbergen, W. M. J. and P. Geschiere (1985) *Old Modes of Production and Capitalist Encroachment. Anthropological Explorations in Africa*. London: Routledge & Kegan Paul.

Ward, C.A. (ed.) (1989) *Altered States of Consciousness and Mental Health. A Cross-Cultural Perspective*. Newbury Park: Sage.

Werbner, R.P. (1973) 'The Superabundance of Understanding: Kalanga Rhetoric and Domestic Divination'. *American Anthropologist* 75: 1414–40.

—— (1977) *Regional Cults*. London: Academic Press (ASA-Monographs 16).

—— (1985) 'The Argument of Images: From Zion to the Wilderness in African Churches'. In W. van Binsbergen and M. Schoffeleers (eds) *Theoretical Explorations in African Religion*. London: Kegan Paul Int.

Zaretsky, I.I. (1966) *Spirit Possession and Spirit Mediumship in Africa and Afro-America. An Annotated Bibliography*. New York: Northwestern University Press.

2

Kings, Spirits
& Brides

In Unyamwezi
Tanzania[1]

Henny Blokland

Introduction

Two sources on Unyamwezi relate a story from nineteenth-century Nyamwezi history which never found its way into the historiography of the region. The hero of the story is *mtemi* (king) Milambo[2] of Ulyanhulu, who can be found in any account of nineteenth-century Unyamwezi and indeed in any history of the wider region. He was a very successful warlord, with extensive interests in the slave and ivory trade with the Coast, for which purpose he raided and subjected large parts of the East African interior, taking home women and children as slaves. Before his rise to power, and immediately after his death, the area was divided into a large number of small territorial kingdoms. The story probably refers to a period of famine around 1870,[3] and runs as follows.

As Milambo was continuously at war with neighbouring people, many warriors died in his wars. The women one day held a meeting and decided to make themselves infertile, as all their children only died in the war: 'Let us all drink sterility medicine, let's stop giving birth, because the king leads all our children into war, where they die, finished off by the Ngoni.' When Milambo realized that he had not seen a pregnant woman for a year, he cried: 'What will become of us, I do not know any woman who has given birth this year. Where should we get people for the army and for labour on the field and in the forest.' He thought of a trick to make the women give birth again. He ordered that, from now on, all women must come and labour for the king. During this project, one day he spotted a pregnant slave. He called the slave and told her: 'Mother, go home, you do not have to perform these male tasks here, because of all women present, you alone are a woman. If you deliver a boy, he will become my Lugaluga[4] in wars, if it is a girl, she will become my wife.' The trick worked. When the women heard this, they decided to take medicine to give birth again, in order to be free from the services of labour to the court. And when Milambo saw the result of his trick, he revoked the order that all women had to work at the court (Bösch 1930: 541; 1946–49 MS IV: 253f).

The same story appears in Carnochan and Adamson (1936). Here, it is explicitly the 'Women's Guild', also referred to as the *Gota* or *Kota* (e.g. Carnochan and Adamson 1936: 275), who

> rebelled, and sent out orders to local lodges that Nyamwesi wives were not to have children for a whole year. These instructions were easily carried out. Every Nyamwesi woman is a member of

the Women's Guild and as such is taught the use of medicines that insure against pregnancy. News of this conspiracy reached Milambo's ears in short order. He immediately issued an edict that if women were to behave like men, they would have to do the work of men in time of war. Women were, therefore, put to such tasks as digging trenches, building palisades and clearing away timbered areas. Then, one day, when Milambo was inspecting some work in a village near Ulambo, he noticed a slave girl who was pregnant. He called her before him and said: 'If your child is a boy, I will make him subchief. If it is a girl, I will marry her to a chief of royal blood and make her a queen.' Accounts of this incident spread like wildfire throughout the tribe and brought the strike against motherhood to an end.

(Carnochan and Adamson, 1936: 223ff).

I am not primarily interested in the historicity of the account, i.e. whether a fertility strike did take place, or a decline in fertility which could be interpreted as such a strike. There are several reasons why women's fertility may have declined. The participation of men in raiding and trading increased the workload of women considerably, and may have caused abortions and/or infanticide. Famine occurred at least twice in the period between 1870 and 1880, which may have aggravated the situation of women's fertility by malnutrition. Whatever may have been its cause, the suggested decline in fertility is presented as a conscious decision by the 'Women's Guild', based on a consideration of costs and benefits of child bearing and rearing. Their decision was perceived as 'rebellion' by Milambo, who claimed it threatened the very basis on which his reign rested. He used a slave woman, presumably ignorant of the agreement amongst her sisters (newly imported, not knowing the language, kept in isolation), to break the women's fertility strike in a classic divide-and-rule strategy.[5]

The Sukuma-Nyamwezi[6] women's guild, called Gota or Kota, *Basana* or *Mabasa*, is usually referred to in the literature on Usukuma and Unyamwezi as a fertility or twins' cult (e.g. Abrahams 1967: 64; Cory 1944). As such it is also characterized in Janzen's profile of Sukuma ngoma based on Cory: 'Mabasa was joined by parents of twins and was concerned with the ceremonial cleansing of twin children' (Janzen 1992: 22). This description hides the fact that nearly all women were members of the ngoma and fails to disclose that the Kota were concerned with many other things, indeed that there was very little in Nyamwezi society in which they were not involved. As well as cleansing twins, they acted as midwives, abortionists, healers, and ritual officers in domestic, village and royal rituals. These rituals varied from weddings and girls' puberty rites, to burial rites (for twins, women passed away in pregnancy or delivery, kings, and other 'special' dead), rituals to ensure good harvests, to ensure good clay for making pots, to ensure victory in wars, the purification of the domestic fire and the protection against lightning and heavy rainfall.

It is not my intention to criticize and correct Janzen on the details of ngoma outside his own ethnographic 'home territory' of Lower Zaire, but to show the shortcomings of the use of the concept 'healing' in the description of the heart of the ngoma institution, which forms the subject of his book. My aim is to answer his invitation to constructive criticism in a shared effort to understand ngoma (Janzen 1992: 9).

It is Janzen's intention to outline ngoma as an African institution transcending the compartmentalized treatment which cults and organizations referred to locally as ngoma have so far received, 'under rubrics as diverse as divination, healing, health care, religion, epidemics, magic, ritual, cult activity, dance, song, folklore, and more' (ibid.: xi). In the course of the book, however, 'healing', 'health care' and 'song' are put at the heart of the institution formed by the ngoma performance, characterized as 'the consciously formulated exchange of song-dance, and ... the movement of the individual from sufferer-novice to accomplished, singing, self-projecting healer' (1992: 109). It is this 'heart' which is said to constitute ngoma as 'a classic – that is, ancient and formative – institution in Central and Southern African *healing*' (ibid., emphasis mine).

In my view, the focus on therapeutics and personal song tends to identify ngoma in general with one particular type of ngoma, taking the part (healing ngoma or drums of affliction) for the whole (the ngoma institution). As a result, other types of ngoma are either neglected (many of these hitherto categorized as 'religion, epidemics, magic, ritual, cult activity, dance, song, folklore, and more'), or regarded as recent developments away from the 'original' (cf. below), or as exceptional cases which do not fit well the generalizations on ngoma, as Janzen argues for the Lower Zaire ngoma (1992: 9).

Throughout his book Janzen implicitly identifies healing, and thus ngoma, with saving lives. On this ground, the Kota cult would not fit well. Its members are depicted as rebels in their exercise of control over their fertility. They chose to block the 'uterine flow of life' rather than to 'enhance fertility', which is often considered to be the main aim of their type of cult (cf. Devisch 1993, Janzen 1992: 161ff). They spoiled lives rather than saved them. This ambivalence in the exercise of power, the ability to give life and to take or withhold it, characterizes all positions of power, including those of the leaders of the cults which Janzen seeks to capture under the name ngoma. Great healers know how to kill as well as they know how to heal. The suspicion that they cause the diseases they heal for commercial or political purposes, simultaneously increases and threatens their reputation. Their power, like that of kings, spirits and witches, is the power to control life rather than save it. The spirits who heal have first caused the very affliction they heal (cf. also Janzen 1992: 23, 66).

To describe ngoma as healing cults would be legitimate only if a definition of health as social reproduction, advocated by Janzen (1992: 6, 82, 153) would be maintained in the concept of 'healing' also. The failure to apply such a broad concept of healing consistently has led to the neglect or exclusion of many cults and organizations from the ngoma concept as proposed by Janzen. These ngoma do not fit the therapeutic model, although they would fit in the health-as-social-reproduction approach. More importantly, it is not only the definition of health as social reproduction which indicates that a narrow concept of healing as therapeutics is deficient; the very Bantu concepts which Janzen translates with 'health', and in which he seeks to embed ngoma, point in the same direction.

The linguistic puzzle

The choice of the name ngoma is argued by Janzen thus:

> The name is no trifling matter, for on the choice of the name will hang much of the identity of the institution. 'Cult of affliction,' 'possession cult,' 'divination,' 'rite of affliction,' 'drum of affliction,' and ngoma have been used more or less interchangeably. The first several are recognized analytical names; the last, an indigenous term that has multiple meanings and is therefore ambiguous. The advantage of utilizing an analytical term is that we can say it exists even if the locals give it another name. However, the advantage of utilizing the African name, ngoma, or another *variant*, ngoma za kutibu ('therapeutic ngoma,' in the words of E. K. Makala in Tanzania's Ministry of Culture), or 'ngoma-type ritual' or therapy ... is that we tie into the conscious level of

awareness of it. ... This perspective helps us overcome particularly the Western preoccupation with 'trance' and 'possession' as the central definers of the institution, which the term cult denotes.

(1992: 175ff, emphasis mine)

In my opinion, this amounts to trading in one preoccupation, trance and possession, for another, healing and therapeutics. The central place which these latter two concepts acquire in Janzen's study is, in part at least, the result of a trifling with names, words and concepts. Of the Bantu concepts which are translated with 'health' and 'healing', many have meanings which go beyond these two concepts. As examples I will look at the Swahili *kutibu* and the Proto Bantu (PB) reconstruction *-pód-*, which are both used by Janzen.

Makala's selection of *kutibu* to characterize ngoma could well be politically motivated. He could have chosen other words. In Johnson's Swahili dictionary, for instance, *kutibu* is not listed under 'heal', where we find only *-ponya* (Johnson, 1989), derived from *-pona* and *-poa*, 'to become cool, and so ... improve in health, become well, be cured'. It is a reflection of the Proto Bantu reconstruction *-pód-*, 'be, become cool, cold', which is the very concept Janzen links to ngoma in his speculations on the deep historical roots of ngoma (Meeussen 1980: 24, Janzen 1992: 63). For *-pona*, its Swahili reflection, Johnson gives the following: 'become safe, escape, be rescued (saved, delivered); get a living, subsist, preserve one's life, live; and esp. get well (from illness), recover health, be convalescent, regain strength' (Johnson 1978). It is also used for things, like cars, which have been repaired. For *-ponya*, Johnson lists: 'save, deliver, rescue, cure, restore to health, evade danger etc.' And for *mpozi*: 'one who cures, a physician, one who gets another out of danger, difficulties, etc. *Mpozi ni Mungu*, God is the (real) physician. Native medicine-men are usually called *mganga*; European doctors, *daktari* or *tabibu*; one who cools, comforts, etc.'

Clearly, there is more about *-poa* and its derivations than healing. Interestingly, we meet *-tibu* here again in *tabibu*, as a variant of *daktari* for European doctors, nowadays also used for Western-trained doctors in general. *-tibu* is a variant of *-tabibia*, 'treat medically, act as doctor to, attend professionally' (Johnson, 1978), and is thus much more restricted in meaning than *-ponya*, and closer to 'therapeutics'.

Makala's choice for *kutibu* can be interpreted in the context of a more general policy of the Tanzanian government to gain control of ngoma. As Janzen noted, the Ministry of Culture supports the organization of healers, in Dar es Salaam as well as elsewhere. Using the term *kutibu* generously acknowledges the skills of African healers, as they share it with their Western counterparts. Still, as Janzen also points out, the organizations of healers are stimulated and controlled by the Ministry of Culture rather than that of Health. The attitude of Western doctors towards African healers remains largely one of disdain, granting them at best the skills to heal psychological disorders caused by beliefs in witchcraft and spirits, beliefs which they neither heal nor share. The use of the concept *kutibu* for ngoma reduces spirits to medicines or therapies for the ignorant believers in witchcraft and supernatural causation of disease. The spirit hypothesis, which is stressed by Janzen as vital to ngoma, is under attack, as spirits are regarded as placebos, controlled by the healers, who are in turn controlled by the Ministry. The use of the term *kutibu* to characterize the healing ngoma is to deny them religious status and, with that, to deny that their healing is based on a worldview at variance with that of the political elite. It must be placed in the context of the governmental efforts to encapsulate ngoma. Janzen's statement that 'a distinction between religion and healing ... is not so useful in the present setting' (Janzen 1992: 4) is therefore questionable, as it opens the door to a reduction of religion to therapy, of healers working for the spirits to healers working for the government. I will return later to the subject of sacred legitimation.

A more concrete disadvantage of using the term *za kutibu* is that it has an Arabic origin, and thus cannot 'tie into the conscious level of awareness' all over the area it supposedly covers, the Bantu-speaking area[7] (Janzen 1992: 57), as it is restricted to the Swahili language. Better candidates would be reflections of Proto Bantu (PB) reconstructions like *-pód-[8] (as in the Swahili reflection -*pona*), which is in fact listed by Janzen in his list of ngoma-related concepts (ibid.: 63). However, his treatment of the concept *-pód- betrays his difficulties in coming to terms with his own definition of health and healing. Despite his suggestion to link health with social reproduction, he reduces *-pód- to a mere metaphor for health:

> Health is identified by numerous metaphors, including 'balance' ... 'purity' ... and 'coolness,' whose most widespread cognate (sic) is *pód*, 'to become cool', or 'cool down' or 'to become well, healthy,' in contrast to the heat of disease or witchcraft.[9]
>
> (Janzen 1992: 64)

These concepts, however, can be directly related to health if Janzen would indeed hold on to his 'health-as-social-reproduction' model. This, in turn, implies that one cannot narrow ngoma down to therapeutics only. Therefore there is no need for Janzen to save the ngoma status of not obviously therapeutic ngoma by describing therapeutics as:

> The metaphor serving to facilitate consolidation of substantial resources, material and human, and to aid long-term reordering of institutions of redress, economic redistribution, and ideological change.
>
> (Janzen 1992: 82)

It seems a complicated and unnecessary operation if 'healing' from the start can be regarded as part of a broader concept, a concept which we propose to formulate as fruition (cf. the introduction to this chapter). The example of circumcision is enlightening for what I try to argue here. Whereas circumcision obviously does not cure anything, it is thought to 'heal' in the sense of 'making whole' or 'purifying', or 'bringing to fruition'.

From that point of view, 'therapeutic ngoma' (whatever the African concept matching it) distinguishes one type of ngoma from others, rather than forming a variant of ngoma. In fact this is what Janzen shows the term *ngoma za kutibu* to mean in other parts of his book:

> [In Dar es Salaam] the term ngoma is widely recognized as connoting performance, drumming, dancing, celebration, and ritual therapy. This understanding of ngoma means that the performances are independent of the healing functions, leading to a distinction between ngoma of entertainment and of healing (ngoma za kutibu).
>
> (Janzen 1992: 21)

Janzen refers to the first type of ngoma also as 'secular ngoma'. He reports that the same drums may be used in ritual healing, secular ngoma and also 'ngoma for circumcision, or any other festival or ceremony' (ibid.: 25). He concludes that,

> The sacrality or secularity of ngoma depends not on the music or dance form as such, but on its function or use, its context ... the secular ngoma 'for entertainment' possibly reflects an evolution of the particular ritual from its original context, focused on a sufferer in the midst of a personal crisis, to a more generalized performance outside that focus and the timing of a crisis.
>
> (Janzen 1992: 32)

The part and the whole

While *ngoma za kutibu* was introduced to distinguish one type of ngoma from others, Janzen uses it as a synonym for ngoma in the quotations above. This forces him to exclude the other ngoma (locally referred to as such), from the 'real' ngoma, identified as therapeutic ngoma. This intervention has a high price. Not only are the modern tourist ngoma excluded, but also ngoma like *Beni*. References to Ranger's study of Beni are conspicuous by their absence. The Beni ngoma is referred to only once: 'Terence Ranger found, in coastal and historic trade-route Tanzania, that the revivalist and dance dimensions of ngoma had followed the trade routes and population movements between early colonial settlements (Ranger 1975)' (Janzen 1992: 2). Beni is a competitive ngoma, described by Ranger as 'team dance', which was widespread in eastern Africa in the first half of this century. There is no indication at all that this form of ngoma should have developed from anything else but preceding competitive dancing, or other forms of regulated competition. Moreover, Ranger explicitly links the 'disappearance' of Beni in Tanzania with the genesis of TANU, the political party which led the country to Independence. As soon as this form of political organization became possible, Beni began to fade away, suggesting it fulfilled a political function in a period in which explicit political organization was forbidden to Africans (Ranger 1975).

It is to these types of developments and relations that Janzen briefly turns in the section on 'social and political variables of a complex institution' (Janzen 1992: 74–79). Here, a number of cults are mentioned which are more evidently political in their outlook than cults of affliction, and which are described in terms of their relationship with such political institutions as the lineage and the state. Consequently, disease moves to the background here, and ngoma is described as referring to 'a cluster of recurring processes and perspectives having to do with the interpretation of misfortune … . The particular source of the adversity, whether it is the impact of foreign trade, twinning, snakebite, or lineage segmentation, is secondary to the fact of its definition as the phenomenon of adversity' (ibid.: 83). Such a description of ngoma, however, clearly should include the lineage and the state, or at least show where they differ from ngoma in their interpretations of and dealings with misfortune. Instead, the state is held to be an independent variable, on whose strength the number and strength of ngoma depends (ibid.: 78ff). This contrasts with Janzen's argument in an earlier publication, claiming that

> Theoretical discussion of the conditions giving rise to new cults should, therefore, compare ritual and institutional phenomena across a broad spectrum, including the formation of states. Once this is done it is immediately apparent that the various theories of cult emergence are the same ones used in accounting for the rise of traditional states, at least in Africa.
>
> (Janzen 1982: 21; emphasis mine)

And this applies not only to the emergence, but also to the history of the relation between cults and states up to the present day. Its history can be described as one of contest, appropriation, suppression, and adaptation of interpretations of (the cause of) adversity, and consequently of how to deal with it. As in the clash between Milambo and the Kota, in which each side acted upon its own interpretation of what went wrong. Milambo blamed the women for failing to cooperate in his project to unify Unyamwezi, while the Kota accused Milambo of paying too high a price for his wealth and power. To Milambo, these women were rebels trying to uproot the order he had established, and he punished them with harsh labour, leaving pregnancy as the only way out. The Kota, bearing the costs of Milambo's career, decided to launch a fertility strike. Their action can be interpreted as an accusation of witchcraft, holding up a mirror to the king, who, in his greed for wealth and power, was sacrificing the yet unborn children to his ends (see Harms 1983: 108ff). A famine would no doubt have constituted an important argument in the hands of the Kota to raise doubts about the legitimacy of the king. Famines are the work of royal ancestors, showing their disfavour. By blocking the rain, they block the fertility of the land, and that of the women. The role of the slave woman aptly describes the loss of influence of the Kota. The king in fact did not depend on their wombs to get people to till the land and fight his wars. He could, and did, import them. The story thus forms a description of an important shift in Nyamwezi politics.

It is his, admittedly vague, description of ngoma as 'dealing with adversity' which I will follow in Janzen, with the explicit understanding that the very definition of adversity itself forms part of the process. Janzen fills in this vague outline of ngoma with a number of core features which together form a synthetic model of ngoma ritual (1992: 87–107), which is supposedly aimed at the personal transformation of the sufferer into the healer (see above). But these features describe in fact the rite of passage in general, used for other types of transformation as well, for instance in enthronement and life cycle rituals. They can therefore not serve to identify ngoma as a unique institution, unless, again, these other types of transformation are included in the institution.

Song versus drum

The substitution of a part (therapeutics) for the whole (purity, strength, wellbeing, fruition, social reproduction) is parallelled by that of the personal song for the drum (ngoma) as *the* core feature of the institution (Janzen 1992: 109). The choice of ngoma for the name of the institution suggests that the drum would at least be present amongst the core features of the institution. While in chapter two the presence of *-goma* in PB is used as an argument for the deep roots of the institution carrying its name (ibid.: 63–69), and efforts are even made to reconstruct a ngoma drum (ibid.: 69–74), the drum is substituted by the personal song in chapters four and five, where it, rather than the drum, is considered to form the core feature of ngoma performance. If the song is at the centre, then the song instead of the drum should be central too in the arguments establishing the deep roots of the institution.

In the Sukuma-Nyamwezi area, songs circulate amongst different types of ngoma, and the same has been described by Janzen to be the case in Dar es Salaam. To take over Makala's view that it is a 'mistake', that is a *misapplication* or change of the *pure* form of the rite from its *original purpose*, when 'in their hired events these [secular] groups might perform a song-dance that had been used for healing' (ibid.: 33; emphases mine) testifies to the awkward position into which Janzen has manoeuvred himself, as now the 'specialists on ngoma', like Makala and Janzen, know better than the members what is allowed and what is not. Again, it is not surprising for a Tanzanian government official to express views like this, as it in the interest of the government to compartmentalize different forms of ngoma, and to establish normative rules governing what is allowed and what not, what is real and what is not. Drums, rhythms, songs and dances have been traded, stolen, repressed, revived, and invented over a long period, and political leaders, themselves more often than not jealously guarding their drums, have always shown interest in ngoma of whatever type.

The substitution of the song for the drum seems to be inspired by Janzen's embarrassment with spirit possession. His embarrassment with possession is shared by Nyamwezi men, who, as will be described below, regard trance behaviour as obscene. This unease seems the main reason to insist on the 'personal song', and stress the *consciously* formulated exchange of song-dance' in ngoma against the many scholars who 'have followed trance behaviour and assumed it is the central point of the ritual' (ibid.: 109, emphasis mine). As mentioned above, one of his arguments for the introduction of the name ngoma is that 'cult' denotes trance and possession as the central definers of the institution, a Western preoccupation which is to be overcome by using ngoma instead. Although I belong to the group of scholars obsessed by trance and spirit possession, the term 'cult' is too general to evoke these in me without the proper and usual specification of 'spirit possession cult'. To substitute ngoma, 'drum', for 'cult' could in fact have the inverse rather than the desired effect, evoking the 'all-night long throbbing rhythm of the drums around which Africans frenziedly dance' images of travel literature on Africa, past and present. If ngoma, however, really refers to song-dance, as Janzen seems to argue, this danger is evaded in a very unusual way, by using ngoma, 'drum', but meaning 'consciously formulated exchange of song-dance'. The substitution of cult by ngoma is argued on the wrong grounds. The argument should, in my view, be that there are also 'secular' ngoma, next to cults or 'religious' ngoma. I will elaborate this distinction below.

The only certainty we have on the basis of linguistic material is that there is a PB reconstruction *-goma* meaning drum. Its presence in the PB vocabulary does not say anything about where and how it was used, nor what it looked like.[10] That there is a reconstruction for 'drum', and several for 'healing' does not imply that these were related.

Janzen's considerations for reducing ngoma to healing and ngoma performance to personal song are understandable. If the health as social reproduction (and therapeutics as metaphor) model is followed, there seems hardly a social activity, practice or institution which falls outside its scope. But this is exactly what he suggests by his insistence that ngoma transcends Western analytical categories of kinship, politics, economy and religion (1992: 81). And this ubiquity parallels that of the drum, which is after all the primary meaning of the word ngoma. As Janzen himself pointed out in his study on Lemba, 'drum symbolism, denoting consecrated leadership, exists across the set of political types' formed by 'centralized kingdom, chiefdom or shrine, and a network-like aggregate of figures in a major drum of affliction such as Lemba'. The shared drum symbolism, he argued, suggests that the distinctions between these political types, to which the lineage may be added, are 'distinctions of degree and not of kind' (1982: 22).

Recapitulating

Ngoma has various meanings. First, it is one of the most widespread Bantu names for the physical drum (reflections of the proto Bantu reconstruction *-goma*, L 9, Meeussen 1980: 22). Second, it is also a widely-used term to refer to the music, singing and dancing accompanied by the beats of the drums, the drums in action, the performance. In this sense it can refer also to music in which no drums are used, as well as to dancing. Third, it is used in a more limited number of Bantu languages to refer to the group of performers and, in case they form or are members of an organization, to their organization. It is obviously this third meaning to which Janzen refers as the Ngoma institution. For the sake of clarity, I will refer in the remainder of this article to ngoma in the first sense as 'drum', to ngoma in the second sense as 'ngoma' and to ngoma in the third sense as 'Ngoma'.

In the following effort to develop an alternative approach to Ngoma, I follow Janzen in his description of Ngoma as dedicated to the interpretation and handling of adversity, or, put in a positive way, to the quest for fruition (cf. the introduction to this volume). Unlike him, I do not take disease as the central or basic manifestation of adversity, but as one amongst many. I follow him in taking the ngoma performance to lie at the heart of the institution, but unlike him, I place the drum at the centre of the performance rather than the song. Where Janzen seems to make no difference between the perception of misfortune as caused by 'spirits or ancestors' (Janzen 1992: 83) on the one hand, and that of misfortune caused by witchcraft (*dòg*: that just as words and intentions by others can afflict, so they can heal', ibid.: 84), on the other, the Nyamwezi material indicates that these are alternative and distinct ways of interpreting and coping with adversity. The drum can shout for revenge or proclaim submission. This distinction is present in each of the three forms of social organization in which the drum is used (kinship, Ngoma, kingship). Ngoma, as an institution, is far from unique; on the contrary, it is strongly related to and often hard to distinguish from kinship and kingship, with which it shares the drum and ngoma. The following account of Nyamwezi Ngoma seeks to contextualise the use of the drum in Nyamwezi society, by tracking it through the three institutions in which it is used. After a short introduction to the Nyamwezi Ngoma, I will sketch the two ways in which ngoma is performed at the wedding, and how one is transformed in the other. Then I will show how these two distinct types of ngoma correspond with two types of Ngoma, sacrificial and competitive (Janzen's sacral and secular ngoma). In terms of dealing with adversity, the first relies on what Janzen calls the spirit hypothesis, the second on witchcraft. In kingship, the same distinction appears in the king's roles as sacred king and big man.

Nyamwezi-Sukuma Ngoma

During my research on Ngoma in Unyamwezi, I have collected the names of 107 Ngoma known to have been active in the past hundred years in the Nyamwezi-Sukuma area. Janzen's 'classic profile of ngoma in Sukumaland, Western Tanzania' (1992: 21ff), which is based on one of Cory's many studies of the subject, mentions some seventeen Ngoma. The passage clearly shows the compartmentalized way in which Ngoma were treated by scholars, and which Janzen aims to overcome, but fails to achieve (cf. e.g. Janzen 1992: 77ff). Abrahams initially had a similar fragmented approach to Ngoma in his monograph on Unyamwezi (Abrahams 1967). But the genesis and fast spread of a new Ngoma in the 1970s, the *Sungusungu*, led him to the following observation:

It is probably significant that there has been historically a wide range of small-scale groupings in the area with a variety of functions. Thus there have been dance societies, cultivating teams, spirit possession and other ritual associations, hunting groups, threshing teams, and more general forms of neighbourhood organization . ... The relation of such associations to the kinship system has generally been one of complementarity rather than conflict, though the potential for the latter is highlighted in the rituals of initiation into some of them. With regard to chiefship and other governmental systems, there has been a more mixed history of symbiosis and conflict . ... The longstanding presence of such groups in the area, and the sometimes uneasy division of labour between the state in one form or another, seems to be a major persistent feature of the Nyamwezi and Sukuma political scene.

(Abrahams 1987: 193)

The relation of Nyamwezi Ngoma to the kinship system on the one hand and the governmental system on the other, is reflected in the fact that the use of drums is limited to these three systems. Ngoma, it is suggested by Abrahams' observation, is related by the drum to the two other contexts in which drums are used: weddings (the kinship system) and royal ceremonies (the governmental system). The drum stands for something which the three systems or institutions share.

In the remaining part of this article I will concentrate on the Nyamwezi area, the area in which I did my own research on Ngoma. Although there are many similarities between the Sukuma and the Nyamwezi areas, and the border between the two is hard to draw, it is precisely in the interrelationship between Ngoma, kinship and kingship that they show differences, which I have analyzed elsewhere (Blokland, forthcoming).

In Unyamwezi, then, drums are beaten almost exclusively in the dry season at weddings, Ngoma performances and royal ceremonies. The only occasion at which drums are heard in the rainy season is at the burial of a woman, man or child belonging to a special category of people who, like the king, are mourned by the drum, instead of by their relatives, neighbours and friends as is the case normally. I will show below that these burial ngoma do not form a special category, but form part of Ngoma and royal ritual.

Various types of drums are used, usually in a combination forming an orchestra of two to five drums. Many drums have their own proper names, especially drums owned by Ngoma and by kings. These names offer opportunities for the reconstruction of historical processes of migration and/or contact, as some can be found back in areas far away from Unyamwezi, and others appear over a very wide area (see Blokland, forthcoming). The drums are seldom the only instruments used: rattles, handclapping, whistles, bells, sticks, and hoes beating stones can be heard at most ngoma performances. There are other percussion instruments which are referred to as drums: 'The Maanga [a diviner's Ngoma] do not have a drum; they use a bell as their drum' (interview; Mwana Mmeja, 20.10.1988).

At first sight, the drum seems to stand for the unity of a group, formed by a family, a Ngoma or a kingdom. Each have their drums, around which people belonging to the group unite, to the tunes of which they dance, whether they are hunters, witches, thieves, healers, relatives, or subjects of the king. The drum would then simply be a sign for the group's identity, comparable to a flag. A first indication that there is more at stake, is the reference to the bride, more specifically to her body, as a drum, 'her drum' as well as 'my drum', are the expressions put in the mouth of the groom to praise his bride in the song quoted below.

The bride as drum

They have brought my colourful bird
Mama, my beautiful bird
her drum shining with oil
You're too late, she's already married
My drum, shining with oil

– Nyamwezi wedding song (Bösch 1946–1949 MS III: 189)[11]

The song is mentioned by Bösch as an example of the songs sung during the wedding ngoma performed on the night preceding the formalization of the wedding. The scene is the homestead of the bride's parents. The preparations which led to this ngoma can be divided in three parts. I follow here the descriptions of a wedding noted down by Bösch, a wedding as it was performed in the 1920s and 1930s in Ndala. In the meantime, some things have changed, others continued. The point I want to make is that there are two types of ngoma danced at the wedding: a competitive and a sacrificial type. This is illustrated most clearly in the wedding as described by Bösch.

Part one of the wedding is formed by the negotiations between the man and the woman. The friend who accompanies the man to the house of the woman, explains their visit by saying: 'We have come to look for a ladle, we wish to be born into this homestead, we want marriage (Bösch 1946–1949 III: 148ff).' The wife's symbol is the ladle (*mdinho*), the tool of mixing. The bow (*buta*) is the husband's. The ladle is held in the right hand, the matrilateral relatives are 'those of the right', in distinction to 'those of the left', the patrilateral relatives, as the bow is held in the left hand. Another corresponding distinction is that between 'the head' (*ku mutwe*; male, patrilateral) and 'the back' (*ku mgongo*; female, matrilateral). The ladle stands for the blending which is the work of the wife. She mixes flour with water when she prepares the staple food, *bugali*, the blessing material, *lwanga* (raw), or beer (cooked). As I will show, she mixes her own and her husband's families into one, as her children are identical to the parents of both man and wife.

If the girl agrees, part two starts, the engagement (Bösch 1946–1949 III: 151–6). Two or three male representatives, *bakombe*, of the groom's family visit the bride's village, and offer their counterparts, the bakombe of the bride's family, the price 'to scare', or 'to split open the homestead', a price the height of which indicates what they are ready to pay in brideprice (ibid.: 153). When they have left, the father of the bride asks her whether she agrees to be married to that man. She can refuse that very day, or at any other time up to the formalization of the wedding.

When the girl agrees to be married, part three starts, the negotiations on and payment of the brideprice. The father of the woman accompanies his bakombe to the groom's home. First a round of negotiations takes place between the two male parties in the absence of the fathers.[12] The groom's party bids, the bride's answers: 'You have injured us (but not yet killed us), increase', and so on until agreement is reached. Then they move to the house of the groom's father, whither also the bride's father comes. Facing each other, they finish the negotiations. The groom's father lists what he will pay: 'Ten for the bow (patrilateral relatives), ten for the back (matrilateral relatives),' and so on, paying for each part of the bride's body, for the suffering of the mother in pregnancy and delivery, for the care with which the relatives surrounded the child in rearing it (Bösch 1946–1949 III: 158–61). This list is similar to the one paid by the family of a murderer to the family of the victim, the bloodprice. I will return below to this similarity.

Once the negotiations between the men are satisfactorily ended, the girl's family's bakombe receive a life goat from the groom's family, together with the necessary tools for killing, skinning and preparing it. When they have skinned the goat, they divide it. The part of the 'head', the upper part, is divided between the fathers of the groom and the bride, the lower part, 'the back' between the mothers of bride and groom. All parties prepare and eat their part of the goat on their own.

There are clear signs of female resentment against the agreement. During the skinning of the goat, a senior woman of the groom's family hits the goat with her ladle, to make it taste bad (Bösch 1946–1949 III: 163). When the bride's party leaves with the cattle or goats which make up the brideprice, they are followed by the senior women of the groom's side who try to stop them and get the cattle or goats back. When the mother of the bride has received her part of the goat, and starts to prepare it, her husband, responsible for the agreement made, is tied with ropes like a criminal (ibid.: 168).

A few days later, the bakombe of the groom's family pay a return visit. They too receive a life goat from their hosts, which is treated in the same manner as the first goat. A date for the formal wedding ceremony is agreed upon, and both families start to collect sorghum and to invite guests for this day.

The goats exchanged before the formalization of the wedding show the symmetry of the relation between the two families: one goat against another, each divided in four parts, a brideprice against a bride. The equal exchange has been brought about by the males of the two families, united in their sharing of the 'heads' of both goats. The women, on the other hand, have united in their resistance against it, each eating half of the 'back', the part of the victim's family in the ritual of the bloodprice.

It is this situation of symmetry which is staged in the ngoma danced the night before the wedding is formalized. It takes place in the evening after the groom with his party has arrived in the homestead of the bride, an arrival in the form of a (mock) battle, resulting in the bow of the groom being fixed in the girls' house, where the unmarried girls of the homestead or village spend the night. After this, the dance starts. Both parties have invited master dancers and poets, who are paid for their services. The guests of the bride dance on one side, those of the groom at the other, in competition. The songs of the dance leaders are of many kinds, old, traditional ones, notably warsongs, as well as new ones composed for the occasion. The wedding songs sung at this ngoma have as main subjects sex and the tensions between man and wife, each side mocking the other, and praising itself. The dance continues deep into the night, in case none of the parties gives up. When one ngoma's vigour weakens, the dancers overpowered by sleep or beer, the winners move to the dance place of the losers and there perform a couple of victorious dances (Bösch 1946–1949 III: 194, 201).

The ritual performed after this ngoma transforms the egalitarian and competitive relation between the two sides into a hierarchical one uniting the families in the asymmetrical whole formed by head and back. I use the concepts egalitarian and hierarchical here as Tcherkézoff, following Dumont, uses them in his analyses of Nyamwezi ritual (e.g. Tcherkézoff 1983, 1986, 1993). An egalitarian relation is one between two distinct parties which are similar. Which one is superior to the other is decided by their ability to gain more of whatever desirable objects they are competing for (women, children, food, arms, money, power, status). A hierarchical relation is one

> between a whole . . . and an element of that whole . . . : the element is part of the whole, is in that sense consubstantial or identical, but simultaneously it is distinct or opposite to it. That is what I mean by 'comprehension of the opposite'. . . . The clearest formulation is obtained by distinguishing and combining two levels: at the superior level, there is unity; at the inferior level, there is distinction'.
>
> (Dumont 1979: 397, 400; quoted in Tcherkézoff 1983: 135)

Ritual constitutes the link between these levels, transforming distinction into unity. In Nyamwezi marriage, the egalitarian relation between the two families is subordinated to the unity of marriage, a unity expressed in the ngoma performed after the ritual.

At the first cry of the rooster, around three or four in the morning, the bride is brought from her mother's house to her man for the actual wedding ritual. All non-married persons leave the house. The ritual is led by the bride's maternal grandmother. The bride sits down to the right of her man, both facing the back of the grandmother, all three facing east from where the new day will come. The grandmother kneads two small balls of *ugali* (thick porridge), sticks a ball on each little finger, and scoops up some raw *mlenda* (Digitalis). Stretching her arms backwards, she crosses them, offering the bride the ball from her left hand, the man that from the right. They receive them with their mouth and let them drop to the ground. The grandmother again kneads two small balls, now scooping up some cooked mlenda, and reaches them backwards in the same fashion. These balls are swallowed by the pair.

It is this ritual which transforms the egalitarian relation of exchange and competition into the hierarchical unity of marriage, head and back. Bösch comments: 'The two balls symbolize the bride because of the shape of the balls, the holes which contain the groom's mlenda. The *tonge* is the woman's vagina, the mlenda the semen of the man.'[13] They thus represent the children of the pair: the tonge may not be chewed as chewing them would amount to eating their own children (Bösch 1946–1949 III: 208). The symmetrical relation, in which the bride was exchanged against wealth, is transformed into a totalizing unity, in which the bride stands for the whole. By handing out the tonge crosswise, the grandmother shows that it is the womb, the back, which transcends the distinction between back and head, giving birth to both. The superiority of the ugali ball is clear. It is the staple food, gained at the cost of many hours spent in preparing the fields, planting, weeding, harvesting, and grinding, labour predominantly carried out by women. Mlenda, on the contrary, grows in the wild, where it is gathered by women. The refusal of the raw mlenda stands for the refusal to continue the pre-marital sexual relation, in which pregnancy is avoided.

After this ritual, the marriage is consummated in the presence of the bride's grandmother. This intercourse, the first performed in marriage, is called the purification of the brideprice. The bride's father's sister knocks on the door with a ladle, asking whether the girl has been married, and the grandmother inside affirms this. Then the groom's father's sister shoots an arrow into the door asking the same question about the man. The affirmative answer of the grandmother is answered by ululations of the women gathered outside and thus the wedding's formalization is made known into the silent night. At that moment a goat is slaughtered by the bride's parents. The mother will serve it in the morning, already prepared, to the groom and his bakombe, who carefully inspect it before accepting it.

Without these two things, the ululations of the women at night, and the goat being slaughtered, cooked and accepted by the witnesses, the marriage has no juridical value, no matter how high the amount of wealth paid in brideprice may have been (Yongolo 1953: 20). There is no obligation on the part of the receivers of the wealth to pay it back in case of a divorce, as it has not been purified. This forms a strong indication that the brideprice does not confer any rights over the woman or her children. In the course of this article, the meaning of the Nyamwezi brideprice will be further explained.

Around three o'clock of that day, ngoma is performed again, to 'proclaim' the formalization of the wedding. This time the dancers are many, often in their hundreds. All youths from the neighbourhood take part, and many relatives are present. Again, the dance is danced in competition, at two sides, danced in a (semi-) circle. But this time, each party is joined and blessed by members of the other. The party of the groom opens the dance. After some time, the sisters of the groom fetch the bride from her mother's house, and lead her to the dance of the groom's party. She is accompanied by her maternal grandmother, her paternal aunt, and two girl-friends. They are 'swallowed' by the groom's ngoma and perform a short dance, bless the dancers with *lwanga* (*kubafupila lwanga*), and return inside. Now the groom, accompanied by his grandfather, friends and some sisters, goes to the dance of the bride's party to 'be swallowed' by it and to give the dancers some beads or money (*kubafupila mabusalu*). The sisters of the groom carry his insignia. The songs this time often refer to the (land of the) joking partners, *bapugo*, who are characteristically described as both 'former enemies' and 'ancient affines', stressing again the transformation from enmity to affinity which took place in the night (Bösch 1946–1949 III: 211–13). The dance shows that the symmetry between the two groups has been ended. The groom's side has become 'bow' to the woman's side; the woman's side has become 'ladle' to the groom's; they have become united in marriage.

That it is the bride who creates this unity is clearly expressed in the beads worn by the bride the following day, when she and her husband are blessed by their parents. At around four o'clock, three to five stools are arranged in front of the bride's mother's house. One of her husband's sisters sits down on the middle stool, and the bride sits down on her lap, holding her husband's bow in her left hand. To her left sits one of her husband's sisters, holding the bride's ladle in her right, on the lap of one of her own sisters, the husband standing next to them. Around her neck the bride wears an ornament representing the collective ancestors (see below). On her forehead she wears double strings of copper beads representing both her own (W) and her husband's (H) parents and grandparents (father = F; mother = M). From her right ear to her left ear:

WFM WMM WM HM HMM HFM

WFF WMF WF HF HMF HFF

She will attach these to the cloth in which she will carry her children on her back, the place where right now, at the wedding, the beads representing herself and her husband dangle. She will store these beads in the *kilindo*, the bridal bark box which she receives at her marriage, and which represents her marriage. It contains also nailclippings of husband and wife, the small pots used for washing after sex, and those containing the oil used before. It will also contain the umbilical cords of her children. The kilindo is the marriage, and may only be opened by the woman. Her husband has to have her consent to open it. Like the drum, which it resembles in both form and material, it stands for the womb of the woman. As long as it remains in the house, the marriage is considered to be valid. If a woman takes it with her when she leaves, a divorce is usually near.

The beads worn by the bride show her status as the one uniting the two families. One by one, the parents of bride and groom bless them, telling them to 'give birth to me like I gave birth to you' (Bösch 1946–1949 III: 220). The parents of bride and groom refer to each other as blenders (Nyamwezi: *basanzi*). At the birth of his grandchild, the father-in-law tells his son's wife: 'Thank you, you have given birth to me.' Nyamwezi grandparents identify themselves with their grandchildren. The relations between alternate generations are relaxed, in contrast to those between proximal generations, characterized by distance, respect and authority.

Until the purification of the brideprice, the two families were distinct: two goats are exchanged, both divided into four parts: two times the head, and two times the back, each family forming the mirror image of the other. The purification of the brideprice marks the moment in which the two are transformed into one: head and back of one family, a hierarchical relation in which the back is superior (allowing for birth). The ngoma taking place afterwards shows this new situation: the husband becomes part of the bride's group and blesses it with beads or money (= semen), the bride becomes part of the husband's group and blesses it with the product of mixing, *lwanga* (= children for whom the family is one, head and back). Where men dominated the negotiations, the transformation has been the work of women.

To understand the nature of this transformation, the purification of the brideprice, I will shortly sketch the main differences with other types of marriage, which, as Tcherkézoff put it, 'carry the presence of death' (Tcherkézoff 1993). The marriage described above is the so-called brideprice marriage, *kukwa*, also called 'sun wedding'. There are other forms of marriage, in which no kukwa is paid, no purification takes place, no goat is slaughtered, and no drums are beaten. These marriages do not result in the blending of the families of bride and groom. Children from such marriages belong to the mother's family only. This is also the case when a girl gets pregnant before marriage. The kukwa marriage differs from these other forms of marriage mainly in what happens after the wife dies as a result of pregnancy, either during pregnancy or during delivery.

In non-kukwa marriages, the man is held responsible for the life of the woman during pregnancy and delivery, until the moment when the afterbirth is delivered. Pregnancy is seen as caused by the arrow of the man, which has hit the woman, causing her to bleed, an image also used in the brideprice negotiations (see above). In the womb, iron and blood are blended into a foetus which is fed by the woman. The afterbirth in particular stands for the blood caused by the arrow of the man. The brothers of a woman tell the man who made her pregnant: 'You have left our sister with your arrow in her body' (Bösch 1946–1949 III: 65), and talion (retributive sanction) will follow if the woman dies during pregnancy or delivery. If the woman dies before the afterbirth is delivered, the man who made her pregnant and/or his sister would be killed by the relatives of the bride. Alternatively, a bloodprice has to be paid. If a kukwa-married woman dies in pregnancy or delivery, no revenge follows (ibid.: 256).[14] Affinity by kukwa excludes talion, just as there is no talion between relatives (ibid.: 67). Kukwa, then, is an insurance against talion being practised in case of the woman's death as a result of pregnancy; it is a bloodprice paid in advance.

The payment of the bloodprice is similar to the kukwa marriage. It too unifies two families, that of the murderer and that of the victim, into a unity consisting of head and back. The bloodprice, as an alternative for talion, was settled in front of and on the instigation of the king. Its arithmetic is the same as that of the brideprice, the killers paying for each part of the body of the victim. When it is accepted, a goat is given by the killer's party. They hold it at the head, the victim's party at the legs. When it is cut in two (alive), the two parties become 'head' and 'back', become one (as) in marriage (see Tcherkézoff 1993). It is the establishment of a relation between joking partners (*bapugo*), a relationship described as resulting from an ancient war and/or wedding. As many generations have died since its institution, marriage between joking partners is allowed but talion remains forbidden. Thus the bloodprice established a marriage relation, and the brideprice is best understood as a bloodprice paid before the act of killing because of the great risk involved in pregnancy and delivery.

This is also clear from the fact that if a woman died from other causes, an amount of wealth was deducted from the brideprice to be paid back to the husband for every child delivered by the woman, including still-born children. Thus, even if a woman would have had only still-born children, they would be deducted from the brideprice (Welch 1974: 127). Clearly, then, kukwa is paid is for the risk taken by the woman in becoming pregnant, and should be translated as bloodprice rather than brideprice.

The risk is a high one. Today, in Tanzania, one out of twenty-four women dies in pregnancy or childbirth (The Progress of Nations 1996: 8ff, 52ff). In a society in which talion would be an option, it would be practised very often, probably most often, after the death of a woman in pregnancy or delivery. Without kukwa, conflict and violence would dominate relations between families seeking revenge for sisters who died in the process of giving birth. By kukwa, women, from being the most frequent cause of talion, become the knots between families, blending them in their wombs.

But, this is only possible if what is prefigured in the brideprice procedures, i.e. the death of the bride in childbirth, does not happen. The resentment of the women precisely concerns this exchange of wealth for a woman, allowing her to be killed, treating her as if she had died already. The role of the bride before the purification of the brideprice is indeed in many respects that of a corpse, buried in her mother's house, covered with a burial cloth, not seen, not heard. Being killed and compensated for by the men, it is amongst the women, the Kota, the mothers, that she recovers her future.

All procedures carried out after the first ngoma are marked by the dominance of women, of both families, in contrast to the preceding ones which were dominated by men. It is the grandmother who presides over the central sacrament of marriage. She taught the girl at her first menses, knew her lovers, advised her on sexual matters and on contraception. It is she who now shows her back to the couple, showing the girl that she is still alive after having given birth and having carried daughter and grand-daughter on that very back they are now facing. It is from her that the bride comes, it is she who makes this marriage possible, it is her marriage.

She teaches them that to her, semen, referred to in the male negotiations as lethal arrows, is only mlenda. The process of generating a child is now referred to as one of cooking, the art of mixing and controlling heat, an art in which women excel, and which the girl fully masters. Like she has been taught to cook by her mother and grandmother, she and her husband will be taught how to give birth safely by the community of mothers around her, which is the Kota community. The united women, represented by the grandmother, reassure the bride and her husband of their control over reproduction, which they will share with them. They reassure the woman that it is not death she faces, but life as a mother and grandmother. She will not die in giving birth to her child. She will die only when her time has come, when her great-great-grandchild is born who will come to see her as a member of the collective ancestors.

The ugali balls offered to the pair and the goat offered to the husband's bakombe are both referred to as *ya buzugu ku nungu*, 'of cooking and stirring in the pot'. The acceptance of the goat by the bakombe is referred to as the 'buying of the male'. By accepting his wife's grandmother's tonge, the groom accepts the guidance of the Kota in the process of giving birth. Pregnancy, delivery and the period up to the weaning of the child are governed by Kota prescriptions ensuring health for mother and child, many of which concern the behaviour of the husband. It is only after he has accepted the tonge, that the bride purifies the brideprice by allowing the man to have intercourse with her. The acceptance of the goat prepared by the mother-in-law for the husband's bakombe signifies their acknowledgement of and submission to this female skill on which the marriage now depends.

In kinship terms, what happens during the night is the establishment of a new stock at the bottom of the cognatic kindred. The Nyamwezi kindred consists of four stocks: the descendants of the four pairs of greatgrandparents of ego, as well as the descendants of their brothers and sisters. These four generations are present in the ritual performed by the grandmother, represented by: grandmother – (mother) – bride and groom – (children). The generations represented by the persons between brackets are implied in the ritual, as explained above. By handing children to the pair, the grandmother calls forth her great-grandchildren, for whom her generation will define the kindred (defining whom not to marry, rules of inheritance, etc.). This relationship continues after death, in what Tcherkézoff has called the 'private ancestral cult', that is the cult paid to 'known' ancestors, those of the second to the fourth generation (great-grandparents, grandparents, parents), known to be of the right or of the left, of the 'parent' or the 'grandparent' generation. From the fifth generation and beyond, the ancestors become united and indistinct and are referred to as *baku-lugenzi*, 'the great extenders'.

The two ngoma performed before and after the purification of the brideprice express the formation of the Nyamwezi kindred. Two unrelated kindreds move from a competitive symmetrical relation (two times head, two times back, exchange of a life against a bloodprice) towards a unity of head and back. It is in the womb of the bride that this unity will be blended, and from which it will be born. The bride's body forms the promise of future wedding ngoma to be performed, of ongoing competition as well as unification, it is 'her drum' as well as 'his'.

Mbina and mioga: competitive and sacrificial Ngoma

Both modes of drumming are essential for the reproduction of the kindred. The opposition between kindreds, which lingers on in the distinction between right and left before finally disappearing in the indistinct mass of collective ancestors, provides the context for the life of the individual: to whom he may turn for a bride, from whom he may expect to inherit, whom to avoid, whom to obey, to whom he may turn for seed, for assistance in a brideprice, for shelter, for food. The unification into head and back of kukwa marriage guarantees the reproduction of these distinctions.

In terms of dealing with adversity, the distinctions between relatives and strangers, left and right, proximate and alternate generations, allow for the identification of the cause of adversity experienced by the individual, and the scenario to be followed to rectify it. Diviners try to trace the cause of the problem to one of the categories of people, either living or dead (limited to the generations of the private ancestors), which can be distinguished at the basis of the oppositions and distinctions mentioned above. Unresolved debts, quarrels, insults, broken promises, lack of respect, acts of witchcraft, theft, murder, greed, etc., are exposed as having led to the use of witchcraft against the victim. Once the cause is identified, the adversity can be rectified. The category assigned to the witch defines the scenario to be followed. For instance, if the witchcraft stems from a private ancestor, he or she will be appeased in a ritual addressed to him or her. In the ritual, the relation between the ancestor and the victim is acted out in the choice of the offering, the hand used in ritual (left or right), etc. (see Tcherkézoff 1983: 29–45). In case the witch is a stranger, depending on their status and reputation, the victim or/and their relatives may opt either for the use of defensive witchcraft, or retaliation, or reconciliation.

Another possible cause of adversity which can be traced by the diviner is the category of collective ancestral spirits, also referred to as *mizimu* ('spirits'). They transcend all distinctions: they are both relatives and strangers, parents and grandparents, right and left, male and female. As they are the ancestors of all, they threaten all, and their intervention calls for a ritual of a different order, that of initiation into a sacrificial Ngoma.

Ngoma organizations are usually based on relations other than kinship. Members of a kindred usually live scattered over a wide area. On a neighbourhood basis, people tend to organize themselves around certain tasks and occupations, like threshing, smithery, pottery, hunting, justice, cultivation, as well as for sacrifice. The initiative to form such an organization is taken by a group of relatives or neighbours, who subsequently recruit others. The geographical spread of such Ngoma varies: some remain restricted to a few villages, others spread over several or all of the many small (former) kingdoms of the Sukuma-Nyamwezi region (and some indeed are spread still wider, see Blokland, forthcoming). The life span of individual Ngoma equally varies: some pass like a fashion, others have a history of three hundred years or more.

Two types of Ngoma are distinguished, which correspond to the two types of ngoma performed at the wedding. The first type of ngoma performed at the wedding, in which the two groups remain distinct and compete for victory, is the type of ngoma performed by competitive Ngoma. The second type of ngoma, in which the two parties have begun to mix, is comparable to the ngoma performed by sacrificial Ngoma. There is one important difference, however: in sacrificial Ngoma, the unity achieved is absolute, there is no distinction at all any longer (between left and right) between the two parties who are in this case, spirits and humans. The ngoma is danced by one party only, that of the spirits. The unity achieved in sacrificial Ngoma, amongst which are a large number of cults of affliction, is the absolute unity of the collective ancestors.

The distinction between these two types of Ngoma corresponds with Janzen's distinction between secular and sacral Ngoma (see above). In Nyamwezi two words are used: *mbina* (pl.: *mbina*) and *moga* (pl.: *mioga*). Mbina's first meaning is dance, and was explained to me as 'simply ngoma' (Swahili: *ngoma tu*). Mioga 'possess special knowledge', the knowledge of sacrifice (interview; Usagali, 30.8.1990). I will give a very short description of a typical competitive Ngoma, the *Puba*, and a somewhat more extensive one of the sacrificial activity of the Kota, which is strongly related to sacred kingship.

Competitive Ngoma

The Puba dance society cannot be conceptualized without its adversary the *Gika*. They are also referred to as *Beni*, of which they form a rural variant. Wherever Puba perform, there are Gika on the other side. They form two teams challenging each other, dancing and drumming against each other each day for a week. The songs they sing are mainly songs of praise for their own group, and abuse of the other. A huge rectangular fence is built, surrounding an area the size of a football field. The gate allows the host (a village or an individual) to gather money from the visitors, who usually come in great numbers. The two groups each occupy one side of the area, where they dance, eat and sleep. The groups consist of some thirty people, mostly young men. Each group also brings some three to four medicine men, who are constantly busy preparing medicines to protect their own group and weaken the opponents. Local boys and men line up with the semi-professional visiting teams. One huge drum, two small ones and one of medium size are played by a variety of men and boys, but there are usually two master drummers, who play when the competition gets hot. The winner is chosen by the public. At the last day of the competition, around six pm, members of the responsible committee count the number of people watching each group, and the group which has more people gathered around it, is the winner. The groups, competing for public attention, are eager to adopt changes in style, dance steps, outfit, songs, and medicines. Football clothes are popular amongst Puba and Gika[15], and so are sunglasses, sports shoes, motor helmets, Koran and Bible as well as genet skins, medicine horns and ancestral spears. Dance competitions are serious business. Many stories circulate about dancers having died from the effects of medicines used against them by opponents. The effect of breaking rules of behaviour may also be disastrous. Dancers are for instance not allowed to have sex during the competition. I was told that the breaking of this rule by a poet I admired very much led not only to the defeat of his group, but also to the death of the woman involved (interview; Ikongolo, 6.10.1988). Puba and Gika performances are dominated by men, although sometimes a group of women performs a shy dance, hardly moving a limb, in sharp contrast to the behaviour of the Kota women, renowned for their obscenity. There is no extensive initiation, lining up with either group marks you as a Puba or a Gika. Both groups have their supporters in each village, and this affiliation is usually inherited from father to son. Young men with the ambition to become a poet or star performer may change sides from year to year, thus educating themselves in the art, before they establish their own group.

The relation between the groups is symmetrical: they use similar drums, medicines, witchcraft and tricks to assure victory, and follow the same rules. The aim is to defeat the other, starting from a situation in which each group has equal chances to win, starting, that is, from an egalitarian relation. The competition never ends, as a loser may win next time. The groups are dominated by men and the rules aim at building up strength (by eating meat, using medicines) and containing strength (no sex) in the group. The group's leader, who does not perform himself, the mtemi (king) is typically a 'big man' whose position rests on his economic achievements. He manages the group and contracts the medicine men. Power is achieved by accumulation of wealth and strength. Witchcraft is the dominant idiom of this type of power and competition. Extraordinary competence is perceived as obtained at the cost of a relative's life.

The Puba form a very clear example of a competitive Ngoma, because their competition is publicly staged. This is not always the case. Often these Ngoma are hired in to dance in celebration of a success perceived as the outcome of a competition, e.g. the positive outcome of a courtcase, or the return from a profitable trade journey. The confrontations between such Ngoma as those of witch-hunters and witches, and of thief-catchers and thieves, are usually hidden from the public. The public ngoma performed by these Ngoma is the victory dance, danced after the losers have given up, and their dancing space has been occupied by the winners. Of course, witches and thieves do not stage such ngoma in public, theirs are danced at night in the forest. Or that at least is what their rivals say. But there are also always rumours that they have a pact between them, sharing both the skills and the spoils of theft and witchcraft between them, that the ngoma performed in the village marks the public as the losers, who have lost their village to the witches or thieves. When these feelings grow strong, the formation of a new Ngoma of catchers is near. Thus, for instance, the urban[16] *Sungusungu* vigilante thief-catchers were born from the popular feeling that police and criminals had become too closely allied. Ten years after their formation, the Sungusungu themselves were perceived by many to have fallen for the same temptations, leading someone to the observation that now, 'police and Sungusungu compete in harassing us.'

Sacrificial Ngoma, the Kota and the sacred king

The relation between spirits and humans is unequal from the start. The spirit always wins. Competition is no option. Sacrifice creates a unity between the afflicted and the attacking spirit. Sacrificial Ngoma are dominated by women, the most important consumption is that of beer (a female product, the preparation of which has sexual connotations), and ritual intercourse is an important feature of all sacrificial Ngoma. Leadership is charismatic, sometimes also inherited, but in either case the power of the mtemi, the leader, is perceived to be forced upon him or her and to become effective only through the installation ritual. There are many sacrificial Ngoma in Unyamwezi, and most of them could be described as cults of affliction, in the sense that people become members because of an illness or other affliction. But their function is not perceived as that of healing individuals. The recovery of the patient is secondary to the sacrificial practice, which links the whole of society to its origins, the spirits or collective ancestors. This link is also the legitimation of the Nyamwezi sacred king, the territorial mtemi, who is a child of the spirits. Kingship and sacrificial Ngoma are closely connected, and nowhere closer than in the relationship between the king and the Kota.

The Kota probably form the oldest sacrificial Ngoma in the area (see Blokland, forthcoming). As already mentioned, all mothers were members of the Kota cult. Membership was compulsory for parents (and siblings) of twins and breeches, but many women volunteered as initiates at the occasion of such a birth. The condition was that they had given birth, and most women became members after the birth of their first child. Thus, the translation 'twins' cult' is deceptive, and 'mothers' cult' would be better. Sacrifice, as already indicated, forms only a part of their activities. As shown in the description of the wedding ceremony, the Kota have the power to unite, and to postpone death. Not only the death of the bride, but also that of society as a whole.

The ngoma of twins and breeches, performed by the Kota, is the same as the royal ngoma. Twins and breeches 'are kings', and the king is addressed with '*Kashindye*', breech-born. The birth of these children is reported to the court, where a royal drum is borrowed to be taken to the place of birth to be beaten in the rituals performed there. Vice versa, whenever a royal ritual (sacrifice, burial of king, enthronement) was performed, Kota leaders fulfilled vital roles alongside (other) members of the royal matrilineage.

Royal ancestors are the collective ancestors of all inhabitants of the country (Tcherkézoff 1983: 29). Collective ancestors, with untraceable links to all, act as nature spirits: they threaten the whole area inhabited by their collective descendants, and a threat to one meant a threat to all, as all were their descendants. Their interventions typically come in the form of natural disaster: either lack of rain, or excessive rains, both leading to famine; lightning, epidemics, locusts, and other threats to the country as a whole, notably the birth of spirit-children i.e. twins and breeches.

As already mentioned above, the Nyamwezi king is addressed as *Kashindye*, 'breech-born'. The price to be paid at the court when returning the royal drum (see above) was higher for a breech than for twins. *Wanangwa* (children of kings who were given a part of the kingdom to rule) could be given the right to preside over rituals concerning twins, but breeches always were to be ritually processed at the king's own court. This all suggests that the status of breeches was higher than that of twins. Twins and breeches disturb the process of reproduction of the kindred described above. They are not named after their grandparents, but are always called *Kulwa* and *Doto* (first and second born of twins) and *Kashindye* (breech). Their personality is not mediated by the grandparents; they are direct manifestations of the collective ancestors. They show the lack of distinction typical of collective ancestors: all have the same names, irrespective of gender, family membership or generational position. Their birth means a threat to all. Hiding their birth would lead to famine, as the rains would be so heavy that they would wash away the plants. The news of their birth should spread over the country, just as the bodies of the collective ancestors are buried all over the country, and their offspring have spread all over the land. Unless the Kota rituals are performed, the mother will die. She, or a neighbour or relative, will be hit by lightning, which will also bring the heavy rains destroying the crops.

The superiority of Kashindye amongst the Nyamwezi spirit-children suggests that their status is related to the risk involved in the delivery of twins and breeches. It is the threat they form to their mother's life which gives them sacred status. Delivery of a breech is a risky affair, and without advanced obstetric care there is a fair chance for the delivery to be fatal for both mother and child. In over forty per cent of twin deliveries, one of the twins is also born in breech position (Beischer and Mackay 1986: 495ff). It is therefore suggested that it is the inverted position, forming a major risk in delivery, which is decisive for the status of spirit-child. These children head in the wrong direction. By pushing up in a desire to be born into the head, they threaten their mother's life, and often succeed in killing her. This is exactly what the grandmother's ritual sought to avoid in handing the *ibanga* to the groom and bride, moving the death of the bride three generations up. This breech-child does, or at least intends to, kill its own mother, instead of its *mkulugenzi* (pl.: *bakulugenzi*). In destroying the mother, it destroys the marriage, and the distinctions on which the kindred is based. Immediately after the birth, the lid of the bridal kilindo is beaten with a ladle to make the birth known in the neighbourhood. A Kota leader is often already present, as they are the expert midwives, called upon in every difficult delivery or complication during pregnancy. When the sound of the ladle beating the kilindo lid is heard, all work in the fields should cease. Its sound makes known that the marriage, contained in the bridal box, has been violated, the lid has been taken off. Killers have arrived, coming directly from that unknown depth into which the kindred disappears, and from where future, yet unborn, generations return. They have come unmediated by the kindred. The destruction of the distinction between the mother's loins or back (from where children are born) and head (where the spirit-children seek to be born) is the destruction of the border between kindred and collective ancestors, and obviously forms a concern to all.

The very complex series of rituals performed after the birth consists of two major movements across this border. These rituals are performed also when the children are aborted or still-born, and also in case the mother died. First, the parents are removed from the kindred, and moved to the category of collective ancestors, joining the children. Second, the 'forgotten' links between collective ancestors and all the living, are retraced, the unity between them is made, the kindred is 'forgotten'.

The movement of the parents to the category of collective ancestors is most clearly seen at their death, when they are 'mourned by the drum', and explicitly not by their relatives. Like the spirit-children, they are buried at night, at a refuse heap, one of the representations of the outside. They do not die, as they have already moved over to the collective ancestors.

The linking up of collective ancestors and living is staged in a variety of ways, reaching its climax in sacrifice. Leading up to the sacrifice, the Kota behave in a way which is generally considered to be obscene. These obscenities, defying all codes of behaviour of the kindred, are characteristic of the collective ancestors, amongst whom there is no difference between generations, left and right, man and woman, whose individual identities and loyalties are long lost and who are remembered only for their sexual activity which brought forth the living.

The much-discussed dominance (at least in numbers) of women in cults of affliction may very well be related to women's procreative capacities and the problems many of them experience in pregnancy and delivery.[17] When I asked why women dominated in sacrificial Ngoma, men answered that women are more apt to carry the heavy load of this ritual work. This statement implies a reference to pregnancy, which is often called 'carrying a heavy load'. Each sacrificial Ngoma has its own particular rhythm.[18] When the right rhythm is beaten, the spirit 'rises into the head' of the afflicted. In describing how it feels to become possessed, my informants said they feel the spirit coming up out of the belly, almost suffocating them when it has to pass the throat, before it enters the head and is born. The similarity with the birth of Kashindye is obvious.

Furthermore, the men said that women had less shame, which made it easier for them to perform the obscenities demanded by the ritual procedures. Shame is a major characteristic of the relations between the various categories of relatives and in-laws, between old and young people, between men and women. It has to be thrown away to link up with the spirits. Possession is obscene because the spirit knows no shame, and in the absence of shame the spirit manifests itself.

The sacrifice performed by the Kota forms the unity between collective ancestors and their offspring, the living. A goat is held to the ground by two Kota, one at the head, holding its mouth shut, the other holding the back legs. Father and mother (or a sister of hers in case she died) fall down with their buttocks on the middle of the goat. Other pairs of Kota repeat the act until the goat has died. As in all sacrifices, the killing method is meant to 'open the door', the division between head and loins, formed by the goat's diaphragm. The violent death struggle of the suffocating goat causes the cartilage linking the breastbone to the diaphragm to bend, resulting in a hole: the 'door' of sacrifice. It is always the first thing scrutinized after the animal has died, and when it is open, 'the spirits smile', the sacrifice is accepted, the unity brought about (Bösch 1946–1949 I: 213, 211ff, 231ff, 241). Only if the door is open, can the sacrifice be prepared and consumed. The treatment of the meat (raw, roasted and cooked) represent the stages through which the passage back to life is followed, and through which the distance to the spirits is re-established: from collective ancestors (raw) to private ancestors (roasted) to the living (cooked). The cooked meat is shared between spirits (i.e. those representing them) and public, who receive it from the spirits. With this consumption of the meat, the borders between the various categories are restored, while the links between them have been retraced.

This unification is repeated again at the royal court, at the end of the ritual, when the drum is returned, and the parents destroy the door to the sanctuary of the royal spirits. They discharge their sacred status there, where it charges the royal ancestry, and return home to a normal life again, to be disrupted only at a new spirit birth in their village or region, when they will participate in the Kota ritual.

At the royal court, the unity between the living and the collective ancestors is permanent. The king is a Kashindye, born from a woman of the royal matrilineage and the collective ancestors. The genitor of the king is unknown as royal women do not marry with kukwa. The 'father' of the king, like that of spirit-children, is variously imagined as a lion, as lightning, the sun, God. The royal drums represent the royal womb, the unity between the living and the collective ancestors, where disaster is domesticated, fruition guaranteed.

The relationship between sacrificial and competitive ngoma

Both forms of Ngoma, sacrificial and competitive, have a long history in Unyamwezi. There is no reason to suppose that one is senior to the other, or one is derived from the other. Competitive Ngoma, with their combination of aggression and egalitarian ideology, promote self-assurance and the will to compete. Sacrificial Ngoma, uniting people with their past and re-ordering it for them, offer them a history on which a future can be built. Neither has as its main aim to heal people. Illness is attributed to various causes, many of which are dealt with outside the context of Ngoma (in the private ancestral cult, by private healers who are experts in herbs and witchcraft, by

Western-educated doctors). As in the dances at the wedding, the distinction between the two types of Ngoma corresponds with that between male and female, with the understanding that the female skill in uniting is an extra, and not an alternative to competition.

At the competitive level, the Kota for instance use their skills in delivery and abortion, in rearing children and killing them, in keeping husbands and poisoning them, against the dominance of the male community as a whole. All these practices imply the use of a liberal amount of witchcraft, which ensures their hold over the men, who sometimes hit back with accusations of witchcraft.

I have introduced the Nyamwezi king as Kashindye, the sacred child of the royal matrilineage fertilized by the collective ancestors, represented by the royal drums. The royal drums are beaten at the seasonal and ad hoc royal rituals staged to reinforce the relation between the king and the royal ancestors, a relationship which ensures the fruition of the land and the people. But the king owns other, competitive, drums as well, notably the war-drum braced with human skin. Possession of the royal drums assures his status as the child of the spirits. The war-drum is beaten in his capacity of leader of the army, in protection of his land against intruders, in wars undertaken to gain more territory, in short, in his confrontations with other kings. He, or she, as many Nyamwezi kings were women, is a big man as well as a Kashindye. As long as the spirits form his ultimate legitimation, he is a sacred king, when they turn against him, what remains is a big man liable to witchcraft accusations. Like the leaders of sacrificial Ngoma who are also involved in various types of competition, the king is supposed to be a great witch.

Conclusion

My major criticism of Janzen's book on Ngoma is that, though advocating a definition of health as social reproduction, throughout his book he implicitly applies a much more restricted definition of health and healing, i.e. as therapeutics in the sense of 'fighting disease' and 'saving lives'. This form of healing, as practised in cults of affliction, functions in his book as model for metaphorical types of healing as practised in political Ngoma. Secular or performative Ngoma seem to fall outside the category of Ngoma altogether, being described in negative terms only, as derivations from the original context, which is the therapeutic one.

I have shown that the Proto Bantu reconstructions for 'health' and 'healing', which Janzen links to the Proto Bantu reconstruction for 'drum', *-goma*, do not have this therapeutic connotation as their primary meaning. These concepts, and their reflections in various Bantu languages, cover a much wider field of meaning which could be translated by '(bringing to) fruition'. Consequently, if these concepts could be linked to the PB reconstruction 'drum' at all, a possibility which remains purely speculative, they cannot pinpoint the use of the drum to an original therapeutic context. Thus, the idea that the cult of affliction is the model for Ngoma is a presupposition for which no convincing arguments are given. When this presupposition is given up, what remains to characterize Ngoma is the central place of ngoma, the public performance of drums and dance, shared by all Ngoma, both 'secular', and 'sacral'. The public performance of drums and dance is not restricted to the cult of affliction, or even to Ngoma, but is performed in the context of other types of social organization as well. It is exactly in this ubiquity of ngoma that Janzen's claim that ngoma transcends categories of kinship, politics, economy and religion is borne out.

Each culture has its own specific set of ngoma contexts, with its own complex history of mutual influence, appropriation and renewal. In his earlier work on Lemba, Janzen argued that the shared drum symbolism suggests that the distinctions between political types (centralized kingdom, chiefdom, shrine, drums of affliction like Lemba, lineage) are distinctions of degree and not of kind. This line of argument accords the drum its proper place at the centre of ngoma, and allows an unbiased approach to various types of Ngoma. It is this line of argument which is taken up and elaborated for the Nyamwezi case.

In Unyamwezi, ngoma is shared by the three major social institutions: kinship, Ngoma, and kingship. It forms the principle of social organization, the drum around which people unite and which proclaims their unity to the world around them. The drum is an artificial womb.

The Nyamwezi distinction between sacrificial Ngoma, on the one hand, and competitive Ngoma, on the other, reveals the presence of two ways of drumming, two ngoma, two ways of organizing, both of which are practised in the three major social institutions. The drum not only links these institutions, it also shows their internal dynamics, expressed and realized in two distinct forms of ngoma. The two ngoma construct two types of interrelation with the outside: one competitive, the other unificatory. Competitive drumming is the expression of and means to construct rivalry. Unificatory drumming is the expression of and means to construct unity, either new or renewed. In terms of dealing with adversity, or with life in general, the distinction is one between witchcraft and spirits, between accumulation and sacrifice. The comparison between the bride's body and the drum, and the more general image of the drum as female body, forms the clearest statement on the drum's capacities. Whereas the male body can only confront, the female body in addition is capable of enclosing.

Notes

1 Research was carried out in 1988–93 on a grant from the Netherlands Foundation for Tropical Research, The Hague. The subject of the research is the history of cults and religions in Tabora region. I stayed in Tanzania for some 18 months, mainly in Kanyenye village, Northeast of Tabora town. Some time was also spent in the archives of the White Fathers and Moravians in Tabora.

2 Milambo is usually referred to as Mirambo in the literature. As there is no 'r' in the Nyamwezi language, this is a variant of Milambo which probably stems from Swahili.

3 Seibt's manuscript mentions two famines during Milambo's rule, one around 1870, one around 1876 (Seibt 1910: 48, 81). The 1870 one would be the most likely context for this story, as it is mentioned in the story that the warriors died in the battles against the Ngoni. These battles were at their height then, just before a peace was made between Milambo and Mapangalala, the Ngoni leader, in 1870 (Seibt 1910: 48).

4 Lugaluga was the name for the soldiers of Milambo's standing army.

5 A strategy also applied by Milambo towards his own influential courtiers, see Blokland, 1985: 64ff.

6 There is no clear linguistic or cultural border between the Nyamwezi and Sukuma, and both terms are used in a variety of ways. Both names have been given to the people living on the plateau covering the greatest part of west Tanzania in the nineteenth century, and have been used mainly to suppress the idea that they would form one 'tribe', which numerically would be by far the greatest of the various peoples in Tanzania.

7 In the second chapter, in which Ngoma is identified both historically and comparatively, Janzen states that 'readers acquainted with African culture history will recognize the 'ngoma' region as

approximately that of the distribution of the Bantu languages' (1992: 57). I think there is limited evidence for a restriction to the cult of affliction or *ngoma* to the Bantu-speaking parts of Africa. The Zar cult (Boddy 1989) and the Bori (Masquelier 1994) form two examples of this type of cult outside the Bantu speaking area.

8 Other candidates would be: *-*gang*- L (Meeussen 1980: 18, 42: -*gang*- L: 'wrap up, bandage, heal'), -*cakud*- (ibid.: 22: *-*cakud*- 'heal, cure'; *-*cakud*- 'weed'); *-*pid*- (ibid.: 11: 'be healthy, well'), all concepts which transcend the narrow 'healing'. Cf. also Meeussen under 'cure', for more *tibu*-like PB reconstructions.

9 Or sex or hunting or war or delivery of a child or the hot season, to mention a few more states which are perceived to need cooling in many areas.

10 Janzen's characterization of the one membrane pegged drum as the 'ngoma-type drum', is pure speculation. Boone, on whom he seems to rely here (1992: 70), does not consider the tom-tom as drum, as it is not technically so, having no membrane (Boone 1951: 3). But doubtless most if not all of the composers of the various Bantu dictionaries, and wordlists used for Proto Bantu reconstructions, did not make a difference between drums (with membrane) and tom-toms (without), even if such a difference would have been made in the specific language, which is equally doubtful.

11 The song mocks another suitor of the bride, who comes too late. The bride is referred to as a bird and her body is called a drum, an image which will be explained below. The bride as bird is a frequently-used image for the mediating position of women, like birds mediate between heaven and earth.

12 The fathers of bride and groom are not the ones responsible for the brideprice. The final responsibility lies one generation higher, and depends on the type of marriage the parents of bride and groom have. If it is a brideprice marriage, it is the father's mother's brother who is responsible, if not, it is the mother's mother's brother.

13 During my stay in Kanyenye, I was often asked whether I had eaten mlenda, one of the 'typical' Nyamwezi dishes and a source of many jokes, because of its sexual connotations. Mlenda is slippery like semen.

14 The only difference for a kukwa-married women between her death in pregnancy (or another form of murder by the man) and another cause of death was that no brideprice was returned to the husband in the former case. If he were to insist on brideprice being paid back, he would become the victim of talion, or would be forced to pay the bloodprice (ibid.: 256).

15 The reader may already have noticed the similarities between the Puba and football competitions. The two are alike. Puba dancers like to wear football outfits. Football teams are known to use witchcraft against their opponents. When asked about the differences between Puba and Gika, I was told there were not any, that their differences were like those between two football teams. Alternatively, the differences were said to be like those between various Christian denominations.

16 The Sungusungu is not only found in an urban environment, it is very widely spread in the rural areas as well, but its history is somewhat different there, due to the absence of police.

17 As already mentioned, the maternal mortality rate of women is still very high in Sub-Saharan Africa. The Tanzanian data mentioned above are below the sad average for the whole region, an average of one out of thirteen women dying in pregnancy or delivery (The Progress of Nations 1996: 8ff & 52ff).

18 As intermarriage has created over the generations a stew of various 'types' of collective ancestors in all families, the right one has to be found. This is done by trying out rhythms on the afflicted. The diversity in sacrificial Ngoma reflects the diversity in origins of the Nyamwezi. Descendants from nineteenth century immigrants share the memory of common ancestry, e.g. the spirit of 'Bisaness', or of the Ngoni, the Rua, the Soonge, etc. Over the generations, these spirits become collective ancestors of more and more people. When one of these is afflicted by this spirit, all are threatened, and a ritual of initiation is performed.

Literature

Abrahams, R.G. (1967) *The Peoples of Greater Unyamwezi, Tanzania (Nyamwezi, Sukuma, Sumbwa, Kimbu, Konongo)*. London: International African Institute.

—— (1987) 'Sungusungu: Village Vigilante Groups in Tanzania'. *African Affairs* 86 (343): 176–96.

Beischer, N.A. and E.V. Mackay (1986) *Obstetrics and the Newborn. An Illustrated Textbook*. London, 2nd British edition.

Boddy, J. (1989) *Wombs and Alien Spirits. Women, Men, and the Zar Cult in Northern Sudan*. Wisconsin: University of Wisconsin Press.

Boone, O. (1951) *Les Tambours du Congo Belge et du Ruanda-Urundi*. Tervuren: Annales du Musée du Congo Belge.

Bösch, F. (1930) *Les Banyamwezi, Peuple de l'Afrique Orientale*. Münster: Bibliotheque Anthropos.

Carnochan, F.G. and H.C. Adamson (1936) *Out of Africa*. New York: Dodge.

Cory, H. (1944) 'Sukumu twin ceremonies – Mabasa.' *Tanganyika Notes and Records* (17): 34–43.

Dahl, E. (1915) *Nyamwesi-Wörterbuch*. Hamburg: L. Friedrichsen & Co.

Devisch, R. (1993) *Weaving the Threads of Life. The Khita Gyn-Eco-Logical Healing Cult Among the Yaka*. Chicago and London: The University of Chicago Press.

Dumont, L. (1979) *Homo Hierarchicus*. Paris: Gallimard, collection Tel.

Janzen, J.M. (1982) *Lemba 1650–1930: A Drum of Affliction in Africa and the New World*. New York: Garland.

——— (1992) *Ngoma. Discourses of Healing in Central and Southern Africa*. Berkeley, Los Angeles, Oxford: University of California Press.

Harms, R. (1983) 'Sustaining the System: Trading Towns along the Middle Zaire'. In Robertson, C.C. and M.A. Klein (eds) *Women and Slavery in Africa*, pp. 95–111. Wisconsin: Wisconsin University Press.

Johnson, F. (1978) *A Standard Swahili–English Dictionary*. Oxford: Oxford University Press.

——— (1989) *A Standard Swahili–English Dictionary*. Oxford: Oxford University Press.

Maganga, C. and T.C. Schadeberg (1992) *Kinyamwezi. Grammar, Texts, Vocabulary*. Köln: Rüdiger Köppen Verlag.

Masquelier, A. (1994) 'Lightning, death and the avenging spirits: Bori values in a Muslim world'. *Journal of Religion in Africa* XXIV (1): 2–51.

Meeussen, A.E. (1980) *Bantu Lexical Reconstructions*. Tervuren: Musée Royal de l'Afrique Centrale.

Ranger, T.O. (1975) *Dance and Society in Eastern Africa: The Beni Ngoma*. London: Heinemann.

Tcherkézoff, S. (1983) *Le Roi Nyamwezi, la Droite et la Gauche. Revision Comparative des Classifications Dualistes*. Paris: Cambridge University Press.

——— (1986) 'Les Amendes au Roi au Pays Nyamwezi. La Continuation du Sacrifice par d'Autres Moyens'. *Droit et Cultures*, 11: 89–111.

——— (1993) 'Une Hypothèse sur la Valeur de "Prix de la Fiancée" Nyamwezi'. In Heritier-Auge, F. and E. Copet-Rougier (eds) *Les Complexités de l'Alliance. Volume III: Economie, Politique et Fondements Symboliques (Afrique)*, pp. 51–80. Paris: Editions des Archives Contemporaines.

The Progress of Nations (1996) *The Progress of Nations. The Nations of the World Ranked According to their Achievements in Child Health, Nutrition, Education, Family Planning, and Progress for Women*. New York: Unicef.

Yongolo, N.D. (1953) *Maisha na Desturi za Wanyamwezi*. London: Sheldon Press.

Unpublished manuscripts

Blokland, H. (1985) 'Two Nyamwezi texts. an exercise in translation and understanding'. MA thesis, Leiden: Leiden University.

——— (forthcoming) *Drums and Sacred Power*. PhD thesis, Leiden: Leiden University.

Bösch, père F. (1946–1949) 'Die Banyamwezi. Manuscript in four parts; I. Religion, II. Magie, III. Recht, IV.Familienleben'. Tabora: White Fathers' Archives.

Seibt, A. (1910) 'Aus der Geschichte Ulyanhulus', MS. Herrnhut: Moravian Archives.

Welch, E. A. (1974) 'Life and Literature of the Sukuma in Tanzania, East Africa'. PhD thesis, Howard University, Washington DC; facsimile by University Microfilms International, Ann Arbor, Michigan, London, 1978.

3

Gender & Ngoma

The power of drums in eastern Zambia[1]

Annette Drews

Introduction

In *Ngoma*, Janzen (1992) demonstrates how ngoma as an institution contributes to the well-being of the community by enhancing the renewal and reproduction of social networks. Rituals of healing and transition, however, do not only restore the health of the ailing and ensure the socio-cultural stability of the community, but at the same time express, reflect and constitute basic contradictions found in a society – for example, the contradictions between women and men and between regional and national politics. Little attention has been paid so far to the discourse of ngoma in connection with the power relations which constitute society. I wish to address this omission by concentrating on ngoma as the locus of social contest, as the major battleground where the struggle between the sexes among the Kunda of eastern Zambia takes place. In this article I wish to emphasize the role of ngoma for the construction and manipulation of gender identities and relations. As well as being constituted and reflected in the discourse of ngoma, gender relations must also be for my argument, a description of the gender system and the conflicting gender discourses, together with, a brief outline of ngoma institutions within Kunda society, are indispensable. In order to demonstrate how the gender identity of women is attacked, redefined and invigorated within the realm of ngoma, I will explore one case which I encountered in the ritual performance of *chinamwali*, the female initiation ceremony among the Kunda. As the only accepted medium of academic communication is a written text, which by its very descriptive nature appears to emphasize the discursive elements of ngoma found in the initiation ceremony, this exploration does not do justice to the perceptual immediacy of the event where non-discursive elements of sound, touch and image prevail. Being aware of the serious theoretical and practical pitfalls of this discrepancy, justified only by our academic bias favouring written expressions, and being unable to choose a different medium, in which movement and the tactile can be represented (like a film, for example), I would like to draw the reader's attention to the inherent limitations of this article for the appreciation of ngoma as a specific cultural performance.[2]

The Kunda and their gender-system

The Kunda are a small matrilineal group who migrated at the end of the nineteenth century from the Congo basin to the Luangwa valley in the Eastern Province of Zambia. Among the Kunda, people from other, mainly matrilineal groups like the Chewa, the Nsenga and the Ngoni have also been incorporated. Their language, Chikunda, is almost exclusively used in ritual settings. Otherwise, the inhabitants of the Luangwa valley speak a local variant of the lingua franca of the region, Chinyanja. As subsistence farmers, the Kunda cultivate maize, beans, groundnuts, rice and sorghum. On an ideological level, they consider themselves hunters. Despite the diminished importance of hunting for the survival of the Kunda due to both general modernization processes and the management of natural resources by the National Park and Wildlife Services, men still hunt buffaloes, wild pigs and different kinds of antelope on a more or less regular basis.

The Kunda trace their descent through women. A child belongs to the clan of its mother and is under the authority of its mother's brother. On marriage, the groom moves to the homestead of his bride where he has to work for his in-laws in order to legitimize his marriage. After the initial uxorilocal residence of the couple, the parents of the wife may allow the son-in-law to take his wife home. In the valley approximately twenty-five per cent of the couples lives virilocally.

Gender relations are structured by two conflicting types of discourse. On the one hand, men and women are considered equal. They fulfil complementary tasks in society which are equally appreciated. Women are central because kinship is organized through them. As wives and mothers, women establish most of the relationships which constitute Kunda society. Women are prominent in the business of healing, in which they can acquire a high status. On the other hand, men are privileged with regard to highly valued political roles. They have more access to posts with formal authority. Within marriage, the man is considered the head of the household.

Age is highly respected among the Kunda, as in most African cultures. Within social relationships, age is the most important factor for the establishment of a hierarchy, generally overruling factors like gender, wealth or professional status.

Current gender relations have been influenced by colonization, modern capitalism and national politics in various specific ways. Ironically, institutions of colonial authority, the national state and mission churches, while strengthening the structural and ideological superiority of men, take away the actual bases of male power by reducing the political influence of individual men within their local communities. As a result, the position of women comes under a double attack. On the one hand, general concepts of gender symmetry and the centrality of women are undermined by the patriarchal ideologies of the modern institutions. And on the other, local men try, with the help of the ideologies of the 'big' institutions, to restrict female power in order to counterbalance their loss of authority within local politics. But women fight both patriarchal ideologies and their actual subordination in many ways. One area in which this struggle becomes especially prominent is ngoma. Contradictions in society 'are embodied in cultural forms and emerge in cultural performance' (Kratz 1988: 4). The tension between men and women unfolds in the contradictory gender discourse just as much as in the performance of ngoma.

Ngoma and power

Contradictions inherent in the Kunda gender system emerge in different cultural performances, like rituals of kingship, initiation rites and healing cults. In all these ceremonies, drums (ngoma) are used. Drums are associated with political, reproductive and healing power. Female gender identity is expressed and created in chinamwali, the girl's initiation ceremony, chitewera, a women's dance with ritual and diagnostic elements, and mashave, a possession cult. Male gender identity finds its expression in what Janzen calls 'political' ngoma, most especially in rituals of kingship and territorial cults. Whereas men have lost some of their power in local politics, their traditional domain of influence, due to the centralizing efforts of a modern national state, women still hold their positions in the area of reproduction and healing. It comes as no surprise that some men, especially those who lack status in the formal sector of employment and who have little power in the 'traditional scene' (through age or posts like headman, etc.), try to make up for their loss by claiming exclusive rights to what they consider the paraphernalia of power: the drums. In all ngoma institutions, with the exception of the female initiation ceremony where no men are allowed, men (mostly young men) play the drums, even when they are not in charge of the ritual as for example in mashawe or chitewera.

Power, gender and the struggle over drums

Terrritorial cults like the ones described by Schoffeleers (1979) where the use of drums was prominent belong to the past. Rain-making ceremonies have only been reinstated in times of severe drought, stimulated by the elders' remembrance. These days, political ngoma has almost lost its influence. In the centralized state of Zambia, as Janzen has said, ngoma cults have become 'less influential, or entirely absent, or transformed into the rituals of statecraft' (1992: 75). In the Luangwa valley, rituals of kingship were revived in the 1980s by the postcolonial government and the ruling party in order to gain the support of the Kunda. *Malaila*, as this ceremony is called, is held once a year, at the end of the dry season. It has turned into a spectacle – with drums, dancing, speeches and beer – in the presence of the paramount chieftainess and her advisers. Also on display are the lion's head and all the other symbols of ethnic unity and glory. The old stories of what the ceremony used to be, how it was held and why, are more numerous than the speakers who proudly tell them.

Beyond the mere politics of nostalgia and the celebration of ethnic unity, it has become a matter of wider national entertainment. The members of the television team sent from Lusaka, the capital of the country, are not interested in the stories that tell of local royal grandeur. What they are interested in is the gaiety of the masses, the beer, the colours and the drums which draw spectators on a national basis. Therefore, at the same time, through the spectacle, the power of the postcolonial state is represented as well. The drums symbolize power, political power, which is perceived to be enveloped and supervised by the state. By using the traditional structures of authority, enticing local chiefs and paramount chiefs into national politics and taking control of traditional rituals, the state secures and expands its power in the rural areas.

The concept of power is essential for the cultural construction of male identity. Men undergo several rituals, mostly to enhance their sexual powers. In the upbringing of boys considerable attention is given to the fact that they are supposed to hold authority in later life, not only with regard to their wives, sisters, children and nephews but also within their clan, village and region. Boys are trained to be leaders. As the Kunda recognize the cultural construction of gender roles, they allow the opposite sex to fulfil (most of) the gender-specific tasks if there are no other candidates. This does not mean, however, that a male task, like leadership, will become less 'masculine' if a woman happens to perform it.

Despite the fact that political ngoma in the Luangwa valley has been transformed into rituals of state formation which seem to foreground the political meaning of drums, drums have still not lost their power in therapeutic ngoma, the domain of women. While few domains of Kunda social life are gender-specific – with the notable exceptions of childbirth and hunting – women enjoy a clear predominance in the healing business. All healer/mediums I met in a period of five years of the mashave, a prominent therapeutic ngoma cult, were women. Central in the mashave is the transformation from sufferer to healer/medium, which is a career mostly followed by women. Women express their control of mashave by beating the drum and they also control other areas of Kunda life, such as female initiation ceremonies, where drums are essential.

The appropriation of drums in different domains hence signal a gendered area of contestation. Drums are about healing and personal transformation, associated with women, but also about the public domain of politics, the arena of male power. It is interesting to notice that although people acknowledge that there is political power and healing power within ngoma, the term *mphamvu* singularly stresses the notion of political power and male strength. The concept of power is associated with men and with their reproductive powers. Mphamvu is the Kunda word for (political) power, physical strength and semen. When women intend to be in charge of drums (as in the secret female initiation ceremony) they have to deal with the ambiguity of drums which express and constitute both healing *and* mphamvu, and a struggle for appropriation seems to take place. Men, on the other hand, seem less confronted by this ambiguous notion and profit from the unequal social power balances.

Gender relations are not only reflected in the discourse of ngoma but gender identities must be defended and redefined in actual struggles about the use of drums. The prohibition imposed by the Reformed Church, operating among the Kunda in the postcolonial setting, against the use of drums by women during the initiation ceremony, while allowing them to use the same drums during the church service, can be interpreted along these lines. Historically, the missionary prohibitions on traditional African institutions like chinamwali, ngoma (here referring to the Ngoni war dance also found among the Kunda) and mashave, did not immediately imply or generate a gender struggle. These prohibitions were first and foremost the result of the effort of the missionaries to purge the Native Churches of what they perceived as 'pagan' threats. Chinamwali and *nyau* (secret societies of Chewa men performing masked dances in association with initiation and other rituals, also found in the Luangwa valley) were banned by the Council of Congregations in 1903 together with all other practices linked to the 'veneration of spirits' (see Verstraelen-Gilhuis 1982: 79). As a cornerstone of social life, chinamwali, however, continued to be practised amongst Christians. 'The ceremony was held very far from the mission, so that the drums could not be heard,' a local source of those days revealed (see Verstraelen-Gilhuis 1982: 183). In order to 'avoid the bad things of chinamwali ' especially its 'pagan' roots, which found their expression in drumming, an effort was made to create a Christian substitution for chinamwali around the 1930s. The Christian ceremony was called *chilangizo* ('instruction'), a name which in the Luangwa valley only appears in official church documents. Otherwise people refer to the Christian initiation ceremony as *chinamwali chachikristu* (the Christian chinamwali). Its main characteristics are the *absence* of drums and the reading from church instruction books on family life, hymn-books and the Bible.

From the 1960s onwards there have been several attempts to review the existing rules concerning traditional ceremonies and the use of drums. It was felt that drums might have been bad in the past, but they may have since become purified. In response, the Reformed Church took a more liberal stance by saying that 'a Christian should not be found at a dance where there is beer or other bad things' (1964 Synod, see Verstraelen-Gilhuis 1982: 239), leaving quite some room for individual interpretation. The process of indigenization of mission churches, always accompanied by the fear of bringing back 'pagan' elements in church life, eventually resulted in the introduction of drums in church services.

In this perspective it may seem that the issue of drums is not primarily concerned with power relations between men and women. I intend to argue, however, that when men in line with the clergy refer to the 'danger of paganism' inherent in the use of drums during chinamwali, as is often heard nowadays among the Kunda, they intend to legitimize their desire to control women's access to social and spiritual power. The selective acceptance of drums (allowed during church services led by men, condemned by them during female initiation ceremonies where women are in charge) points in that direction. The 'purified' use of drums in church services, ('purified' in the sense that it is said to be free of any connection to the spirit world) may otherwise also have been conceivable in the context of chinamwali, but men resist the development of a perception along those lines. They rather maintain strong feelings against women using drums. This influences the views of the clergy who work among the Kunda, as the following case may show.

The secretary of one of the biggest Protestant churches in Zambia, who once visited the Luangwa valley, asked me about the drums he heard in the neighbourhood. I told him that the drumming came from a chinamwali ceremony. He got very agitated and said:

> They can go ahead. They can drum as much as they want. But if they think they can be bigger than men, they are mistaken. Once I heard an old woman tell that young girl behind the fence of the seclusion hut: 'Now you can handle any man.' That's too much! They have to stop that, otherwise we, I mean the church, will forbid this kind of activity.
>
> (Fieldnotes, August 1990)

'They can be bigger than men' is a rather free translation of the Nyanja expression the church official used: *Ngati afuna kudiaka pamutu pa wamuna* (If they want to step on the heads of men). While saying that, he was moving his hands as if he were beating the drums. At the same time he was holding his head low as if to avoid the claps coming from those hands beating the drums. Beating the drums, you draw on the powers of the ancestors and with that power you can 'step on the head of somebody', make him small and make yourself bigger. You are in control. This is what the old woman told the neophyte: 'Now you can handle any man.' According to the church official that was 'too much'. He felt threatened by the power of drums in the hands of women and expressed his desire to restrict that power by forbidding 'this kind of activity'. In saying so he reflected very similar opinions and attitudes which I was able to record from groups of men of different socio-economic backgrounds. The expression of this kind of sentiment clearly cuts across male class positions and their location in society. Some of them had completed primary school and found employment in the lower and middle segment within the formal sector of the Zambian economy (clerks, dressers, auxiliary teachers, the lower ranks within the police force, army, game guards).

I hope to have established that in the present gender system the issue of the drums, as it is discussed for instance in the context of the church in relation to a discourse of 'purity', becomes a subject of negotiation in the power struggle between men and women. While many men lost their traditional political areas of prestige and influence, due to the intrusion of the state, drums associated with such power are felt to be inappropriate in the hands of women. I am not claiming, however, that this contestation about the appropriation of drums is part of a *conscious* effort on the part of men to restrict women's access to power where personal and spiritual matters are concerned that signal transformation. The ritual exclusion of men in beating drums is crucial, but its interpretation is beyond the scope of the present contribution.   CAN'T INTERPRET EXCLUSION

Chinamwali as a ngoma ritual

On a symbolic level, the Kunda perceive chinamwali, the female initiation, as a healing rite. Menstruation, and especially the first menses, is considered a kind of sickness. A menstruating woman *wadwala* (is sick) and should, like any other sick person, be isolated from normal social life. A menstruating woman is not allowed to sleep with her husband or put salt in the relish. The idea is that the heat of her 'disease' will 'cut' others (cause them to be sick) through contact with the medium of salt or her blood (see Drews 1991, 1994, where I discuss Kunda disease aetiology in more detail). The heat makes her potentially dangerous to others and makes her at the same time more vulnerable to the sickening influence of other beings in 'colder' ritual states (like corpses). For a girl menstruating for the first time especially the latter point is emphasized. Her 'disease' calls for protection and ritual healing. She is so vulnerable that she needs to be secluded from village life. In the initiation-hut, the neophyte enacts the role of the patient. She can hardly walk, takes very small, shaky steps and needs to be supported by two women on either side. When she has to sit down these women help her. Seated, the girl looks extremely ill, near to death: her shoulders are sagging, her head is bowed, her eyes staring expressionless. The neophyte is not supposed to show any physical signs of reaction; smiling, laughing and speaking especially are forbidden. She is sick. She will stick to the role of patient during the whole period of seclusion and the day of the final celebration itself. She will only 'get better' after the rites inside the hut are over. Then she will change her cloth and after being led outside to the yard by her personal adviser, she will show her 'recovery' (or transformation) to the whole community by dancing for them. In the yard, her coming out, her healing and her transformation are celebrated with clapping and singing or preferably drumming when there are no church restrictions.

Through the symbolic link with disease and healing, chinamwali becomes a ngoma ritual as defined in the introduction of this book. Chinamwali is a way of articulating and commenting on the process of transition from childhood to adulthood and ritual transformation. It claims an authority based on a specific association and communication with the world of the ancestors through the performance of the traditional teachings of *miyambo* (see below). Furthermore, its power is embodied, expressed and effected in rhythm (drumming, singing, dancing).

The bringing about of healing in a proper healing ritual like mashave and the ritual transformation of the neophyte is intimately linked to the Kunda concept of disease aetiology. To the Kunda, most diseases are the result of a clash between different ritual temperatures. Different persons in different stages of their life cycles have different (ritual) temperatures, which also vary according to their activities. The activities that influence a person's temperature are mainly located in the area of reproduction. The basic concept is that people with a different temperature should not come into contact with one another via touch or the mediums of salt, blood or sexual fluids lest one of them will fall sick or even die. Sickness can be avoided by at least one person involved in the *mdulo*-contact ('cutting'- or injuring-contact, from *ku-dula*: to cut). When it comes to healing, the Kunda are not so much concerned to establish guilt in either the patient or the community, but rather to communicate norms of conduct through which the clash of different ritual temperatures is avoided. The moral responsibility for a mdulo-disease lies with either person that can or could avoid that clash – either the patient, or the one who causes sickness in others, or both. The communication of proper social behaviour through the performance of miyambo aims at the protection and healing of the patient and the community alike. As such, in ngoma, healing and ethics are two sides of the same coin. The healing and transformation of the 'sick' neophyte is effected through the ritual performance of certain miyambo which teach the girl (and at the same time the community) to protect herself or to protect the community from her own 'sickening' influences, such as selfish behaviour for example. The discourse of Kunda ethics is the discourse of health (individual and communal).

Chinamwali as female tradition and practice

Chinamwali or *chisungu*, the female initiation ceremony, is the most prominent institution among the Kunda concerned with the fruition of life. As there is no such ritual for boys, chinamwali is the only place where historical and cultural continuity is produced in a systematic, that is to say institutionalized, way. In chinamwali, the miyambo (plural of *mwambo*, customs or traditions) are handed down and reformulated in a most explicit way. Miyambo, however, are not taught discursively but performed and celebrated. Certain procedures, informed by received wisdom, are also called miyambo, like the little sketches with negative moral outcomes enacted by the participants of the chinamwali to instruct the young woman about proper behaviour. The participants in the chinamwali enact the situation that constitutes the mwambo. Mwambo in this sense is perceived as an act in which people engage either to strengthen the good course of life or to counteract its hazards by drawing creatively upon the received wisdom. Chinamwali serves to teach the initiate about the behaviour she is supposed to display as a grown-up woman and full member of her community. Yet, as Richards (1956) claims, the message is not new at all, not even to the neophyte. The instruction is more like a repetition. The repetitive nature of the ceremony, which marks at the same time the girls' transition from childhood to adulthood, is also expressed and emphasized by the beating of the drums, known to the girl from a time probably prior to her birth. Chinamwali functions to re-emphasize and recreate the social norms and moral knowledge for all participants. Teaching the neophyte springs from, and is directed at, the wisdom of the ancestors which constitutes and inheres in the mwambo. A mwambo is intimately linked to the explanation of the moral and to the rhythm and rhyme of the song which assists memory and intensifies the drama of the performance. As the core of moral knowledge in the Kunda society, the miyambo do not form a timeless, rigid system of encoded prescriptions for proper behaviour and evaluation but rather serve as 'the store of reference points from which a people, as individuals or as collectivity, judge their own predicament, their own conditions, themselves as persons' (James 1988: 145–6). As a store of reference points, miyambo function as a 'working fund' to which people continuously contribute as history moves on and upon whose heterogeneous (re-)sources they can draw to understand themselves. Through the performance of miyambo in the initiation ceremony, Kunda women can draw on the traditional value of gender equality in order to redefine their womanhood and strengthen their position *vis-à-vis* men.

Somewhere after her first menstruation, every girl has to undergo the initiation ritual which consists of three main parts. The first part is the seclusion. In the past, the girl was locked up for two to three months in a house where she was instructed on matters concerning family relations, sex, marriage, health, fertility and household activities. These days, the seclusion lasts for the period of a holiday, on average three weeks. The *ndola*, the neophyte, sits barely dressed with a ragged cloth around her hips on the floor with her eyes cast downwards, while the participants perform their teachings. The *anamkungwi*, the mistress of ceremony, orchestrates the different genres of teaching. There is dance, drumming, songs and little spots of drama. Often these genres mix.

Although the *phungu*, the personal adviser of the neophyte, has the task of explaining the message of a certain song or play to the ndola, all women can give their interpretation of the mwambo, the 'tradition', the teaching to the girl. Often this leads to a very lively discussion about norms and morals. After the period of seclusion, there is 'the big day.'

On a Saturday, all girls and women from the area gather to celebrate the final coming out of the neophyte. The morning is filled with dancing and singing. The drumming is felt to be essential because it establishes the relationship with the realm of the ancestors and the spirits from which all life springs and to where everything eventually will return. The powers of beyond manifest themselves in the beating of the drums, as in the beating of a heart. The experience of these powers emanating from the socio-cultural event of chinamwali effects the transformation process and legitimizes its performance. On hearing the drums, many girls and women volunteer to demonstrate their aptness to perform sexually provocative dances and also the ndola has to show what she learned in this respect during the time of her seclusion. A lot of songs and dramatized performances are then repeated in the presence of the mature, initiated women. This is also the time of the public humi-lation of the neophyte. If she has displayed anti-social behaviour in the past, people are asked to ventilate their complaints about her and the neophyte will be reproached in a harsh way, water will be thrown on the floor of the mud house, and she will be kicked in the mud by the other women. They will step on her, seemingly mercilessly, even kicking her in the face. After this symbolic killing, the neophyte will be helped to get up again and the party continues. Towards the end of this instruction period, some women, the 'outsiders', will be asked to leave the hut for the performance of the *mwambo wamkulu*, the ritualized seduction. The mwambo wamkulu, literally 'the great teaching' can be considered the core of the initiation ceremony. After the solemn instruction and celebration of the secret sexual techniques, only the phungu and the anamkungwi will stay with the neophyte. The other women gather outside in the yard, where also the men are waiting, for the final part of the chinamwali: the bringing out of the neophyte. The elders will come out dancing with the ndola covered with big pieces of cotton material. The ndola is then placed on a mat with her mother and the instructresses next to her. She is now said to 'be like her mother' and many speeches, especially from the male folk, follow. In former times, this was the moment of shaving, (which, by the way, is still done at the end of a mourning period or after the recovery of a serious disease). Today, shaving the 'healed' ndola is only remembered by putting scissors on her head. The visitors then have to bring their gifts, mainly money, to the girl and her teachers, which they place at their feet. This is also the moment when the girl gets new clothes from her father. While the audience is dancing, the girl will go and change and then dance for everybody in her new clothes. The chinamwali comes to an end with a *phwando*, beers and a big meal, for everybody.

Chinamwali and female gender identity

Before formulating abstract, and basically anthropological comments on the cultural practices of others, I would like to focus on what participants acknowledge as their ceremonial ends. According to the Kunda, chinamwali makes a girl 'like her mother.' As the girl has not given birth yet, this is an important statement about the gender identity of Kunda women. A girl becomes a woman, a mature member of her community, not through motherhood, as in many other cultures, but through her ability to be a wife, socially, practically and above all sexually. This perception of womanhood is in line with the general gender identity among horticulturist-hunter groups as outlined by Collier and Rosaldo:

> Women's rituals, by contrast, have much less to do with the creation of life than with health and sexual pleasure. It is not as mothers and nurturers that women win ritual status, but rather as sexual beings; cultural conceptions of women acknowledge their role as participants in the heterosexual relationships through which adults organize and manipulate mundane cooperative bonds.
> (1981: 276)

'In chinamwali we teach the girl how to please a man; how to be a good wife, and how to make a man enjoy sex with her,' an old woman once told me. On the one hand, this statement can be interpreted as an affirmation of women's subordination and servitude with regard to men. The construction of female gender identity as sexual beings and partners, however, emphasizes at the same time the complementarity of gender roles, women's centrality and the core value of reciprocity. After her 'coming out', the ndola is 'like her mother'. She has achieved her status not through procreation but through the proof she has given of her social and sexual abilities. She will contribute to the growth of society not through politics – which is ideologically the domain of men – but through the establishment of heterosexual relationships. She will gain access to male labour and goods important for herself, her matriclan and society at large through the successful handling of her sexual powers. By wearing the cloths of her father, the ndola acknowledges the role of men as providers. In chinamwali, the ndola 'earns' the father's cloths through the proof she has given of her social and sexual abilities, just as in later life she will earn a man's financial support through sex. In the West a woman loses status and respect through this kind of exchange because of the devaluation of the body (with regard to the higher qualities of the mind) and the negative moral connotations of female sexuality. Among the Kunda, however, a woman gains status through her sexuality. If she does her job well, she energizes her husband who will be motivated to work harder in order to please her and her relatives. Female sexuality is a source of pride and power which enables women to transform society through the establishment of alliances.

Although women use the power of drums to establish a positive gender identity and enhance their status in the community, especially within the female initiation ceremony, where men are excluded, chinamwali cannot be interpreted as an exclusive stronghold of female power. As in other cultural forms and events, chinamwali carries contradictory purposes and interpretations simultaneously. Contradictions between men and women, as well as contradictory norms and values inherent in the discontinuous gender discourses, are expressed and celebrated within chinamwali. The age hierarchy structuring women's relations among themselves is also articulated within the ritual performance of chinamwali, where only elderly women hold formal authority. The two conflicting gender discourses, one stressing female dependence, subordination and servitude, the other affirming women's autonomy, centrality and equality, are articulated at the same time within one ritual performance. The degree to which one or the other gender discourse contributes to the construction of female gender identity entirely depends on the performance. The message which is communicated evolves through the communication process itself (see Schipper 1983: 19). The actors, the miyambo, the tune and rhythm of the accompanying songs, the audience and the multiple interaction occurring between all the other communicative components constitute one whole: the communicative event (see Ben-Amos 1972: 10). The telling is the tale! And the tale is that there is a struggle within a struggle: the women's appropriation of the drum for the purpose of transition is in itself experienced in contradicting modes, in acts of communication filled with opposition and conflict. The following account of an initiation of a young woman named Lucy presents and explores this communicative struggle within the struggle.

Lucy's chinamwali

I chose Lucy's chinamwali, a Christian ceremony, as the basis for the present analysis, because of the clear articulation of the women's self-perception. The need for self-definition is intimately linked to the Christian character of the ceremony, as I will show later on. I will refer to Jeannette's chinamwali, a 'pagan' ceremony I observed at another occasion, mainly for reasons of contrast. Furthermore, comparing the two ceremonies, I will show *how* the context of Lucy's chinamwali and the performance of the actual *mwembos* shape and constitute its specific meaning and its communicative struggle.

At Lucy's chinamwali there were no drums allowed because Lucy's mother 'prayed with the Dutchies' (was a member of the Reformed Church of Zambia). As we saw, backed by official church doctrines, men tend to prohibit drums during female initiation ceremonies if the girl and her family belong to one of the Protestant mission churches (see also Verstraelen-Gilhuis, 1982: 181–9). Sometimes Protestant women ignore this church order. At other times, women accept the restriction and replace the drumming by clapping with their hands. In this case, however, they made sure, as we will see, that they defended their gender identity by drawing on traditional values affirming reciprocity and women's autonomy.

The reverend's wife came to the occasion and there was extensive Bible reading and praying before the actual ceremony could start. Hostility and resistance quickly grew, however, towards the patriarchal norms of female servitude and charity enforced by the church. Women felt that they had to defend their 'traditional' gender identity, which they felt was attacked on two counts. On the one hand they were not allowed to evoke the presence of the ancestors and spirits who give power and life to the transformational process of the ceremony. And, on the other, the church's one-sided emphasis on charity and female servitude was perceived to weaken the women's traditional gender identity where autonomy and reciprocity are equally appreciated as female qualities.

The participants at Lucy's chinamwali reacted towards this attack in a variety of ways. One of the most evident reactions was their rather unconventional performance of the sketch 'Smarty and the Fool'. In order to show how the women understood, defended and redefined their role as women in society I would like to describe the actual performance of 'Smarty and the Fool' during Lucy's chinamwali, analyse its content and interpret its impact for the construction of gender identity within the context of (denied) ngoma.

Setting and participants

The chinamwali always takes place on a Saturday morning, in the house of the ndola's parents. Together with my research assistant, Mary Ndhlovu, I went to Lucy's chinamwali on a hot Saturday morning in October 1990. As usual, the rather small hut offered far too little space for the numerous participants. Everybody tried to find a place next to the wall, leaving some space for dancing in the middle of the room. Doing the polite thing, most women sat down. The ones who only found a standing place, were rebuked for their lack of respect. One wall was reserved for the main actors of the ceremony: the initiate Lucy, a girl aged about fifteen years, and a middle-aged woman, the phungu. Phungu (literally teacher) and ndola were both seated on a mat.

Though all the miyambo are performed *for* the neophyte, she is not supposed to react in any visible way. The place of the main instructresses, the anamkungwi, was to the phungu's left. These two highly respected elderly women are the specialists of the chisungu. They lead the ceremony, sing, dance and act. Sometimes they delegate tasks to other participants. For this job they are paid by the initiate's family. The phungu 'translates' the teachings by explaining the moral of the instruction to Lucy. All participants are women: schoolgirls hardly older than Lucy but already initiated, young mothers with their babies on the back, middle-aged hard-working farmers and a few highly respected elders. Because of the lack of space only a few schoolgirls are allowed inside the house; their classmates are peeping through the windows.

Components of communication

Annotated translation of the recorded initiation song: 'Smarty and the Fool'.

Stella, one of the instructresses (namkungwi) suggests: Let's perform another mwambo (teaching/tradition)!

The women start clapping. Stella sings: I am going to the fool, mother!

The participants sing in unison: To the fool!

Stella, playing Smarty, sings: Yeah, I am going to the fool.

Everybody echoes: To the fool!

Stella: Perhaps we could cooperate a bit to sing nicely together? A participant: First, let's join forces!

Namkungwi Elisa: Yeah, they can do it for us right now!

Participant replies: But clapping is painful. My legs are numb.

Everybody laughs.

Stella sings: Yeah, I am going to the fool!

Everybody echoes: To the fool!

Stella appoints the other actors: This one and that one over there are playing. Now we need two more. Let's start, mummy, this is your child. Go over there! Mummy, please give me some salt.

The actress playing the mother of Smarty, says: There is none. Elisa is still sleeping. The hunger becomes worse, my child.

Smarty sings and dances towards the other actors: I am going to the fool, to the fool!

Smarty says: Hello, hello, darling!

Namkungwi Elisa, playing the fool, answers: Yeah, darling, you have come my friend!

The audience laughs about the fool.

Smarty: You, my darling!

The fool: Good morning!

Smarty: My mother sends me for sugar and bread, is that alright?

The fool: Here you are; sugar and bread for your mother to eat.

Smarty: What about coffee?

The fool: Here is the coffee and the chocolate. And this meat is also for your mother. Here is some corn flour, now go!

Smarty: Isn't this flour the one you bought a long time ago at Banda's shop?

The fool: No, do not worry, it is new one.

Smarty is satisfied. She dances home singing: I am coming from the fool!

The audience echoes: From the fool!

The song is repeated a few times.

Somebody from the audience remarks sarcastically: She made friendship with a thief!

Everybody laughs.

Mother Smarty: Oh, heaven, she is just coming, my child!

The fool sings and dances towards Smarty's house: I am going to Smarty today! To Smarty, I am going today.

Fool: Hello, hello, everybody!

When Smarty notices the fool's arrival, she immediately feigns sickness.

Smarty's mother: Come in, my love!

Smarty groans with pain: Oh, oh, eh, eh.

Smarty's mother: It is malaria! Since she left your house yesterday, she has not eaten anything. She is seriously ill.

The fool: My friend, what is wrong? You cannot even see me? You should go to the hospital.

Smarty's mother: But for heaven's sake, now they are charging money, ten Kwacha! Fifty Ngwee for a bed and ten Kwacha admittance.

The fool: You cannot ask her fifty Ngwee?

Smarty's mother: No, we are starving. How can you ask anything from your suffering chum?

Mother gets angry: How could she manage? Go, go away!

Mother chases the fool out of the house.

Smarty continues to simulate illness: Ai,ai, ai, have you seen my leg, mummy, mummy!

They laugh together about the fool.

The fool sings: I am coming from Smarty!

The audience repeats: From Smarty!

Smarty's mother: We have fooled her. We have not given her anything! Go and get some other things from her home!

Smarty: Yes, let me go and get it!

Smarty's mother: But will your friend believe you?

Smarty gets up like a drunk commenting on it: It is the dizziness. Yeah, it is because of the shock.

Smarty sings: I am going to the fool, yeah!

The audience echoes a few times: To the fool!

Smarty: Hello!

The fool: Yeah, hello, come in!

Smarty: What an attack of malaria when you came! This was really bad!

The fool: I have noticed, my friend, I have noticed!

Smarty: Malaria will finish this country. Well, my mother sends me for salt.

The fool: Yeah, yeah, your mother!

An old woman asks the phungu (personal adviser) to explain the moral to Lucy, the neophyte: You should tell her everything, so that she knows!

The phungu hesitates. Suddenly there is a lot of commotion.

The phungu shouts: Shut up, everybody!

The play is continued.

The fool: Here you are: salt! And this is the sugar. I give it to you so that your mother may eat from it. And the child of that mother should also eat well, yeah! There is nobody in the world I love as much as I love you, no!

Smarty: Mmmh, give it!

Everybody laughs.

Smarty dances towards her house singing: I am coming from the fool, yeah!

The audience repeats: From the fool!

Smarty comes home: Oh, mummy, it is true, it is real love that my friend showed to me!!

Here the play ends and the phungu starts to explain the moral: This is only their 'honeymoon', Lucy! Lucy, you got food from your friend's place, but when she comes, it is 'no', you just become shrewd, you refuse to give your nice things to her. . . .

Now everybody gives her own interpretation, all are talking at the same time. The phungu gets angry: If you all talk at once, you think that Lucy will hear anything? An elderly woman shouts back: Very much! With her ears she will hear!

Interpretation

The message, form and language

Several languages are spoken in the Luangwa valley in the Eastern Province of Zambia. Whereas in daily life Chinyanja, as a standardized lingua franca, becomes more and more important throughout Zambia, Chikunda, the language of the Kunda, prevails in rituals and ceremonies. Especially in the initiation songs, Chikunda is employed in its 'purest' form.

Within the communicative and ritual event different registers are used, however. First, the language of the play is colloquial: all languages spoken in the area are freely mixed, the speech resembles in almost every aspect the informal encounters 'outside' in daily life and there is less aesthetic surplus to be traced. Second, the style of the initiation song is highly poetic. The poetic use of language among the Kunda can be characterized by a communicative device called 'parallelism'. 'Parallelism' involves the repetition with systematic variation of phonic, grammatical, semantic or prosodic structures, the combination of invariant and variant elements in the construction of an utterance (see Jakobson 1970). It is generally agreed in the literature that such parallelism serves as a mnemonic aid to the performers (Lord 1960). Third, in the explanation of the plays the phungu speaks exclusively Chikunda, perhaps to emphasize the ceremonial character of her sayings. Non-vocal channels by which the message is 'conveyed' are the dances, facial expression, all the action of the play, and so forth.

The initiation songs are part of the vast body of oral literature defined by Mineke Schipper as 'the aesthetic use of the spoken word' (Schipper 1983: 18). The recorded and transcribed initiation song is related to the vast corpus of songs on the one hand and to dramatic performances on the other. These songs accompany most activities of Kunda daily life. There are songs associated with pounding, harvesting, worshipping and hunting. All major life events call for certain songs. Birth, initiation, marriage and death all have their specific songs. The majority of songs, however, are sung for sheer pleasure: children sing when playing, elders when drinking and relaxing, youngsters and adults when dancing. Songs are for leisure use. Most Kunda music is vocal music. The call-and-response form of songs is very common. Whenever possible, songs are accompanied by drums, clapping and stamping. Occasionally other instruments like beating sticks, whistles and bells are heard. The recorded initiation song is part of the corpus of Kunda songs as it shares common elements such as tune, rhythm, movements (clapping and dancing) and the call-and-response form.

On the other hand, the performance is differentiated from other songs by its emphasis on drama. Drama, which occasionally can also be part of folk narratives, is nowadays mainly a teaching genre. Apart from its use in initiation ceremonies, drama is performed during pre-marriage ceremonies, health talks and religious ceremonies.

The combination of song and drama as found in the described event, however, is unique for the kind of dramatic poetry used during the initiation ceremony. As a mwambo, 'Smarty and the Fool' is representative as it contains the proper song, accompanied by drums (at Lucy's chinamwali, clapping) and dance, the drama-play in-between and the moral of the teaching whispered afterwards in the ears of the neophyte. The term mwambo can be used in two ways: either to refer to a well-circumscribed genre or to the concept of tradition in general. Genres are culturally definable, traditional types of verbal communication (Enkvist 1973: 20). As a genre, mwambo contains the song, accompanied by drums and dance, the drama-play and the moral. The distinction, however, is not always clear. Some miyambo are performed without explanation, or like the mwambo wamkulu (the ritualized seduction) even without a song, drums, words or any sound whatsoever. Because the mwambo wamkulu is performed under circumstances similar to those of the other miyambo, it is both part of the teaching genre and of tradition in general. The ambiguity of the term mwambo is not entirely due to polysemy, but above all inherent in the subjectivity of context interpretation.

Context of perception

For the interpretation of the present initiation song, it is important to notice that the performance above all sets up a distinctive interpretative frame.

Because the material objects of the miyambo commonly used in 'pagan' intitiation ceremonies were missing at Lucy's *chisungu*, different communicative means were needed to 'key' the performances.[3] At the level of the initiation ceremony as a whole, meta-communication centred around special dances, beats and the use of religious language. The directives for the interpretation of the song were given in the announcement: *visango viakene*! which is the Nsenga-variant of *mwambo wina*! (Another teaching!). By naming the genre itself this formula can be taken as the marker of the miyambo. Money was not only offered to the dancers, the ndola, and her mother, but also to a church congregation. The wife of the local minister was present and a song from the Reformed hymnbook was sung. Together with some evaluative remarks from participants I perceived the differences between Lucy's and Jeannette's chisungu as indicating varying degrees of Christian influence on the ceremony. I will come back to this differences later on.

Norms of interpretation

In a mwambo one of the actors represents the initiate. During the act the 'initiate' displays the unwanted behaviour. In this case Lucy is identified with the fool by the audience. This is exactly what Drake (1976: 94), referring to the Chewa initiation ceremony of girls, called 'enacting the negative'.[4] Through the identification with the ridiculed fool, the initiate feels the shame put on such behaviour by the community. The lessons taught should reach further than an intellectual understanding only.

Ideally, the participants agree on the personage who is to 'enact the negative' and who simultaneously represents the neophyte. In Lucy's chisungu, however, this was not very clear. The fool's improper behaviour attracted most of the audience's attention, which they expressed by comments and laughter. The audience's reaction to the fool's behaviour anticipates their criticism of the possible 'foolish' behaviour of the neophyte in the future. The phungu, however, does not fully share the audience's and the actors' choice of the leading actress. This uncertainty is expressed by the phungu's identification of Lucy with Smarty: 'You got food from your friend's place, but when she comes it's "no".:.'!

Interpreters

The actors

The core of the mwambo is the song which focuses on the contrast between notions of brightness and stupidity. The actors at Lucy's chisungu choose to emphasize the naivety of the fool. This naivety is ridiculed by the use of irony. Remember Smarty saying to her mother: 'It's real love that my friend showed to me!' Smarty does not think it is love, but simply dullness. She echoes her friend's opinion who said: 'There is nobody in the world I love as much as I love you, no!' Naivety is also ridiculed by means of exaggeration. Smarty asks her friend whether she bought the maize flour a long time ago, indicating that she would only accept fresh flour. As this breach of the minimal rules of politeness is not met with indignation by the fool, it severely offends her dignity as a person. The shame of this loss of dignity is sharply felt by Lucy who is supposed to identify with the fool. Lucy was on the verge of tears.

But the condemnation of naivety is not the only perspective possible in this mwambo. During Jeannette's chisungu the actors stressed the wickedness of Smarty. In this case, Smarty, relying on her friend whenever necessary, refused to help her friend in need. Consequently, Smarty fell seriously ill. This performance evoked more explicitly the notion of illness causation prevalent among the Kunda. Illness and misfortune are thought to be primarily the consequence of one's own misbehaviour in any field, of life. The actors at Jeannette's chisungu drew the audience's attention to the connection between the violation of the principle of reciprocity and illness. In this case, Jeannette was told to identify with Smarty, inducing the fear of misfortune because of her 'own' selfishness. The identification as prescribed by the phungu is of vital importance for the understanding of the song.

The participants

The actions and reactions of the audience are an essential part of the performance. Their remarks, approval and disapproval are part of the message. At Lucy's chisungu they successfully contested the phungu's interpretation of the moral! The participants showed their adoration for Smarty's brightness in various ways: they were rejoicing with her whenever she achieved her goals, clapping hands, dancing and shouting enthusiastically. The audience also took great pleasure in the tricks Smarty used to fool her friend such as the simulation of malaria. The sarcastic remark about the fool 'making friendship with a thief' can be interpreted as another criticism of the fool. She is so dull that she even trusts somebody who only wants to exploit her. The contempt for the fool is expressed in various ways: especially by irony and scornful laughter. She is a despicable figure who does not get any chance of social rehabilitation. At Jeannette's chisungu, on the contrary, she eventually realizes the 'fraud' and chases her friend out of the house. Here, she is *chipusire* in the sense of 'still being ignorant'. At Lucy's chisungu she is the 'fool ever since'.

At Jeannette's ceremony, the participants were celebrating the mwambo, they were instructing the ndola, but at the same time they were reminding themselves of the origin of evil and misfortune.

The dancers at Lucy's chisungu were more clearly instructive. Passionately they were dramatizing their message. Teaching the moral, they were shouting their interpretations all at the same time. This performance was not just a negotiation of meaning but a real struggle of relevance. Here we may return to our original proposition which claimed that the women's appropriation of the drum is a contestation of male power, but that within the women's initiation, ritual internal struggles over meaning, influence and power take place. Women therefore need to defend themselves in a variety of ways, as will be highlighted in the following, final paragraph.

The women's defence

As most of the women perform this mwambo up to ten times a year and half of the actors were the same in both ceremonies, the differences in performances can hardly be due to failing memory. Differences, even essential ones, are inherent in the very nature of the mwambo as oral poetry. Bauman notes in this respect:

Every performance will have a unique and emerging aspect, depending on the distinctive circumstances at play within it. Events in these terms are not frozen, predetermined models for
performance but are themselves situated social accomplishments in which structures and conven-
tions may provide precedents and guidelines for the range of alternatives possible but the possibility of alternatives, the competence and goals of the participants and the emergent unfolding of
the event make for variability.

                                                                        (Bauman 1986: 4)

The interpretation of the mwambo by the actors is bound to textual features of the
song on the one hand and the actors' perception on the other hand. The ethical and
moral ambiguity towards cleverness and stupidity in Kunda society is expressed in a
song such as *kachenjedwe na chipusire* ('Smarty and Fool'), but also created by the very
performance of the song.

At Lucy's chisungu meaning was not only negotiated but actually struggled for. As
I perceived the main differences between Lucy's and Jeanette's ceremony as being
related to the degree of Christian and patriarchal influence on the initiation, I
interpret the struggle for meaning in that perspective.

Although Christianity was introduced to Eastern Zambia a long time ago, influencing deeply its social structures, culture and religion, its domination has never
remained uncontested. The substitution of a purified, Christian ceremony for a
'pagan' initiation rite, started around 1930, has not been a great success (Verstraelen-
Gilhuis 1982: 181–9). Sheridan (1980: 185), citing Foucault, reminds us that wherever
there is dominance, there is both subordination and resistance. The power relation is
constructed, maintained and transformed through discourse.

In the Christian ceremony women used the 'traditional' discourse of the mwambo
to defend their 'traditional' gender identity, stressing autonomy and 'toughness'.
Within this 'traditional' discourse women negotiate ethics, among other things.
Love, charity and generosity as advocated within a 'Christian' discourse are scorned
and ridiculed. 'Lucy, it's only the honeymoon,' the phungu told the initiate. My
research assistant explained this to me as follows: 'Generosity is but a sweet, short
illusion you cannot build on. It is reciprocity which is important'. Kunda women do
not hide their ethical judgement of generosity and naivety in the presence of the
church. They made their point very clear. They fought with a strong weapon, oral
poetry, using dance, rhythm, music, irony, sarcasm and exaggeration. Chipusire got
no chance of rehabilitation, she remained the fool for ever. The audience directed its
scorn relentlessly against her. The adoration of the cunning Smarty used to fool her
dull friend prevailed during the whole performance. Even the reverend's wife was
rejoicing in her tricks! This specific performance of 'Smarty and the Fool' recreates
the traditional value placed on prudence and mutual exchanges safeguarding
women especially from (male) exploitation. For this performance, the participants
could draw on the received wisdom as expressed also in the proverb *Chifundo
chinapha nkhwali* (Generosity has killed the francolin), which is derived from the fable
of the python and the francolin. A snake wanted to cross a river, but he failed to
swim. So he asked a passing francolin whether he could carry him across. In the first
place the francolin refused, but when he heard the python whining, he felt sorry and
changed his mind. When the francolin had taken the python to the other side of the
river, the francolin was eaten by the snake. The python, however, was not to be
blamed for the francolin's death. Generosity killed the francolin. In order to survive
you have to be cautious and you have to find ways to ensure that the services you
offer (to your friend, your husband or neighbours) are reciprocated. If you don't, you

are not 'a good wife' (as some husbands would have it) or 'a good Christian' (as the church would have it), you are just a fool who will have to pay for it dearly. The sin of the fool is not so much that she allowed herself to be exploited, but that she – at the same time – allows precious spiritual, emotional and material resources which also belong to the community to be simply drained. The mwambo and the proverb should serve as a shield against outside pressure to strengthen the woman's autonomy. The cure for 'sick' Lucy lies in her self-defence and protection. In Jeannette's chisungu, the neophyte will only recover if she gives up her wicked ways of exploiting others. This specific message finds its expression in another Kunda proverb: *Choipa chitsatha mwini wake* (Evil follows its owner).

The two occasions where the mwambo 'Smarty and the Fool' were performed emphasize two sides of the same coin: love and self-love. As reaction to the Christian character of Lucy's ceremony, which the participants perceived as weakening their position within the society, the women of Lucy's chinamwali emphasize self-love as the core moral of the mwambo. The participants of Jeannette's ceremony, however, less bound to 'gender ethics', highlight the message of love and respect through their performance. Love and self-love, however, are intimately linked.

With the objective of making women more self-confident in how and where they draw their own social and moral boundaries and those of others, striving for female autonomy in the Kunda version is ultimately based on the altruistic goal of transforming the world into a better place for all (see Schrijvers 1994: 7). Will Lucy understand that message? According to a participant she surely will: 'With her ears she will hear!'

Conclusion

With reference to the performance of the mwambo (dramatized instruction) 'Smarty and the Fool' during Lucy's chinamwali, A Christian female initiation ceremony, it was shown how the Kunda of Eastern Zambia construct and manipulate gender identities in the context of ngoma. As the Kunda perceive the neophyte as 'sick' and in need of ritual healing, chinamwali, the subsequent rite of initiation, can be considered a ngoma ritual. Contradictions in society like those between men and women and national and regional politics are reflected, created and manipulated in ritual performances like ngoma. Drums through which the communication with the ancestors and the powers of the beyond are effected play an important role in chinamwali. Therefore it can be expected that the prohibition of drums as required by the church for their followers will have an effect on the way women understand the world (norms, values, power relations) and themselves (gender identity) and how they express their interpretation of the given situation through the actual performance. In this respect, it is important to notice that the prohibition of the drums through the church also has a bearing on the struggle between the sexes. The interest of (some) men in enforcing church orders and hence limiting women's access to spiritual and emotional power through ngoma can be linked to the process of marginalization which many men experience as a loss of their traditional sphere of influence. In defence, women might feel a greater need to articulate a gender-identity stressing autonomy in a ceremony without drums. For the purpose of contrast and full appreciation of the elements influencing Lucy's chinamwali, the message of a performance of 'Smarty and the Fool' during a 'pagan' initiation ceremony was also described. As expected, the 'pagan' ceremony paid less attention to gender issues, and instead concentrated on general ethics, as expressed in the rejection of selfishness, and on the origins of evil and misfortune.

In order to understand the position which the participating women took in the 'Christian' initiation through their particular performance of 'Smarty and the Fool', a rough outline of the Kunda gender system was given. The relationship between men and women among the Kunda is structured by two conflicting types of discourse, one stressing male superiority and female servitude, more in line with the 'Christian' discourse as practised in Zambia today, the other affirming gender symmetry and female autonomy. Which discourse is articulated, how and by whom is highly context-dependent. In Lucy's chinamwali, through the performance of 'Smarty and the Fool', women established their identity as bright, knowledgable and autonomous. In this part of the ritual they defended and recreated social and moral values of reciprocity and mutual dependence as opposed to charity and one-sided female servitude, thus enhancing sound social relationships among women and among the sexes. For the cure of the neophyte (and the community), the participants of chinamwali brewed a medicine which responded to the specific needs of the parties involved. The healing was effected through the performance of the mwambo, the yeast of their medicine. Drums are a vital element in effective ritual performance, but in their absence the believers can still have access to their powers by singing, clapping and dancing. As I hope to have demonstrated in this article, it is the performance itself rather than the drums which embodies, expresses and effects the power of ngoma.

I would like to emphasize that this chapter on chinamwali among the Kunda should be understood as a contribution to Janzen's attempt to describe and analyze ngoma institutions rather than as a critique. As he admits (Janzen, 1992: 3), the field of scholarship relating to healing in community settings in Central and Southern Africa is not well defined. In addition, there are innumerable conceivable perspectives on ngoma institutions. Therefore, it would be unfair to criticize Janzen for the choices he made, which led him to concentrate on the health restoring and community-stabilizing functions of ngoma. In order to balance this view of ngoma, I have tried to demonstrate how the basic contradictions found in a society – such as those between women and men and between church norms and 'traditional' ethics – are expressed and shaped within a ngoma-like ritual. The performance of the initiation song 'Smarty and the Fool' during Lucy's chinamwali expresses and at the same time aggravates the antagonism between the sexes rather than enhancing the stability of the community. Furthermore, the performance, although – or maybe because – it is the Christian version of the ritual, emphasizes the more 'traditional' – as opposed to Christian – norms concerning the role of women. As such, the performance marks opposition between rather than reconciliation of conflicting segments of the Kunda society. The interpretation of Kunda female initiation presented in this chapter should broaden our understanding of ngoma as a possible locus of social contest.

Although the present study was carried out along different methodological guidelines, it can be compared to Janzen's Chapter 4 (1992) where he describes and analyses a single ngoma session in depth. The centrality of song to ngoma – claimed by Janzen for the 'washing of the beads', a ngoma ritual in the Western Cape –

is also apparent in chinamwali. The analysis of the interpretations offered for the same song during two initiation ceremonies, as attempted in this study, confirms Janzen's conclusion that the variations in communicative structures of ngoma provide important clues to the understanding of the institution.

Notes

1 This article is based on fieldnotes, recordings and transcriptions from the author's fieldwork in Kamoto, Eastern Province of Zambia from March 1989 until January 1993, financed by the Netherlands Foundation for the Advancement of Tropical Research (WOTRO). Part of the argument with respect to the Kunda gender system is developed in the author's doctoral thesis *Words and Silence: Communication about Pregnancy and Birth among the Kunda of Zambia* (1995).
2 For a discussion of the scientific analysis of orality and ritual performance, see Kersenboom 1995.
3 Goffman's term 'keying of performance' refers to the process by which frames, including performances, are invoked and shifted (Goffman 1974).
4 Drake (1976: 94) states in this respect the following:

> There is a certain ambiguity in the *chinamwali* rituals. Ostensibly the neophyte learns that she should not do certain things. But in the instructions for teaching these rules, the emphasis in the drama is a negative expression of positive ideals: instead of showing a monogamous situation, it shows a girl with many boyfriends. The tenor of the ceremony is to embrace that which it preaches against.

Literature

Bauman, R. (1986) *Story, Performance and Event: Contextual Studies of Oral Narrative*. Cambridge: Cambridge University Press.
Ben-Amos, D. (1972) 'Toward a Definition of Folklore in Context'. In A. Paredes and R. Bauman (eds), *Toward New Perspectives in Folklore*. Austin and London: University of Texas Press.
Collier, J. and M. Z. Rosaldo (1981) 'Politics and Gender in Simple Societies'. In S.B. Ortner and H. Whitehead (eds), *Sexual Meanings: the Cultural construction of Gender and Sexuality*, pp. 275–329. Cambridge: Cambridge University press.
Doke, C.M. (1872) *Bantu Linguistic Terminology*. London: Longmans, Green & Co.
Drake, M.A. (1976) 'Illness, Ritual and Social Relations among the Chewa of Central Africa.' Unpublished PhD thesis, Duke University.
Drews, A. (1991) '"In de borst gesneden": Een taalpragmatische benadering van ziekteverklaringen bij de Kunda in Oost-Zambia'. *Medische Antropologie*, 3 (1): 85–96.
—— (1994) 'The Sense(s) of Suffering. Social Relationships and Khombola: Illness among the Kunda of Zambia'. *Medische Antropologie*, 6 (1): 52–60.
—— (1995) *Words and Silence: Communication about Pregnancy and Birth among the Kunda of Zambia*. Amsterdam: Het Spinhuis.
Enkvist, N.E (1973) *Linguistic Stylistics*. The Hague: Mouton.
Finnegan, R. (1970) *Oral Literature in Africa*. Oxford: Clarendon Press.
—— (1977) *Oral Poetry in Africa. Its Nature, Significance and Social Context*. Cambridge: Cambridge University Press.
Goffman, E. (1974) *Frame Analysis: an Essay on the Organization of Experience*. New York: Harper and Row.
Jakobson, R. von (1970) *Poesie und Sprachstrauktur: Zwei Grundsätz Erklärungen*. Zürich: Die Arche.
James, W. (1988) *The Listening Ebony: Moral Knowledge, Religion and Power among the Uduk of Sudan*. Oxford: Clarendon Press.
Janzen, J.M. (1992) *Ngoma: Discourses of Healing in Central and Southern Africa*. Berkeley and Los Angeles: University of California Press.
Kersenboom, S. (1995) *Word, Sound, Image: The Life of the Tamil Text*. Oxford: Berg Publishers.
Kratz, C.A. (1988) *Emotional Power and Significant Movement: Womanly Transformation in Okiek Initiation*. Unpublished PhD thesis. Austin: The University of Texas.
Lord, A.B. (1960) *The Singer of Tales*. Cambridge, Mass.: Harvard University Press.

Richards, A. (1956) *Chisungu: a Girl's Initiation Ceremony Among the Bemba of Northern Rhodesia*. London: Faber and Faber.

Salaun, N. (1969) *Chinyanja Chichewa: Intensive Course*. Lilongwe: Likuni Press and Publishing House.

Schipper, M. (1983) *Afrikaanse letterkunde*. Utrecht: Spectrum.

Schoffeleers, J.M. (1979) 'The Chisumphi and Mbona cults in Malawi: a Comparative History'. In J.M. Schoffeleers (ed.), *Guardians of the Land: Essays on Central African territorial Cults*. Gwelo: Mambo Press, pp.147–87.

Schrijvers, J. (1994) 'Reflections on Reproduction; a Feminist-inspired Research Approach'. Paper presented at the Manila Workshop of the Collaborative Project on Gender, Reproductive Health and Population Policies , 7–10 April 1994.

Scott, D.C. and A. Hetherwick (1929) *Dictionary of the Nyanja Language* (various reprints). London: Lutterworth Press.

Sheridan, A. (1980) *Michel Foucault: the Will to Truth*. New York: Tavistock Publications.

Sperber, D and D.Wilson (1986) *Relevance: Communication and Cognition*. Cambridge, Mass: Harvard University Press.

van Leeuwen, T.M. (1981) *The Surplus of Meaning: Ontology and Eschatology in the Philosophy of Paul Ricoeur*. Amsterdam: Rodopi.

Verstraelen-Gilhuis, G. (1982) *From Dutch Mission Church to Reformed Church in Zambia*. Franeker: Wever.

4

The 'Wounded Healer' as Ideology

The work of ngoma in Swaziland

Ria Reis

Introduction

When Janzen's book *Ngoma* was published, it seemed to answer my search for a perspective on Southern African healing that would take seriously its historical depth and its spread beyond local, national and ethnic boundaries. In my research on medical plurality and epilepsy in Swaziland (Reis 1994, 1996), I had come to the conclusion that a description of Swazi traditional medicine as a 'local' tradition not only unjustly devalues the Swazi discourse on healing, but also serves Western biomedicine's expansionistic tendencies.

The need for more insight into local perceptions and practices is often formulated in relation to communication problems or in the context of educational programmes. Its aim may be the preservation of the traditional healers' important roles in their local community (cf. Green and Makhubu 1984: 1074; Green 1987: 93), which in the light of Swaziland's rich oral medical tradition is an applaudable aim indeed. However, the question is why 'modern' health care officials would be interested in local perceptions, while they seem already unable to cope with general and well-known traditional ideas and practices concerning illness and healing in Southern Africa. Most officials in the field of medicine in this region are probably well aware of notions of witchcraft and evil medicine, or of the role of ancestors in healing. Therefore, it is difficult to believe that efforts to communicate or cooperate with healers are hampered mainly by lack of knowledge. The construction of Swazi traditional medicine as a local tradition conceals the fact that in general health care policy makers simply do not wish to take traditional perceptions and practices as the starting point for their dealings with traditional medicine.

In this context, a focus on the regionality of Southern African perceptions and practices, as it emerged in religious anthropology from the late 1970s and in medical anthropology from the 1980s onward, may be interpreted as an emancipation of African medical traditions.[1] For me, Janzen's book *Ngoma* was especially welcome, since he partly founds his thesis on data from Swaziland. I was exhilarated reading his description of these data as among his 'best full accounts of ngoma' (Janzen 1992: 8).

In his book the term *ngoma* stands for a discourse on misfortune and healing connected with an institution which is, among other things, characterized by the fact that the healers who constitute and produce ngoma through their practices have become part of it through a transformation of someone who suffers into someone who heals. Illness and misfortune are characteristically interpreted in terms of problems in human relationships, and healing results in a fundamentally different relationship with the interhuman and superhuman world. Ngoma's central feature is the *ngoma* song-dance, the performance context ' within which the meaning of individual lives, among the *ngoma* practitioners, is articulated and where these individuals are urged to create a song of their own. It is through this creative and musical process, through doing *ngoma*, that the healing transformation is realized' (Janzen 1992: xii, 86, 128, 174).

Eliade called this type of healer the *'wounded healer'* (Eliade 1951, see Eliade 1959: 195–6). Swazi diviners, *tangoma* (sg. *sangoma*) in siSwati, certainly fall within this category. Experiencing a serious illness later divined as being sent by the ancestors is the core of all autobiographies produced by healers in response to the question of how one becomes a sangoma. However, despite my admiration for Janzen's thesis, his presentation of data on Swazi healing left me dissatisfied. In this chapter I will maintain that his description of Swazi ngoma does not do justice to Swazi traditional medicine in several respects.

I will argue that the core of ngoma in Swaziland is not the reproduction of the institution, but the discourse on suffering and healing produced in clinical encounters of healers with lay patients. This discourse centres on evil which is added to the body and has to be expelled. I will maintain that by concentrating on tangoma and the wounded healer complex, Janzen overlooks the characteristic multi-dimensionality of the Swazi discourse on healing, its simultaneous interpretation of illness in material, social and political terms.

Janzen pays no attention to an important diagnostic ritual of Swazi *tangoma*, called *ukuvumisa*, in which ancestral power – the power to diagnose evil and its causes impartially – is realized through trance. This ritual belies his thesis that trance is not essential to ngoma other than as its legitimation. If 'doing ngoma' denotes the transformation process of sufferer into healer, I would like to put forward 'the work of ngoma' as a designation for the diagnostic and curative process through which lay patients are purified of harmful substances and dangerous spirits.

The difference between these two aspects of Swazi ngoma, between the 'doing of ngoma' and the 'work of ngoma', and the relation between them will be illustrated by describing a Swazi healing ritual which is indeed also mentioned by Janzen, the *femba*. As I will maintain, the femba forms part of a widespread Southern African idiom of possession by foreign spirits, which came into being in the first decades of this century and which, following Ngubane (1977), may be interpreted as a reaction to historical processes of social and cultural fragmentation. The transformation of illness caused by foreign spirits into healing capacities of tangoma represents and deals with these processes. As such the ritual is an excellent example of Janzen's concept of 'doing ngoma'. However, in the actual performance of the ritual the powers inherent in the 'wounded healer' complex are employed to identify and expel evil forces causing illness and misfortune in the lives of lay people. In this process tangoma sustain as well as comment upon changing social relationships. The wounded healer complex, that is the complex of ideas pertaining to ancestor illness in chosen people and the transformation of sufferer into healer, authorizes this micro-political work.

The 'work of ngoma' is effected as well as ideologically underpinned by the 'doing of ngoma'. For only the impartial can be trusted with diagnosing evil within the community. Having 'done ngoma' – having proved to have been accepted and empowered by the ancestors – testifies to this impartiality.

The argument will be substantiated by my own research data. My fieldwork in Swaziland took place between June 1987 and November 1988, but I had lived in Swaziland since August 1985. My investigations formed part of a combined medical/medical-anthropological research project focused on people's quest for healing epilepsy in a situation of medical pluralism. The study focused on Swazi perceptions and practices concerning illness and healing, specifically epilepsy, and tried to suggest alternative strategies for Western health care policies to improve the situation of people with epilepsy.

Although healers' and lay people's experiences with epilepsy formed the central subject of my investigations – I have reported on these elsewhere – this article deals with a more general level of perceptions and practices related to illness and healing. My data are derived, among other things, from my contacts with traditional tangoma training centres in the North of Swaziland, and more specifically from the healing rituals which I attended.

Illness in three dimensions

Although Janzen's region-wide project certainly encompasses a larger area than my study, which was limited to Swaziland, within this local context my subject seems to have been the more encompassing one. After all, Janzen is only interested in healers producing ngoma. However, if the Swazi traditional discourse on illness and healing is to be described, another type of healer has to be taken into account: the herbalist, called *lugedla* or *inyanga yemitsi* (specialist in medicines) in siSwati. This type of healer receives his medical knowledge through a learning process. Although he needs the support of his ancestors to become a successful healer, he is not chosen by them. Usually a herbalist has no history of an ancestor calling in the form of a serious illness, nor one of transformation through initiation. Therefore, herbalists do not fall within the category of 'wounded healers'. On the face of it Janzen seems right to exclude herbalism from the discourse on suffering and healing denoted by the term ngoma.

On the other hand, herbalists and diviners do not produce separate discourses on illness and healing, but contribute in different ways to what may be called a Swazi discourse on illness and healing. While Janzen describes *ngoma* as explaining illness in terms of problems in human relationships, the Swazi discourse is dominated by a perception of illness as originating from the interaction with a dangerous natural and social environment. Ngubane's description of Zulu concepts of illness (1977, 1986) applies to the Swazi as well. People fall ill by contact with traces and tracks of living entities (plants, animals, people), with traces of medicines left in the atmosphere after treatment, or with harmful substances which are therapeutically removed from a patient. These tracks and traces are as dangerous as the mixtures of herbal, animal, and sometimes human substances which are concocted and manipulated by witches and sorcerers. Naturalistic and personalistic concepts of causality are often inextricably intertwined. An explanation of illness in terms of problems in human relationships more often than not implies a concept of evil substances added to the body.

All this concerns illness and misfortune at the micro-level, that is, in the lives of individual people and their immediate social environment. There is a third dimension to the Swazi discourse on illness, however. Nationwide suffering, for instance in epidemics, disaster or drought, may be interpreted in terms of social disharmony or the breach of moral rules. This national interpretative dimension is closely connected with the theme of Swazi sacred kingship, in which the well-being of the Swazi king and the well-being and fertility of nation and land are deeply connected.[2] I will not go into this here. Suffice it to say that in the dominant interpretative idiom of illness and healing political, moral and substantial aspects of illness are intertwined.

Berglund's description of Zulu thought patterns applies to the Swazi as well. According to Berglund the Zulu acknowledge a concept of power (siZulu: *amandla*) inherent in material. He contrasts this concept with two other notions of power: power inherent in people as members of a patrilineage, i.e. the powers originating from the ancestors; and power derived from God (Berglund 1976: 248). If the concept of God is perceived as an ultimate form of the power of the king as it is embedded in the royal ancestors of the nation, this description closely fits the Swazi three-dimensional image of human illness and suffering.[3]

It is herbalists who have the most specialized knowledge of the working of powers inherent in material – I prefer to speak of substantial powers – and on how to deal with them. It is tangoma who embody the powers of the ancestors to fight these powers. However, tangoma healing practices cannot be described without taking this 'substantial dimension' of Swazi perceptions of illness and healing into account. For one thing, most diviners also practice some herbalism, the knowledge of which they claim to derive from the ancestors. Secondly, ancestors are seldom divined as the cause of illness, even if the symptoms point to the possibility of such a diagnosis. Seizures, for instance, are among the class of possible signs of an ancestor calling. I interviewed 164 people with epilepsy and/or their caretakers. They reported 172 visits to traditional healers. Only seven of these visits (4 per cent) led to a diagnosis of ancestor-illness and the advice to undergo *kutfwasa*, the training for sangoma. In 75 contacts (44 per cent) the diagnosis was spirit possession caused by evil medicine. If this is added to the 15 diagnoses of contagion by the fumes of traditional medication, it comes as no surprise that in most cases the therapy provided was aimed not at a transformation of patient into healer, but at the expulsion of harmful substances from the body.[4]

Although the autobiographical narratives of Swazi tangoma are dominated by the transformation of sufferer into healer, in their own healing practices the power of the ancestors which they embody is used to counter substantial powers which have entered their patients. Janzen's 'doing ngoma' describes how tangoma become what they are; it doesn't describe their work as healers. If in Swaziland 'doing ngoma' involves self-transformation, 'the work of ngoma' should be conceived of in terms of diagnosing, and purifying people of, substantial powers added to the body.

Communicating with ancestors: Ukuvumisa

If we concentrate on tangoma healing practices, we face another problem with Janzen's description of Swazi ngoma. Janzen is inclined to hope, in the conclusion of his book, that his perspective on ngoma may help to overcome the trance and possession definition of this type of cult of affliction. He sees the so-called 'spirit hypothesis' mainly as a framework that sets up and legitimizes the institution. Fixation upon trance hinders the analysis of the context, structure, history, intent and change in the institution (Janzen 1992: 176–7). In line with this, Janzen argues that among Swazi diviners 'trance' in divination is a relatively recent phenomenon, and that their divining practices need considerable training (and are therefore not 'really' mediumistic, as he seems to imply) (Janzen 1992: 48).

However, he only refers to *pengula* (bonethrowing) and *kufemba*, the diagnostic and therapeutic ritual during which the diviner is possessed by a foreign spirit, even suggesting some sort of historical progression from the former to the latter. Yet all diviners I spoke to agreed that the core of Swazi divinership is a healing ritual called *ukuvumisa*, in which a *sangoma* is typically possessed by ancestors. Hilda Kuper has described this ritual in Swaziland, for example in her rather famous play on witch-craft accusations *A Witch in my Heart* (Kuper 1970: 46–52). Even Makhubu, who is quoted by Janzen to prove his point, describes trance as part of divination practices (Makhubu 1978: 38).

Janzen's Swazi ethnographic data seem to be based mainly on contacts with one school of tangoma during, as may be concluded from his description, a rather limited period. This school is established in a more urbanized area than the tangoma training centres I had contacts with in the northern part of the country. It could be argued that what Janzen describes is simply a specific manifestation of a more general discourse. However, in his introduction he argues, as I mentioned before, that his experiences in Swaziland and in South Africa provided him with the *'best full accounts of Ngoma'* and he also maintains that this may be explained by the fact that the institutions in these areas' *may represent a more generic manifestation'* (Janzen 1992: 8). But how is it decided which elements are 'generic', and which are not? On the basis of a comparison of my own data on Swazi traditional healing and the literature, I believe Janzen claims central status for what may be described as idiosyncratic manifestations of Swazi divinership.

In Swazi divination the power of the ancestors is demonstrated in the healer's knowledge of things which remain hidden from common people. Being consulted to find out the causes of illness or misfortune, the ancestors perform their diag-nostic labour in different ways. For one thing a sangoma has her ancestors with her all the time. They whisper in her ears and may give diagnostic indications during or even before the first encounter with the client. Most tangoma know the art of bonethrowing, a divinatory technique in which the ancestors control the pattern in which the bones fall, and direct the sangoma's interpretation. Some diviners may give diagnostic medicine to patients who are suspected to be possessed by evil spirits, so that these spirits will be forced to make themselves known. Patients with epilepsy who were submitted to this trial recalled fright-ening hallucinations.

Trance is not necessary for any of these divinatory methods. In fact healers who do not claim to be chosen by ancestors, such as herbalists, may also make use of them. Diagnosis through ukuvumisa, however, is reserved for tangoma. This ritual is valued as more effective than other diagnostic techniques. For in ukuvumisa (*kuvuma*= agree, confess) the diviner is possessed by an ancestor who will start a conversation with a patient. This conversation is of a specific character, since it is the diviner who should tell the patient his or her symptoms and not the other way around. A diviner who needs to be told the patient's symptoms is not truly possessed by an ancestor. Therefore, the sangoma is the active party in the diagnostic ritual. In trance she names the symptoms of the patient. The patient will admit to these in chorus with the other people present. That is, every pronouncement of the healer will be met with a loud *'siyavuma'*: we agree, indeed!

The following extract from my field notes gives an impression of the diagnostic process in ukuvumisa. This particular session involved a patient who suffered from several physical and social problems.

The *sangoma* covers her shoulders with a black cloth. Noisily she inhales the fumes of the herbs which she heats over live coal. She growls and talks to herself, but suddenly she sets up a cry at a high-pitched voice: the ancestor has arrived. Then she starts a song at which all those present join in: 'The stars are playing with animal bones'. It is astonishing to see her gentle appearance change into that of a severe looking man. Slowly the diviner dresses herself in the attire and jewellery which belong to this specific ancestor, and which had been hanging among other cloths on a rope tightened between two sides of the round ancestor hut. With an impressive headdress of feathers, a spear and a cowtail staff the metamorphosis is complete. In front of us, a wild warrior takes the floor. But then he suddenly claps his hands and kneels.
Diviner: 'I am greeting all you people in this room. My name is Malunge Dlamini.'
They all politely acknowledge him. He starts another song: 'Let him divine', and while the spectators join in he takes a big leap towards the patient and greets her.
Diviner: 'Now you must listen carefully, so that you will not say: "I didn't understand". Let us start with your feet. Your feet are swelling, and they are also itching as if there is something pinching you like a needle.'
The patient and all others present say *'siyavuma, siyavuma'*, we agree, we agree. (This chorus will be repeated after every sentence.)
D.: 'Sometimes your feet become very hot.' Chorus. D.: 'And then even your kidneys are hurting'. Chorus. D.: 'When you feel pain in the kidneys it comes up to your heart and you feel palpitations. After that you don't like food. Sometimes when you eat you feel like your womb is also paining, and there is moving inside. And you feel like vomiting.'
   Now the diviner waits a little, while the patient hastily agrees to everything which the ancestor has said. D.: 'You feel the pain in your chest, sharp pain in your chest. Even at night you do not sleep well. At the hospital they even suspect TB. Then your heart goes down and down, and you do not want to talk to people. You feel like seeing no one, to be alone. And this goes up to your head.' Chorus.
D.: 'And sometimes you feel headaches. If it is severe you touch your temples. If you push there the headache will stop. Then you don't feel like being with other people. You want to be alone.' Chorus. D.: 'Sometimes you feel a big weight on your shoulders. If you go to the Zionists they might say you are going to have the Holy Spirit but it is not. Sometimes your breasts are itching. And you cannot sleep at night.
The patient loudly agrees to everything and adds that sometimes she would even take sleeping pills.
D.: 'When you sleep at night your dreams are very bad. You dream being in a dark forest. You dream staying with people who are long dead. That is why you do not sleep well at night. If you are sitting down on a mat you are moving around, sitting then this way then that way.'
Chorus.

At this stage the sangoma, still in trance, started prescribing remedies for the ailments that had been described: medicine to drink so that her womb would be purified and medicines to swallow and vomit to clear her head. No direct reference was made to a specific disease, nor to specific causal factors. The sangoma told me later that it was clear that the woman was suffering from sorcery, but that the ancestors didn't want her to tell the patient. Naming the evildoers would only cause further suffering; it would not serve healing at all.

A written account of such diagnostic conversations do not show the essential contribution of the patient and his or her party to the success of the diagnostic process. In ukuvumisa clues are offered in the manner in which people answer 'siyavuma'. By reading these clues, healers sense if they are on the right track. These clues pertain to the tone and raising of voice, as well as to nonverbal expressions of agreement or denial. Janzen is right to point out that sensitivity to these consciously or unconsciously given clues is developed by training. This is done by hiding articles for novices which they have to discover while in trance by performing ukuvumisa. I have observed how neophytes are helped by the exaggerated vocal and facial expressions of spectators while they formally agree to anything the novice says. This doesn't necessarily mean that there is no expectation of clairvoyance, but it certainly has to be brought out by training. This was made particularly clear to me by an incident which I unintentionally caused myself.

> During the final ceremonies of a *sangoma* initiation I was asked by Make Mdluli, an accomplished *sangoma*, to hide some article for one of the neophytes. She promised to do the conversation with the possessing ancestor spirit. I hid a handkerchief in my blouse, but then reconsidered and hid the article in my sleeve. My change of mind, however, was not observed by Make Mdluli. She called a neophyte in trance, who knelt in front of me, and who started giving indications. Mother Mdluli agreed to everything that she said. After some time the neophyte rather violently searched my blouse, at which I started, took out the handkerchief from my sleeve and explained: 'No! It was later hidden here'. The novice snatched her trophy out of my hands and I was scolded by Make Mdluli: 'You have been cheating!' Because she thought the handkerchief to be in my blouse, she had unwittingly misled the neophyte.

However, this aspect of training cannot be taken as proof of a culture-specific 'bridging of the apparent distinction between spirit possession and the learned skills of apprenticeship', or more specifically as evidence of 'structural comparability with divination without trance', as Janzen maintains (Janzen 1992: 49). This could indeed be concluded for any mediumistic trance. It is generally accepted in the ethnography of trance that mediums have to learn how to handle the powers of the spirits possessing them.[5]

Contrary to Janzen, I maintain that trance is a core feature of Swazi divinership. It testifies to the source of healing power of the diviner, but it also realizes this power. As the testimony of what Janzen calls the 'spirit hypothesis', trance legitimizes the work of ngoma; but it is also through trance that this work is done. In ukuvumisa, healing power entails the power to diagnose illness and, if necessary, to point at its human source. If trance had disappeared from the healing practices of Swazi healers, the work of ngoma would have disappeared from Swaziland. In the setting of ukuvumisa trance is an aspect of healing sine qua non.

Communicating with enemies: kufemba

Ancestral powers enable healers to point out and counter evil. However, in the ukuvumisa ritual from which I quoted, the diagnosis offered was rather vague. While the diviner explained this by referring to the wishes of her ancestors, this may also be explained by the fact that diagnoses of evildoing are in fact punishable by law.

Before Swaziland became a British protectorate ukuvumisa was not the ultimate divinatory method. If someone was seriously suspected of being a witch – for instance, if a diviner had pointed at someone as guilty of another person's death – a chief could order *umhlahlo*, a public seance. He would assign several healers to this task. The whole community would be compelled to attend the ritual, and if all diviners pointed to the same person this man or woman would be put to death immediately, unless he or she escaped in time to seek asylum at the queen's kraal (Kuper 1961: 167–8; Marwick 1966: 246). However, at the end of the nineteenth century the colonial regime issued a law which prohibited the execution of criminals by the traditional authorities, and which also made witchcraft accusations punishable by law.[6]

This has changed the position of diviners fundamentally. Rituals publicly exposing and punishing witches and sorcerers are not possible any more. In fact the social embeddedness of divinatory practices has been taken away from tangoma. As far as evildoing is concerned their diagnoses through ukuvumisa can no longer lead to effective counteraction. If the aim of this colonial intervention was to separate healing power and political power, it was certainly successful. The tangoma have lost their key role in processes of social control: they have lost their power to order and reorder social relations. They themselves, and their activities based upon ancestral power, have been declared illegitimate.

Relatively recently, however, a new divinatory method has emerged in Swazi divination which, like umhlahlo, is employed mainly when evildoing is suspected. This ritual is called femba. Kufemba (the verbal form of femba) means 'to sniff' and 'to divine', 'smell out' (as a diviner) (Rycroft 1981).[7] Makhubu, who as far as I know was the first to report on this divinatory method in the context of Swazi traditional healing, describes diviners who make use of it as a specific type: umfembi (Makhubu 1978: 5, 23).[8] Her observation may well have been correct at the time when this ritual started its advance in Swazi divination, and when it was experienced as a new development. Nowadays the femba has become as common among diviners as it has become popular among lay people. A decade after Makhubu's publication, Gort (1987: 113–21) described the femba as the most precise diagnostic technique which is available for tangoma in general. In my own research, healers practising the femba did not come to the fore as a specific type. The point seems to be that any diviner may practise the femba only if she happens to have among her spirits the specific type needed for it.[9]

In the femba the sangoma is possessed, not by the spirit of an ancestor, but by the spirit of an enemy slain by the ancestors. Such a spirit is called lindzawe (pl. emandzawe). It is not clear how the presence of such a spirit manifests itself in a novice. In Makhubu's experience the career of a healer who practises the femba has not by definition started with a serious illness (Makhubu 1978: 23). All diviners I met, however, professed to have suffered from an ancestor illness. They told me that a lindzawe usually manifests itself as just one of the many others that make an appearance during the training process of a diviner. But sometimes its manifestations may be among the first signs of an ancestor calling. Healers told me that certain types of epileptic seizure may be interpreted as the presence of a lindzawe. During the training these seizures should disappear. Accepting the spirit and giving it a chance to manifest itself removes the need for it to cause further suffering.

The femba is unique in that the possessing spirit will locate evil spirits in the body of the patient by smelling them out, and will remove them from the patient by inhaling them into the body of the diviner. For a short while the evil spirit will take over the body of the diviner, so that the patient directly faces his or her enemy. The sangoma who performs the ritual functions as a medium not only for the spirit of an ancestor victim, but also for the enemies of the patient. The following excerpt quotes from a femba for a female patient whose only child had died at toddler age and who suffered from secondary infertility since. Recently she had lost her job as well.

Beneath a black cloth the sangoma softly speaks with her spirits. Before that she had warned the people in the hut: 'I'm the only one who speaks.' Therefore all attention is directed to the diviner, who loudly inhales the fumes of medicines which help her to open up to the spirits. We are startled when she suddenly claps her hands over the fire and says: 'Please open up everything to me so that nothing remains hidden.' She tells the patient to sit down in the middle of the hut with her back to the ancestor shrine, facing the door. She is told to uncover herself from her waist upwards. At the doorpost on her right hand side a gourd with honey water is placed, at the doorpost on her left hand side a plate with medicine. The mother and the diviner's assistant smear her with the sweet water at those bodily areas which are considered 'open': fingertips, earlobes, toes, breasts, back and sides of the body. The honey will attract the spirits.

The atmosphere in the ancestor hut is relaxed: there is chatting and laughing. Now and then the diviner coughs and growls, but nobody pays attention. Then the sangoma casually greets the spectators and they acknowledge the spirit which has obviously arrived. This spirit will not introduce himself. Since he is a slain enemy of the ancestors his status is much lower than that of an ancestor spirit.

The diviner starts a song in Shangani, which is the native group of the spirit. Here the audience start shaking cans filled with stones on the rhythm of the song. Then the sangoma rushes to the left doorpost, hovers over the plate with medicines and growls with a deep voice. She dips a small tassel of cow hair in the medicines. Then she wipes it under her nose and starts sneezing violently. With her deep voice she starts humming a melody, and all others join in. She dives at the patient who waits quietly in the middle of the room and moves the tassel with speed over the body of the patient. With tremendous speed over and over again something is wiped from the body to her nose, which is then noisily inhaled. Starting at the patient's feet she systematically wipes her way upwards: until she reaches a spot where she meets an evil spirit.

When this happens she drops her tassel and with great emphasis touches the spot with both hands. With the power of the *lindzawe* the evil spirit has been inhaled into the body of the diviner and now speaks through her mouth. From her high pitched voice and her affected bearing it seems we are meeting a lady here.

Diviner: 'Greetings.' Patient: 'Greetings.' D.: 'How are you?' P.: 'I am fine, but who are you?' D: 'What are you going to do, that you ask me: who are you? I won't tell you.' P.: 'You must tell me who you are.' D.: 'I won't tell you, I am leaving now.'

The diviner pulls the patient's hair with both hands and after that her earlobes, she shakes the patient's shoulders, pulls every one of her fingers and toes and then the evil spirit leaves the body of the diviner. The foreign spirit takes over again and the whole cycle is repeated, starting with the inhaling of medicines at the doorpost and the wiping of the patient's body.

The second evil spirit is a man, who greets the patient angrily.

D.: 'Do you feel that your breasts are itching?' P.: 'Yes, they are.' D.: 'It is us who are breastfeeding at your nipples. You are proud, if we meet you at the road, if we want to talk to you along the way, you refuse to talk to us.' P.: 'But you have been found today.' D.: 'But we will come back again.' P.: 'No, you will never!' D.: 'We will meet again.'

In this way eleven spirits appear and are removed from the patient, each one from another part of her body. Two more are presented here:

A woman spirit has entered the diviner and greets the patient. D.: 'Why are your hands itching?' P.: 'I know they are itching.' D.: 'You think that someone is going to write you a letter, but it is not like that, it is me. Could you please give me some money?' P.: I don't have any money, why don't you go and look for a job?' D.: 'I want money from you.' P.: 'No one is working for another person, everybody works for himself, so I won't give you any money.'

Without replying the diviner stretches the body of the patient and this evil spirit leaves too. Now a lady spirit shows herself. The spectators laugh because she is obviously walking on high heels. She speaks siZulu.

P.: 'Why do you pretend to be a Zulu?' D.: 'You are snobbish, you think you are better than me, you wish to know everything.' P.: 'Yes, I am better than you.' D. (clapping her hands): 'Where are they coming from, all these nice people. They look nice, they look like people that are living in houses with electricity!' P.: 'Yes, and they are even better than you. Who are you anyway?' D.: 'I am in a hurry to go to the bank.' And she stretches the patient and leaves with greetings.

Although sometimes *tilwane* (animal spirits sent to a victim with the help of evil medicine) are smelled out, i.e. in this episode all the evil spirits which were diagnosed and expelled presented themselves as people with malicious intents. None of them was actually called by its name, although the patient later told me that she had recognized several people near to her. Gort (1987: 119) attended more than twenty femba rituals at one healer's homestead, during which one or more evildoers were always identified. The evil spirit would mention the reason why he or she took possession of the patient (for instance, jealousy of the patient's wealth). The spectators would start shouting names, until the sangoma would acknowledge a name, after which this evildoer, embodied by the diviner, would be forced out of the ancestor room.

More specific research on the Swazi femba probably would yield more differences and idiosyncratic forms, but I believe the femba can be described by its core features of the involvement of a foreign spirit in healing, the functioning of the diviner as a medium for the evil spirits located in the patient, and the therapeutic aim to expel these spirits.

The transformation of a foreign spirit

The colonial laws which made witchcraft accusations liable for punishment are considered very unjust by those Swazi who believe evildoing to be a reality. Since these laws have come into being, witches and sorcerers cannot be fought by legal means. If ancestors diagnose witches, it has become impossible to confront them. According to many this is why there are many more evildoers at present: they have nothing to fear. The prohibition of the public seance caused a serious gap in the effectiveness of Swazi traditional healing.

Even if the femba points out specific culprits, this does not distinguish it from other divinatory practices. Any divination may lead to the naming of an evildoer. But even if no culprit is named, the femba partly fills the gap which was created by the prohibition of umhlahlo. Patients and their parties are enabled to name the causes of illness themselves, since they may recognize their enemies in the manifestations in the body of the diviner. Also, in contrast with ukuvumisa, but in accordance with umhlahlo, the femba answers the need to confront the enemy, maybe not as large as life, but certainly as a substantial being. It is not an ancestor who diagnoses evil: evil may be seen with one's own eyes, and may be spoken with. In some way it answers the need of riposting aggression, just as this was the case in umhlahlo. Kufemba not only diagnoses, but also effects a cure. The ritual removes the evil spirits.

Indeed the femba could be interpreted not as a transformation of medical practices into something completely new, but as an old practice which is created anew within restrictive socio-legal structures. On the other hand the emergence and popularity of the ritual among Swazi diviners may also be explained by its capacity to provide symbolic answers to structural changes in society. If we follow this lead, we may take a look at the region-wide idiom of possession by foreign spirits which emerged in Southern Africa during the first decades of the twentieth century.

For the concept in femba of a foreign spirit that manifests itself in the diviner, and which may assist in divination, is not unique in the Southern African context. It has some likeness to phenomena of epidemic spirit possession specifically among the Zulu, for instance *ufufunyane*, possession by a mass of foreign spirits caused by evil medicine concocted from cemetery earth. That also goes for *indiki*, i.e. *amandawe*, which involves the spirits of men for whom no funeral rites have been performed to unite them with their ancestors, the fate of many labour migrants in Southern Africa (van Nieuwenhuijsen 1974: 12; Ngubane 1977: 144; Hammond-Tooke 1986: 162–4). According to Hammond-Tooke the Shona *shave* spirits may be considered to belong to this idiom as well. As against the lindzawe which will assist the sangoma in healing, the treatment of indiki and ufufunyane is through expulsion of the spirit. Someone who has been healed of indiki will try to replace it by an ancestor spirit (Ngubane 1977: 142–4). However, Ngubane mentions that in a victim belonging to a healing church the indiki may in fact strengthen healing power. Van Nieuwenhuijsen (1974: 12–15) mentions that some of his informants among the Nyuswa Zulu believed that an indiki will protect its victim after treatment. In relation to the powers of foreign spirits the notion of expulsion seems to be rather ambivalent. In any case, healing of epidemic possession is accomplished, in line with Turner's 'cults of affliction' and Janzen's ngoma, by an initiation in a sisterhood of healers, who may heal others who have fallen victim to the same type of spirits.

Ngubane interprets this type of possession as an expression of the social disorder in South African society (1977: 147). In this line she also interprets the Swazi femba (quoted in Janzen 1992: 49). She argues that the Swazi pacific character (in contrast to that of their Zulu brethren), is reflected in their divination rituals which use – in considerate memory of those they killed in former wars – slain enemy spirits. I agree that it is plausible that the incorporation of foreign spirits among healing ancestor spirits in Swazi divination is a culture specific transformation of a typical Southern African idiom of epidemic possession. The phenomenon of *emandzawe* spirits causing seizures in neophytes and their transformation into healing spirits therefore can be fully understood within the contours of the discourse on misfortune and healing which Janzen coined ngoma.

Kufemba: The work of ngoma

In Swazi traditional healing possession by a lindzawe is healed through training for divinership, just as in the cases of ufufunyane and indiki. However, the foreign spirit in the Swazi femba does not assist in treating people who have become possessed by the same type of spirit. The femba heals people of evil caused by living human beings. The patient treated through kufemba is not initiated to divinership.

Kufemba resembles umhlahlo in that it is simultaneously diagnostic and thera-peutic, and that its aim is the smelling out and expulsion of evil. But umhlahlo would be ordered by a chief. The classical anti-social witch involved in the traditional witch-smelling seance would represent problems in the field of jealousy in structurally tense relationships, such as between co-wives, or about cattle and territory (see Gort 1987: 121). Umhlahlo pointed to evildoers who would threaten the safe structures of society. Problems were solved by physically eliminating the witch, thereby purifying the community. The femba, on the contrary, represents the victim as successful but vulnerable, surrounded by enemies. The problem is solved by the purification of the victim. There is no action upon the community.

The concept of a living person possessing his victim as an evil spirit does come close to the classic Swazi concept of the witch who with psychic powers can attack from a distance. Neighbours sucking at the breasts of their victim remind us of the image of the witch who steals his victim's life power (*umoya*, breath). However, the image of the witch produced in the femba is more ambivalent than the witch which was expelled through umhlahlo. In the femba a person is not sick because of the one witch in the community, but because of the jealousy of many of his neighbours. Expelled from the body they may be met as living persons the next day. Evil in kufemba seems to be located somewhere between the witch and evil medicine.

It is only appropriate that the femba is performed not by an ancestor, but by a marginal spirit, the spirit of a slain enemy. Ancestors represent society's order, in the same way as umhlahlo affirmed and strengthened the social order. In the femba there is no return to a stable order of society. It is rather the individual who is supported in his efforts to escape from this order. The surrounding community is depicted as full of jealous people. Healing activities do not surrender individuals to the needs of the community here. In the femba, social relations are sacrificed to foster individual growth. The marginality of the lindzawe could be interpreted as a reflection of the marginality of the individual in a new social order.

Unlike umhlahlo, kufemba cannot enforce the reordering of social relationships. Diagnosed evil cannot be physically controlled. But the fact remains that like umhlahlo it points out evil within the community, even if this evil is not the same as that confronted in the past. While in umhlahlo the impartiality of such an important diagnosis was guaranteed by the involvement of more than one wounded healer – that is, by the involvement of a group of ancestor spirits – in the femba this equity is ensured by the fact that the diagnosing spirit is a slain enemy, a stranger who is above local parties by definition (see Spierenburg, Chapter 5 in this volume). As such the femba does redress the colonially induced break between the healing of illness and the reordering of social relations which was effected by the prohibition of umhlahlo. The fact that the evil which is pointed out in the femba is tuned to modern developments in Swazi society only underlines this point of resemblance. When social relations change, the dangers threatening these relations change.

The wounded healer as ideology

Janzen maintains that the transformation of someone who suffers into someone who heals is central to ngoma. In Swaziland healing through transformation is indeed a core feature of biographies of initiated tangoma. The incorporation of foreign spirits as part of such a transformation demonstrates how the explanation of individual suffering may reflect and express problematic social processes and how it may be transformed to the advantage of society.

It is also clear, however, that this core is found in autobiographical accounts of other healer types such as of the Swazi healers reported by Gort (1989), the 'transitional' healers actually practising herbalism but claiming to be tangoma, and 'modern' healers combining traditional and modern therapeutics. Similarly prophets of African healing churches speak of serious suffering as sign and commencement of their vocation. The recurrence of the theme of the 'wounded healer' among such diverse types of healing alerts us to the meaning and function of the theme in relation to healing as such.

The fact that self-transformation is a core feature in the biographies of diviners does not imply that it is the core feature of healing activities in Swaziland. Within Swazi traditional medicine healing by transformation is reserved for a few chosen ones. Restricting the Swazi discourse on suffering and healing to the dramatics of the 'wounded healer' would devalue the important role of tangoma in society. In their diagnostic and therapeutic activities diviners expel and protect against evil forces and dangerous influences originating from the human or the non-human world. Both ukuvumisa and kufemba demonstrate how the ideology of the 'wounded healer' is used in a battle against this surrounding evil. The moral purity attained by the sangoma through her ancestrally inspired self-transformation is the touchstone of the evil she diagnoses. This is particularly clear in the femba, since the healer temporarily serves as a medium for the evil spirits that possess the patient. Only a morally pure person is sure to recognize evil as an alien element. Only a pure person may embody and expel evil without negative consequences for themselves.

For those who consult diviners as patients, a history of ancestor illness testifies to the true calling and legitimacy of these healers. Such a history testifies to the involuntariness of divinership. It clears healers of selfish motives, such as greed for power or money. It is necessary to have suffered a serious illness to be able to claim that one's healing power originates from the ancestors. Suffering certainly is a lived reality for diviners, but as sign of a calling it is also an ideology.

The literature and my own ethnographic data give cause to perceive the 'wounded healer' complex as an ideology, in the neutral meaning of the phrase: as a complex of ideas at the basis of a philosophical system pertaining to certain social and political relations. Accounts of personal suffering and salvation through transformation legitimize as well as giving effect to a certain type of healing power. In kufemba this power pertains to the diagnosis of a modern evil, namely jealousy, aimed at a person who has successfully adapted to modern goals of individual advancement. As such 'the work of ngoma' sustains the fundamental changes in social relations that are taking place in Swaziland.

Notes

1 Schoffeleers 1979; Janzen 1992; Ngubane 1981; Ranger 1993; van Binsbergen 1994.
2 See, for a key publication on this theme, Schoffeleers 1979; for Swazi sacred kingship Stevens 1967: 192; for the role of the king in procuring fertility of the land Van Binsbergen 1981: 123.
3 It is rather surprising that there is no reference to Berglund's important publication in Janzen's book, since this publication is the first full description of the Zulu wounded healer complex.
4 Explanations offered by traditional healers:
   no explanation – 27 (16%); cause unknown – 9 (5%); falling illness – 25 (15%); 'just an illness' – 5 (3%); heredity, pregnancy etc. – 4 (2%); contagion by traditional medicines – 9 (5%); evildoing – 75 (44%); ancestor calling – 7 (4%); snake in the stomach – 8 (5%); other – 3 (2%); total – 172 (100%).
5 Leacock and Leacock (1975: 171–3) describe such a learning process in the Afro-Brazilian Batuque cult, and confess that it took them some time to accept that controlled trance behaviour is the most convincing. I believe this to be true for Swazi tangoma as well. Experienced tangoma will smile over the sometimes not very impressive divination efforts of neophytes, calling them 'children' but never doubting the presence of the ancestors in them.
6 Crimes Act 1989, No. 6, Statutes of Swaziland, Ch. 4.
7 And not 'to possess' as Janzen (1992: 37) claims.
8 A decade earlier Polanah (1967a, b) described the ritual as the diagnostic method of a certain type of traditional healer (nhamusoro) in the south of Mozambique, thereby affirming the suggestion that the femba has been adopted by Swazi diviners from their Mozambican neighbours.

9 Janzen (1992: 38) maintains that healers who practise the femba accept the title sangoma, but that the technically correct name for them is *takoza*. Moreover, such healers would differ from common tangoma by a specific hairdo: oiled and ochred 'dreadlocks'. However, according to the healers I spoke with, *thokoza* (in official siSwati *(ku)tfokota* means to be happy) is the way one addresses the spirit who performs the femba, that is the smelling out. Also, the hairdo is the usual one for Swazi and Zulu tangoma when they receive the ancestors (cf. Kuper 1961: 164). In his monograph on Zulu thought patterns Berglund explains the meaning of it extensively (Berglund 1976: 131–4).

Literature

Berglund, A.I. (1976) *Zulu Thought-Patterns and Symbolism*. London: C. Hurst & Co.

Eliade, M. (1951) *Le Chamanisme et les techniques archaïques de l'extase*. Paris: Payot.

—— (1959) *The Sacred and the Profane. The Nature of Religion*. New York, London: Harcourt Brace Jovanovich.

Gort, E. (1987) 'Changing Traditional Medicine in Rural Swaziland. A World Systems Analysis', PhD thesis. Columbia University.

(1989) 'Changing Traditional Medicine in Rural Swaziland; the Effects of the Global System'. *Social Science and Medicine* 29(9): 1099–104.

Green, E.C. (1987) 'The Integration of Modern and Traditional Health Sectors in Swaziland.' In Wulf, R.M. and S.J. Fiske (eds) *Anthropological Praxis; Translating Knowledge into Action*, pp. 87–97. Boulder, London: Westview Press.

Green, E.C. and L. Makhubu (1984) 'Traditional Healers in Swaziland: Towards Improved Cooperation between the Traditional and Modern Health Sectors.' *Social Science and Medicine* 18(12): 1071–9.

Hammond-Tooke, W.D. (1986) 'The Aetiology of Spirit in Southern Africa'. *African Studies* 45(2): 157–70.

Janzen, J.M. (1992) *Ngoma. Discourses of Healing in Central and Southern Africa*. Berkeley, Los Angeles, Oxford: University of California Press.

Kuper, H. (1961) *An African Aristocracy*. London: Oxford University Press.

——(1970) *A Witch in my Heart*. London: Oxford University Press.

Leacock, S. and R. Leacock (1975) *Spirits of the Deep. A Study of an Afro-Brazilian Cult*. New York: Anchor.

Makhubu, L.P (1978) *The Traditional Healer*. Kwaluseni: University of Botswana and Swaziland.

Marwick, B.A. (1966) *The Swazi*. London: Frank Cass & Co.

Ngubane, H. (1977) *Body and Mind in Zulu Medicine; an Ethnography of Health and Disease in Nyuswa-Zulu Thought and Practice*. London: Academic Press.

—— (1981) 'Aspects of Clinical Practice and Traditional Organization of Indigenous Healers in South Africa.' *Social Science and Medicine* 15B: 361–5.

—— (1986) 'The Predicament of the Sinister Healer: Some Observations on "Ritual Murder" and the Professional Role of the Inyanga'. In Last, M. and G.L. Chavunduka (eds) *The Professionalisation of African Medicine*. Manchester: Manchester University Press.

Polanah, L. (1967a) 'Possessao Sagrada em Moçambique: I. Patologia religiosa.' *Geographica* 11: 17–33.

——(1967b) 'Possessao Sagrada em Moçambique: II. O Nhamussoro.' *Geographica* 12: 71–91.

Ranger, T.O. (1993) 'The Local and the Global in Southern African Religious History.' In Hefner, R.W. (ed.) *Conversion to Christianity: Historical and Anthropological Perspectives on a Great Transformation*, pp. 65–98. Berkeley: University of California Press.

Reis, R. (1994) 'Evil in the Body, Disorder of the Brain: Interpretations of Epilepsy and the Treatment Gap in Swaziland'. *Tropical and Geographical Medicine*: S40–43.

——(1996) *Sporen van ziekte. Medische pluraliteit en epilepsie in Swaziland (Traces of Illness. Medical Pluralism and Epilepsy in Swaziland)*. Health, Culture and Society: Studies in Medical Anthropology and Sociology. Amsterdam: Het Spinhuis.

Rycroft, D.K. (1981) *Concise SiSwati Dictionary*. Pretoria: J.L. van Schaik.

Schoffeleers, J.M. (ed.) (1979) *Guardians of the Land: Essays on Central African Territorial Cults*. Gwelo: Mambo Press for the University of Salisbury.

Stevens, R.P. (1967) *Lesotho, Botswana and Swaziland. The Former High Commission Territories in Southern Africa*. London: Pall Mall Press.

Van Binsbergen, W.M.J. (1981) *Religious Change in Zambia: Exploratory Studies*. London/Boston: Kegan Paul International.
—— (1994) 'Divinatie met vier tabletten; Medische technologie in Zuidelijk Afrika'. In Van der Geest, S. *et al.* (eds) *De macht der dingen: Medische technologie in cultureel perspectief*, pp. 61–110. Amsterdam: Het Spinhuis.
Van Nieuwenhuijsen, J.W. (1974) *Diviners and their Ancestor Spirits: a Study of the Izangoma among the Nyuswa in Natal, South Africa*. Amsterdam: Universiteit van Amsterdam, ASC.

5

Social Commentaries
& the Influence of the Clientele
The Mhondoro cult
in Dande, Zimbabwe[1]

Marja Spierenburg

Introduction

While doing fieldwork in Dande, in northern Zimbabwe, I read John Janzen's book *Ngoma*, which at that time had just been published. I was very enthusiastic about his attempt to link together a number of cults that hitherto often had been described as separate and highly localized. This effort arose out of his work on the Lemba cult. It became clear to him that local descriptions and explanations made little sense of the continuities and variations in this cult. Janzen argues that one has to take both the regional view of the cult and a long-term historical perspective of the economic, political and social climate to understand its emergence and duration (1992: 4). Through comparison of several cults Janzen wants to clarify the 'layered ontology' of the cults he proposes to group together under the name of 'ngoma'.

From the cults he describes, Janzen distils some essential characteristics, which he refers to as 'core features' (1992: 86–106). Looking at the *Mhondoro* cult, with which my research is concerned, I could recognize many of those core features. The main characteristic of the Mhondoro cult is the interpretation of adversity and change – of drought and the introduction of cash cropping, for example. Spirits do play an important role in interpreting and coping with adversity; rain is believed to be withheld by the royal ancestors if people anger and insult them; Mhondoro mediums all claim to be 'sufferers-transformed-to-healers'. Nevertheless, like the other contributors to this volume, I soon started to wonder whether these core features actually describe the 'core' of the Mhondoro cult, what the cult is about. In his search for essential characteristics, the economic, political and social context – which he considers important in understanding 'ngoma' – soon disappears from sight. Only in his descriptions of the Lemba cult in Zambia and the Amagqira cult in South Africa does he refer to the socio-political and economical backgrounds of the participants although he does not report on how these cults respond to or reflect on the circumstances in which their patients live.

Janzen does not want to distinguish between healing and religion, nor does he follow Werbner's (1977) distinction between 'regional cults' and topically focused cults of affliction (1992: 4, 76). Nevertheless, he still focuses primarily on healing and affliction. Janzen even appears to limit the concept of ngoma further by focusing predominantly on the healers themselves, the community of 'fellow-sufferers-turned-healers', instead of on the problems ngoma is concerned with or how these problems are dealt with. Most of the 'core features' he describes refer to the process through which sufferers turn into healers. The role of 'lay' adherents is ignored completely. Yet, in many of the cults which can be recognized as 'ngoma' the majority of participants will never be transformed into healers, nor is this always the ultimate object of these cult.

The remark which probably precipitated the writing of this article is one which very specifically refers to the cult with which I am concerned here. It reads as follows: 'In a few instances, centralized shrine cults have persisted over centuries, defining primary values and social patterns for generations of adepts. The ... Korekore and Chikunda in Zimbabwe are well-studied examples that continue into the present' (Janzen 1992: 76). Perhaps it is not fair to react so strongly to a single remark on one specific cult in a book which deals with so many different cults. Nevertheless, I think that this remark is rather symptomatic of the limited way in which Janzen deals with the relationship between politics, 'ngoma' and the influence of lay adherents.

Maybe this neglect partly has to do with the fact that not all political reactions are very open and direct. For instance, the Lemba cult Janzen describes accepts members of a new merchant elite on an individual basis and apparently treats their individual problems without overtly relating their problems to their position in society (Janzen 1992). Yet, the cult may be 'tuning in', as Pels (1993) would have put it, to social and political changes: reconciling cult members with their new position and creating a new social network for them. Perhaps one should not focus too much on politics in the form of resistance, innovation and revolutionary statements. It could prove more valuable to focus on a cult's commentary on society. Certain developments in society can be rejected and resisted, accepted, adapted, supported or even initiated by cults; all these are possible reactions.

In my contribution to this volume I will argue that the operation of the Mhondoro cult in Zimbabwe cannot be understood without taking into account the economic, social and political context in which it operates. Nor can it be understood without analysing the role of lay adherents of the cult. Contrary to Janzen I argue that the cult does not define primary values and social patterns but, on the contrary, serves as a platform where the adherents of the Mhondoro cult discuss values and social patterns. I will do so by focusing on: 1) the nature of problems presented to Mhondoro mediums; 2) the process of acquiring and preserving legitimacy as a medium; and 3) the influence of the clients/adherents of the cult. I will present the case of a Mhondoro medium who was involved in the resistance against a land redistribution project to illustrate the complex situations in which Mhondoro mediums operate, as well as how fluid their reputations are as a result of attempts by adherents to influence their pronouncements. And I will show that what Janzen distinguishes as one of the most important core features of ngoma, the wounded healer complex, is in fact part of a power struggle between different groups of adherents and Mhondoro mediums.

The Mhondoro mediums of Dande

Before I discuss the Mhondoro cult, let me first give a brief description of the area in which I conducted my research. Dande is situated in the Zambezi valley in northern Zimbabwe. The people who consider themselves the original inhabitants of the area refer to themselves as Korekore. The climate in the valley is hot and the soil is not particularly fertile. In the past people in the area depended on trading and hunting as well as agriculture. When the area was effectively brought under control of the white settler regime of Rhodesia, trading and hunting became increasingly difficult. Due to the unfavourable conditions for large-scale commercial farming, virtually no land was alienated to white settlers but the availability of virgin land attracted large numbers of immigrants from overpopulated communal areas in the south east of Zimbabwe, as well as retiring farm labourers who originally came from Mozambique and Malawi to work on the big commercial farms on the plateau of Zimbabwe. Nowadays, most people in Dande depend upon agriculture, often supported by household members who are (temporarily) engaged in wage labour on farms and in the cities of Zimbabwe. Until the introduction of a major land redistribution project (see below), land was communally owned in Dande. The main crops grown in Dande are maize, cotton, sorghum, groundnuts and sunflowers.

Mhondoro are the spirits of royal ancestors, the great rulers of the past. All present-day chiefs of Dande claim descent from one of the Mhondoro. The Mhondoro of Dande are considered to be related to each other and placed in genealogies of two main families, one autochthonous, one an invading lineage. The hierarchy among Mhondoro mediums is partly based on their place in these genealogies. The Mhondoro spirits are believed to continue to look after the territories they ruled when they were still alive. In Dande, these areas have relatively clear boundaries which are known by most inhabitants. Garbett introduced the term 'spirit provinces' to refer to these areas (1969, 1977). The size of a spirit province varies. Some spirit provinces encompass only a few villages, while others may extend into different chiefdoms. Every tract of land in Dande belongs to one of the Mhondoro. The land and all other natural resources in a spirit province ultimately belong to the Mhondoro of that province. The Mhondoro take care of their lands by providing rain and ensuring the fertility of the soil (see also Lan 1985).

Mhondoro spirits are believed to communicate with the living through mediums. In theory Mhondoro mediums can be either male or female, but in Dande most mediums are male. The very important Mhondoro Nehanda, however, who is famous almost nation-wide, usually has a female medium.

Mhondoro mediums claim to have been called to their profession in a painful way, similar to the process described by Janzen as one of the core features of ngoma. They suffer from an illness (often a mental illness) which cannot be cured. When suspicions arise that the illness is caused by spirit possession, a *n'anga* (healer-diviner) is called upon to confirm this and diagnose the type of spirit involved. The n'anga, in cooperation with the relatives of the patient, organizes a ritual to induce the spirit to reveal its identity. It may take several rituals before the spirit finally reveals him or herself. Once the spirit possessing the patient is diagnosed as a Mhondoro spirit, the patient is instructed to go to the spirit province of the Mhondoro possessing him or her. The spirit is believed to direct the patient to the spirit's home. Upon arrival the aspirant medium has to contact the (senior) ritual assistant, the *mutape* of the spirit. In many cases this assistant will direct the aspirant medium to a senior Mhondoro medium who will help the aspirant medium to come to grips with his or her possession and prepare for the tests which they have to undergo.[2]

Mhondoro mediums move from one ngoma modality to another in the process of establishing themselves as mediums. Divination by a n'anga, who belongs to a different tradition from that espoused by the Mhondoro mediums, is a necessary step in the career of a Mhondoro medium.

Collective problems and possibilities for social commentaries

The Mhondoro cult is mainly concerned with rain and fertility. Each year, two rituals are conducted for the Mhondoro. These are *huruwa* (or *mbudzirume*) and *tsopero* (or *doro retsepero*). The huruwa ritual is conducted before the onset of the rainy season. Its purpose is to beg the Mhondoro for rain and protection of the crops. After a prosperous harvest, the ritual of tsopero will be held to thank the Mhondoro. Each village, or cluster of villages, has its own shrine (*dendemaro*) dedicated to the Mhondoro of the spirit province at which the rituals are conducted. The Mhondoro mediums need not be present at all the rituals which are held in their province. The rituals will be conducted by the local assistant of the medium (*mutape*, pl. *vatape*). Each village, or cluster of villages, which has a shrine will have a resident ritual assistant; even if the Mhondoro of the spirit province has no medium. Unlike the mediumship, the mutapeship is patrilineally inherited. In many cases, the mutape is also the village headman, or at least a close relative of the headman.[3] Apart from organizing the biannual rituals, the vatape also mediate between adherents who wish to consult the Mhondoro and the medium.

In general a Mhondoro medium is concerned with the collective problems of the community living in his or her spirit province, whereas a n'anga is concerned with the problems of an individual and his or her immediate family. Mhondoro mediums are consulted by village elders in times of drought, when locusts or other plagues threaten crops and in the case of epidemic diseases threatening large groups of people. In practice, however, the distinction between n'anga and Mhondoro mediums is not all that rigid. People claiming descendance from the Mhondoro may also consult the Mhondoro's medium when suffering from individual or family problems. Some Mhondoro mediums may acquire such good reputation that they also attract individuals and families living outside of their spirit province who consult them for more personal afflictions.

Nevertheless, collective community problems are the major concern of the Mhondoro mediums. The Mhondoro spirits are supposed to provide rain and fertility of the soil. However, it is believed that they only do so when the inhabitants of their territories follow their rules. Schoffeleers (1979) refers to this as 'management of nature through the management of society'. Many of the Mhondoro's 'rules' concern moral values of the community; incest, murder and theft are believed to provoke droughts. Other rules concern the observance of 'traditional' resting days (*chisi*), respect for sacred places, etc. When village elders consult a Mhondoro medium for an explanation of drought, they can be told that individuals committing offences against the Mhondoro's rules are responsible. Today, in most such cases, no actual perpetrators are identified.

However, the explanation of climatological mishaps also offers possibilities for Mhondoro mediums to deliver social commentaries. Natural disasters can be, and often are, attributed to social and political problems. The introduction of new cash crops which may upset existing differentiation patterns or abuse of authority by local leadership can be identified by Mhondoro mediums as potential causes of natural disasters. But Mhondoro mediums do not confine their judgement to local situations. For example, the nationwide drought of 1992 was attributed by most Mhondoro mediums in Dande to the Zimbabwean government's failure to fulfil the promises made during the struggle for independence and the introduction of the Economic Structural Adjustment Programme. This expansion of scope may have been facilitated partly by the fact that the 1991/1992 drought was nationwide and therefore required a 'nationwide explanation'. However, even before this event, Mhondoro mediums in Dande had been issuing critical remarks about the Zimbabwean government. When doing so, many mediums referred to the role played by Mhondoro mediums in the armed struggle for independence (see Bhebe and Ranger 1995; Ranger 1967, 1985, 1991; Lan 1985). They seemed to claim authority *vis-à-vis* the government on the basis of their alleged role as criticizers of the pre-independence state and as allies of the guerrilla fighters who helped putting the present government in power. Furthermore, the policies of the present government are certainly affecting the lives of the people in Dande. They cannot live independently of the state, and neither can the Mhondoro mediums.

Apart from offering 'political explanations' for natural disasters, Mhondoro mediums can become involved in socio-political issues in a number of other ways. As the Mhondoro are the 'real owners of the land', they have to be consulted on all major developments introduced in their territories. The introduction of new cash crops; immigration of large numbers of people; the foundation of a new village – these are just a few examples of cases that should be presented to Mhondoro mediums for approval. Furthermore, when a chief dies, his successor should be appointed by the medium of the senior Mhondoro of the chiefdom.

Adherents of the cult

The possibility of Mhondoro mediums offering social commentaries while explaining droughts or other threats to the community renders their position precarious. They are dealing with large groups of potential adherents which are far from homogeneous. Participation in the Mhondoro cult is based on the following two principles: lineality and territoriality. Those who are considered lineal descendants of a Mhondoro, may consult a medium representing their ancestor regardless of where they are living. But the majority of the potential following of the Mhondoro cult is formed by those who are simply living in and, even more important, are cultivating land in a particular spirit province (see Garbett 1977). The communities that mediums are serving are rather large and far from homogeneous. The position of the mediums *vis-à-vis* the different interest groups is complicated.

Chiefs are the leading members of lineages that claim descent from a Mhondoro spirit (see also Bourdillon 1987a: 100; Lan 1985: 19). The land within the chiefdom is 'owned' by the lineage of the chiefs, through their link with the Mhondoro. The lineage of the chief usually forms a large group within the chiefdom, but most subjects of a chief belong to other lineages. Village headmen may belong to the chiefly clan, but this is not a prerequisite for headmanship. Usually headmanship is granted by the chief to the family which is believed to have founded a village. Sometimes these families migrated into a certain chiefdom; others broke away from another headman in the same chiefdom.

The relationship between Mhondoro mediums, chiefs and headmen is rather complicated. Mhondoro mediums derive some right to criticize chiefs from their position as representatives of the chiefs' ancestors. The boundaries of the spirit provinces are independent of the political boundaries of the chiefdoms, which also contributes to a degree of autonomy of the Mhondoro mediums. Yet, the ritual assistants of Mhondoro mediums often serve as headmen as well, which ties them to the chiefs under whose jurisdiction the headmen serve (see also Lan 1985: 63–6).

Chieftaincy was passed on by what is referred to as adelphic succession (see Bourdillon 1987a; Lan 1985: 57). A chief should be succeeded by a younger brother. This continues until there are no more men of that generation left alive, upon which the chieftaincy should pass on to the next generation. In this next generation there were often several candidates claiming the chieftaincy. The senior Mhondoro mediums of a chiefdom were involved in the selection of the successor of a deceased chief. However, after the arrival of the white settlers, things changed.

During the colonial period, chiefs and headmen became government employees. Colonial administrators sometimes tampered with the succession procedures of certain chiefly lineages. They could veto a certain candidate in favour of a more cooperative candidate. In Dande some critical chiefs were demoted to headmen. Some chiefs lost their status as they found it difficult to respond to the interests of their employers as well as those of their subjects, while others were more successful in maintaining a certain balance (see Holleman 1969; Weinrich 1971). Chiefs were made to relinquish the greater part of the authority they once held. Officially, they could no longer try criminal cases at their own courts. Furthermore, their role in the distribution of land was diminished. Chiefs and their headmen became responsible for the collection of taxes which their subjects had to pay to the state. Today, chiefs still receive a government salary, but are no longer responsible for the collection of taxes. Village headmen no longer receive government salaries. There is some talk about restoring the 'traditional' duties of both chiefs and village headmen again.

The principle of territoriality almost 'ensures' that the potential adherents of the Mhondoro cult constitute a heterogenous group. It contains many different people occupying different places within the power equation. First of all, there are those who are related to the chiefs and headmen, and those who are not. Those who do not belong to the chief's clan are referred to as *vatorwa*, strangers (see also Lan 1985: 19). Though the chief's lineage usually forms the largest single lineage, the members of the different 'stranger lineages' together outnumber the chiefly lineage. After independence in 1980, migration to Dande has increased rapidly, introducing even more 'strangers' into the area.

Other distinctions which can be made among the potential supplicants of the Mhondoro cult, and have received quite some attention in the literature, are based on age and gender. Furthermore, potential adherents occupy different places within the pattern of socio-economic stratification. Some are mere subsistence farmers, others successfully grow cash crops, some supplement their income from farming with income derived from wage labour or other off-farm activities. Some farmers have cattle while others have not. Furthermore, there is also a local elite of shop owners, teachers, nurses, etc.

Lastly, there is a group of people who are part of the new local administration structure which came into place after independence in 1980. Democratically elected Village Development Committees (VIDCOs) are the basic units in this new system of local government. Each VIDCO represents about 100 households. The VIDCO submits its plans on an annual basis to the Ward Development Committee (WADCO), which ideally represents about six villages. In each ward a Ward Councillor is elected. The Ward Councillors of all Wards within a District serve on the District Council, assisted by a ministerially appointed Senior Executive Officer and District Administrator. Chiefs and headmen are not officially represented in this institutional structure, though chiefs are often invited to attend District Council meetings as ex officio members. Relations between those participating in the new system of local administration, on the one hand, and chiefs and headmen, on the other, differ from village to village and ward to ward.

The reason I speak of 'potential adherents', is that there are alternatives in the religious field in Dande. Several so-called independent churches are active in Dande, among which the Apostolic Faith Church, the Apostolic Church of Johane Marange, and ZAOGA. Of the mainline churches, only the Catholic Church is still active in the valley. The Methodist mission stations were abandoned and destroyed during the struggle for independence, and have never been rebuilt.

According to Daneel (1977) processes of individualization and stratification were important factors leading to the emergence of the independent churches in Zimbabwe. As early as the 1960s Garbett noticed that some people in the Zambezi Valley who earned some cash through wage labour withdrew from the Mhondoro cult and joined, for example, one of the Apostolic churches, to escape the levelling forces of the Mhondoro cult. Another category of members of independent churches, according to Garbett, is constituted of people who are not able to obtain a position of status and power within their own communities. They hope to attain a position of status and influence within the churches (Garbett 1967). The churches create a new 'brother- (and sister-)hood' in which people offer help to each other in times of need without the conditions and constraints implied by the kinship system. Furthermore, the practice of brideprice was denounced by many independent churches. This often resulted in large polygamous households having abundant family labour available.

Many of the independent churches in Zimbabwe are strongly based in the rural areas (Daneel 1977). Most leaders are farmers themselves. The churches often conduct rituals to ensure rain and fertility of the soils, and engage in witchcraft eradication. By this they provide an alternative to the Mhondoro cult, more so than the established mission churches (see Daneel, ibid.).

Legitimization of mediums

Mhondoro mediums need to present a strong case to establish and uphold their positions. In my view, many of the core features Janzen describes, especially the transformation of the sufferer into the healer, serve more as legitimization of those who 'do ngoma' than as the core of the cult itself. I do not wish to repeat Ria Reis's statement (elsewhere in this volume), but I would like to draw attention to some aspects that may serve as ideological legitimization for Mhondoro mediums.

In most accounts of the way people have become Mhondoro mediums (see also Lan 1985), much stress is put on the medium's initial resistance against the possession by the Mhondoro. People do not voluntarily become mediums; on the contrary, it is described as a very painful process. For instance, the new medium of Badzabveke told me how the Mhondoro was fighting inside him with another, lesser, spirit which had been diagnosed earlier as the cause of his health problems. As a result of this battle the medium said he had become dizzy and fell into the cooking fire. I met him while I was visiting the local mission hospital where he was treated for his burns. He said he disliked his possession, but 'there is nothing you can do once the Mhondoro chooses you'. Both adherents and mediums say that mediums do not choose a career as a medium, but that the Mhondoro choose their medium.

It might very well be that the tales of sickness are to show that initially the medium was not receptive to signs from the Mhondoro and that only through the force of sickness is the Mhondoro able to draw attention to its wish to possess someone. By stressing that the medium did not choose to become a medium, did not consider it a career option, the mediumship may become more genuine and credible.

Nevertheless, even if one accepts that the concept of the wounded healer is ideological, this does not exclude the possibility that some mediums actually did experience sickness or adversity prior to their establishment as mediums. Burck (1989) found that many male n'anga received their 'calling' while facing problems with their careers and a considerable number of female n'anga were either divorcees or widows. Burck suggests that embarking upon a career as a n'anga is a socially acceptable option to escape financial misery without losing face. The life histories of some Mhondoro mediums in Dande suggest similar problems prior to possession. Quite a number of them told me that they experienced the first signs of possession while they were working outside of Dande. They lost well-paid jobs due to social conflicts which were followed by bewitching, employers selling farms and companies, or accidents at work. I am not in a position to judge whether stories of illness and misfortune are 'true' or not. Bourdillon (1987a) states that quite a number of mediums in his research area had long been destined for mediumship regardless of any affliction, and that some of them had been trained for mediumship from an early age. The fact remains that it is socially accepted and culturally 'logical' to explain health problems and other afflictions in terms of spirit possession.

Most mediums I have spoken to emphasize that they consider the mediumship a personal burden. The mediumship disrupts their lives and prevents them from working hard in their fields or building up an enterprise. Mhondoro mediums are supposed to work for the good of the communities in their spirit province. Unlike n'anga, Mhondoro mediums are not expected to use their position to acquire personal wealth (see also Garbett 1977; Lan 1985). Small amounts of money are paid to the mediums for the performance of rituals and personal consultations, but a large part of that money has to be spent on the upkeep of the shrine and providing hospitality for the many visitors to the shrine.

Aspirant Mhondoro mediums have to undergo certain tests in the presence of senior Mhondoro mediums, vatape, headmen and villagers. They have to recite the history of the Mhondoro possessing them and the genealogy of the Mhondoro of Dande. Often, they also have to select the ritual staff and axes which belonged to either the Mhondoro or the preceding medium from a heap of staffs and axes. Sometimes they have to recover things which were hidden by a previous medium. A new medium may need several rituals before he or she passes the tests. Most people I have spoken to adhere to the theory that the mediums are outsiders and therefore all knowledge they show of the history of their Mhondoro, the staffs and the things hidden must come from the spirit. Mediums are not supposed to belong to the same clan as the Mhondoro, and thus the chief of the area. That would mean that mediums, as persons, are classified as vatorwa (strangers, see also Lan 1985; Bourdillon 1987a). The emphasis on the medium as a stranger may serve to enhance an image of impartiality: the medium has no personal interests to defend. However, I found that nearly all the mediums I interviewed were born or grew up in Dande. I also discovered that quite a number (nearly half of all the mediums I have spoken to) actually do belong to the same clan as the Mhondoro possessing them.

Mediums need to show a convincing possession 'performance'. Their voices are often distorted, they cough, spit, and growl like a lion,[4] they writhe around on their mats in half-dark *dendemaro*. After witnessing many possession seances I could not help but notice that younger mediums who had been established fairly recently usually put up more of a 'show' than the older mediums who had been functioning for a much longer time. The popular and long-established mediums of Negomo and Nyahuma hardly change their voices when possessed.

'The past' also plays an important role in authenticating mediums. Most seances start with the reciting of the heroic acts of the Mhondoro in past wars and the history of the area. The problems of the present are compared with problems of the past. Possessed Mhondoro mediums often deal with modern developments, issue social commentaries that have to do with 'modern' conditions, and certainly do not oppose all forms of 'modern development'. Yet they often claim they have no knowledge of the present. Before entering the medium's hut, shoes and watches have to be removed 'as the spirits do not know these things'. To give an example, the first time I consulted the possessed medium of Karembera, I asked him if I could tape the seance. The spirit then asked me to explain what a tape-recorder was. I did so, and he agreed that I could use it. Towards the end of the session he asked me how I was going to get the words out of 'that little black box' again. I replayed part of the tape for him and he roared with laughter. He sang one of his favourite songs 'to put in the little black box'. After the session, the mutape took me to the hut of the medium, where he asked me to wait as the medium himself (and not the spirit) wanted to ask me something. Entering the hut, somewhat to my surprise, I discovered a huge ghettoblaster displayed on an elaborately decorated shelf.[5]

This brings me to another issue. Both adherents and mediums alike stress that the medium and the spirit possessing him or her are completely separate. Mediums cannot be held responsible for the pronouncements that spirits make using their voices. When I started interviewing Mhondoro mediums about the land redistribution project which was introduced by the government, I found many of them reluctant to speak to me when they were not possessed. Often they seemed relieved when I asked for consultation with the Mhondoro spirit. While possessed they would criticize the project without hesitation. The separation between medium and spirit is usually made more clearly by younger mediums who have not been practising for a long time. They often, after a seance, ask their vatape what the spirit has said. Older, more established mediums were more likely to answer questions about their spirits' opinions while they were not possessed once they got to know me better.

Fluid reputations of Mhondoro mediums:
The case of the Mid-Zambezi Rural Development Project

The possibility of Mhondoro mediums' ability to issue social commentaries as well as the boldness and openness of their statements depends upon their reputation. Indeed, one can observe that the older and longer-established mediums make the most daring statements. However, their reputation also depends upon the popularity of their statements. Adherents may try to influence Mhondoro mediums by subjecting the mediums' reputations to discussion. Reputations of mediums are very fluid. Even long-established Mhondoro mediums can lose respect, as will be shown below.

The case I wish to present here to support my argument concerns the involvement of the medium of Chidyamauyu in the opposition against a land redistribution project. In 1987 the Mid-Zambezi Rural Development Project (or Mid-Zambezi Project) was introduced, taking in a large part of Dande. The project is a follow-up to an EEC-funded project to eradicate the tsetse fly in the Mid-Zambezi Valley. The idea behind this eradication scheme was that, once the fly was controlled, farmers would be able to move into the area with their cattle and start farming this hitherto marginal and scarcely inhabited area. The EEC commissioned the Food and Agriculture Organisation of the United Nations (FAO) to make plans for the development of the valley once the tsetse fly infestation was controlled and people and livestock could move into the valley. The Mid-Zambezi Rural Development Project was one of the projects the FAO proposed (see Derman 1993). The African Development Fund assisted with funding the project. The actual implementation was the responsibility of the Department of Rural Development (DERUDE, a department of the Ministry of Local Government and Rural and Urban Development of the Government of Zimbabwe) and Agritex (the national agricultural extension service).

The aim of the Mid-Zambezi Project was to resettle all inhabitants of Dande in newly created, or reorganized, nuclear villages. All arable land was to be redistributed into 12-acre plots which would be allocated to all resettled households (ADF 1986). In addition to land reforms, the plans envisaged the improvement of infrastructure and services: construction and upgrading of roads, building of schools and clinics, and the construction of water points.

With the implementation of the Mid-Zambezi Project, the communities' control over the land has been greatly reduced. Communities had no say as to where land for cultivation and grazing areas would be situated. The designation and demarcation of these areas was done by Agritex on the basis of aerial photographs and not existing settlement patterns.

The main reason for resistance to the project was the fact that not enough twelve-acre plots had been demarcated to provide all those living in the Mid-Zambezi area at the time with land. Initially, it was assumed that the area was only sparsely populated. There were even plans to resettle about 3000 families in Dande from other overpopulated communal areas in Zimbabwe. But when the project was introduced the implementing agencies discovered that more than the 7600 households catered for in the plans were already residing in the project area. Nevertheless, the project was to go ahead as planned, and no extra plots were demarcated. As a result, a considerable number of households will be rendered landless if the project is ever to be completed, Derman (1993) estimates this to be about a third of the present population in the project area.

Chief Matsiwo's chiefdom is divided into several administrational wards, among which Matsiwo A and Matsiwo B ward.[6] Matsiwo B ward was one of the first wards where the resettlement exercise was introduced. Arable plots and residential areas were pegged and allocated without much consultation with the inhabitants. It was in this ward (and the Muzarabani area) that the consequences of the project first became visible to the people subject to the project. When it became clear that not enough plots were demarcated to cater for all present inhabitants, conflicts broke out within communities about land rights. People tried to stall the project by refusing to move to their new fields and homesteads. The project staff realized it had grossly underestimated the practicalities of getting people to move from one place to another. As initially no landlessness was expected, it was not clear to the project staff what should be done with people who stood to lose their land. News about the consequences of the project quickly spread to other wards. Resettlement officers and other project staff came under great pressure.

The project proved more difficult to implement than the planners had envisaged. The implementation was supposed to have been completed in 1992, but by that time Matsiwo A ward as well as several villages in some other wards had not yet been resettled. Additional funds were arranged for another three-year period and the project staff set out to resettle the people in Matsiwo A ward. When I arrived in the field, in late 1992, new plots in a few villages in Matsiwo A ward had been demarcated, but these had not yet been allocated. In other parts of the ward no demarcation had taken place at all. In the face of the difficulties with implementing the project, a change of strategy was decided upon. This change entailed the involvement of the hitherto ignored 'traditional' leadership, the village headmen and chiefs. The idea behind the new strategy was that once the support of 'traditional' leadership was obtained, its subjects would follow and implementation of the project would be facilitated. As will be shown, however, this idea proved to be erroneous.

Early in 1992, before I arrived, chief Matsiwo had been approached by a delegation of the project staff. He was asked to give permission for the implementation of the resettlement exercise in Matsiwo A ward. I was told by the chief that at first he refused any cooperation with project staff on the grounds that a large part of his chiefdom had already been subjected to the implementation of the project without prior consultation. Later, he advised the project manager to approach the medium of Chidyamauyu, under whose spirit province most land in Matsiwo A ward falls. The chief argued that the Mhondoro are the real owners of the land in Dande and therefore they are the only ones who can give permission for resettlement.

The project manager persuaded the chief to visit the medium of Chidyamauyu on behalf of the Department of Rural Development (DERUDE), the department responsible for implementing the Mid-Zambezi Project. The project manager provided the chief with a piece of black cloth, the usual fee for consulting a spirit medium on such an important issue. When the chief visited the medium of Chidyamauyu, the medium told him that he did not accept the piece of cloth. He could not be sure that it actually came from DERUDE. The chief was ordered to inform the project manager that he should personally visit the spirit medium and bring another piece of cloth. Furthermore, the medium stated that his Mhondoro refused to give permission for the implementation of the project. The project activities were to halt at Sapa stream (which forms the boundary of the spirit province, and is situated a few kilometres south of the ward boundary). Like many other Mhondoro mediums in Dande he blamed the drought of 1991 to 1992 on the introduction of the project. The project was taken as an example of how the present government was betraying the promises they had made during the struggle for independence.

After some delay, the project manager, accompanied by the chief, decided to pay a personal visit to the spirit medium and donated the required piece of cloth. At the meeting with the spirit medium the project manager got the same verdict as the chief.

The chief was in a difficult position. On the one hand, he was receiving a salary from the government which wished to implement the Mid-Zambezi Project. On the other hand, he was very much aware that by that time most of his subjects opposed the project. My feeling is that he handed over the responsibility of judging the project to the medium of Chidyamauyu partly because the Mhondoro indeed are considered the 'real owners of the land' but also because he himself found it difficult to openly condemn the project. The medium could more easily condemn the project in the name of the Mhondoro, as he could not be held accountable for the Mhondoro's judgement.

During that time the medium of Chidyamauyu was very popular. Part of his popularity may have derived from his behaviour during the struggle for independence. He joined the guerrilla fighters who operated in the area and became caretaker of the medium of Nehanda. Nehanda is a Mhondoro spirit who is famous nation-wide. Her medium joined the guerrillas in Mozambique where she died before the end of the war. In the hierarchy of Mhondoro, based on the genealogy of the two main 'Mhondoro families' in Dande, Chidyamauyu occupies a rather junior position. His original spirit province is rather small. After the death of the medium of Nehanda, he claimed responsibility for her spirit province, and many adherents agreed with this. His opposition to the Mid-Zambezi Project may also have played a role in his popularity, which seemed to have increased even further after his denouncement of the project. Often when I asked people why the medium of Chidyamauyu was so important they referred to his pronouncements concerning the Mid-Zambezi Project. His junior position was now taken as an advantage. As the vatape of another Mhondoro medium said: 'Chidyamauyu is very important, as he is the grandchild of all the Mhondoro of Dande, he has access to all of them.' Increasingly people living outside Nehanda's (and thus Chidyamauyu's) territory went to consult the medium of Chidyamauyu instead of the medium of their own spirit province. When a dry spell occurred, the vatape of the village where I stayed went to consult the medium of Chidyamauyu instead of the medium of Chivhere, in whose spirit province the village was situated.

In October 1992 Bill Derman, a visiting professor from Michigan State University, had asked his research assistants to interview people in Matsiwo A ward about their ideas on how the land in the ward should be used. The plan was to develop, in cooperation with local farmers, an alternative landuse plan which would be presented to the staff of the Mid-Zambezi Project.

Most people who were contacted by the research assistants refused to give any information. They accused the assistants of being 'spies' for the project management, whose goal was to find out if there was any resistance to the project. The research assistants were told to visit the medium of Chidyamauyu, to ask permission for their research. Early in November I was invited to join Derman and his assistants on their visit to the medium. We spent a long time discussing the issue with the medium and had a difficult time trying to convince him that we were not associated with the Mid-Zambezi Project but, on the contrary, wanted to help the people in Matsiwo A ward to counter the negative effects of the project. At last, the medium said he believed us and that he would arrange a meeting with all VIDCO chairmen[7] and village headmen of the ward at which Bill Derman could explain his plans. If all would agree to cooperate with the exercise, the medium promised he would ask the spirit of Chidyamauyu to give his opinion on what would constitute a proper landuse plan.

The meeting took place about a week later.[8] The village headmen were present as well as many other people, mostly village elders. It was very early in the morning and the medium was possessed. After Bill Derman explained his plans, the medium referred the problem to those present: 'It is the duty of the people to give opinions on how they want their land used. I am a spirit. I have nothing to do with today's living.[9] Let us ... hear what the people ... have to say.' After some deliberation, one of the village headmen said that he and his colleagues refused to cooperate with the creation of an alternative landuse plan, because they still suspected that Bill Derman and his assistants were working for the Mid-Zambezi Project and they '[did] not want the difficulties that have been experienced by other villages'. Then the possessed medium gave his opinion on Derman's plans:

> Village headmen and people, is there anything that you have grasped from these people? As I can see from these three men, they bring no trouble into your villages. If you cooperate with them, no trouble will befall you. But if they are roots that supply water to the trunk to allow the leaves of the tree to grow [if they want to pave the way for the introduction of the Mid-Zambezi Project], that is where we will disagree. I see the future of your villages bright if you cooperate with these people. Village headmen, you need to observe carefully and learn if you can benefit from them or if it is [they] themselves who benefit. What I do not want is you, village headmen, to cry later, saying Chidyamauyu did not warn us. But as I foresee, the future has no tears. If you do not work with them, what happened in Hwata will also happen here, you will be forced to move against your wishes. These three men will come later and say 'did we not tell you to work with us?' Listen carefully everybody, I will not be happy to see my children from Mukombe ... and Mamhuri moved to Chidodo, Karusanzi or Gonono.

Though he had been quite decisive about the Mid-Zambezi Project, in this case the medium was less eager to make a definite pronouncement. He first asked those present for their opinion. His own opinion about Bill Derman's plans was more positive and he tried to persuade the audience to cooperate. However, he did not enforce his opinion upon his followers and in his pronouncement paid attention to their worries. In the end he concluded: 'My final answer is: we did not say yes or no to work with you. Give us more time to discuss the subject of landuse plan[ning], alone. We will tell you later.'

By March 1993 no decision had been reached to cooperate with the creation of an alternative landuse plan. At this time, the manager of the Mid-Zambezi Project decided to pursue the matter of resettling the people in Matsiwo A ward again. After mediation by the chief, a meeting was organized with the medium of Chidyamauyu and the village headmen. The meeting was held at Tsokoto, one of the most sacred places in Dande. About fifty villagers, young and old, were present as well. During the meeting the possessed medium asked the chief why he had called

Chidyamauyu. The chief answered that he is the leader of the people, but that the Mhondoro is the owner of the land. When the project manager and the resettlement officer asked whether they could get permission to start the demarcation exercise, both the chief and the spirit medium told the village headmen to discuss the matter in a separate meeting. The village headmen withdrew from the meeting and discussed the matter amongst themselves elsewhere in the village. The rest of the audience stayed close to the dendemaro, waiting and discussing the issue amongst themselves. There was a general atmosphere of opposition towards the project. When the village headmen returned about half an hour later, they told the project manager and the resettlement officer that they did not want the resettlement project introduced in their area. This was greeted with enthusiasm by most people in the audience and a group of older women ululated. An older man in the audience remarked that in the previous week elephants and buffaloes had been spotted close to his village and that this was a sure sign that Nehanda disliked the project. Then the possessed medium said:

> You people from DERUDE are just tempting the mediums and the Mhondoro, but you do not satisfy our needs. The first time DERUDE came to Dande the Mhondoro were not consulted. Now that you are facing problems you consult the Mhondoro. I already told you that Sapa stream is where you should stop demarcating. And still you come to ask me permission to continue. I cannot accept that. Mugabe [prime minister and president of Zimbabwe] and Nehanda did not agree on this demarcation project. In the areas that have been demarcated sacred areas of the Mhondoro have been allocated to people. I am not happy about that and the other Mhondoro are not happy with it either. DERUDE is using power so they can demarcate without my permission. I am refusing and if you want to put my medium in prison, that is fine, I dislike the demarcation. DERUDE will have to pay a fine for the areas they have already demarcated without my permission. You will have to wait for Nehanda and ask her permission. The Mhondoro of Zimbabwe have caused last year's drought because Mugabe is not listening to them.

Upon this statement from the possessed medium, the chief publicly remarked that he too opposed the project. The project manager turned to the audience and asked them to say yes or no to the project. The medium answered: 'Tell your seniors that Chidyamauyu has refused and that they should wait for Nehanda to come to Dande. Matsiwo [the chief], report to me any trouble you have with DERUDE.'

Here again we see the spirit medium openly consulting the audience before he issues a statement. The people he specifically asked for their opinion were the village headmen, among whom were vatape of Chidyamauyu and Nehanda. He then provided supernatural legitimization to their objections. He also seems to shift some of the responsibility to the new aspirant medium of Nehanda. This aspirant medium was living outside of Dande, in Hurungwe District. Since 1991 every rainy season there have been rumours that she was to come to Dande to perform her tests, but up to this date she is still residing in Hurungwe.

On the following days, the project manager and the resettlement officer organized three meetings in different villages of the ward, at which the chief was also present. Many people attended these meetings. The project manager tried to obtain support for the resettlement project by focusing almost entirely on the project component of infrastructural development. The audience was told that only if they accepted the project would schools and clinics be built and roads improved so that buses could start servicing the area.[10] The project manager also informed people that the project would provide them with boreholes.[11] He stressed the importance of the availability of clean water, especially in the light of the cholera epidemic that had hit some villages in the ward. At one meeting, the audience openly objected to the project.

However, when the chief then said that he thought people should accept the project because of the development it would bring, a few people started to doubt whether they should continue their resistance against the project. At the other two meetings some young men asked the elders to accept the project, citing as a reason that it would bring development to their area. One young man told the project manager that the only reason why the audience at the meeting with Chidyamauyu had refused the project was because they were afraid of the medium.

At these meetings the chief publicly supported the Mid-Zambezi Project, urging his subjects to accept it. Earlier, faced with all village headmen and the spirit medium opposing the project, the chief had objected to the project in the presence of the project manager. Village headmen no longer receive government salaries and seemed more free to object the project. Authorities at District level were pressuring the chief into supporting the project. At the meetings organized independently by the project manager he actually did so. Yet, in a private interview I had with him the next month, he stated that he opposed the project as it was causing a lot of conflicts:

> The people dislike the project but they are forced by the government. The Mhondoro do not want these pegs [used for demarcating plots and residential stands]. ... In Chitsungo one person was killed because of [a fight over] the boundaries of the pegs. Long ago we did not have such things.

In an interview I had with the project manager, he complained that nobody in Matsiwo A wanted to take responsibility to allow his team to go ahead. After the meetings he had organized himself, he felt confident that the people were actually supporting the project and that he could set the demarcation team to work in April or May. But then the chief changed his mind again and said that he did not dare to give his permission as long as (the medium of) Chidyamauyu refused:

> No one wants to take responsibility. The village headmen refer the problem to the chief and the chief refers the problem to the medium of Chidyamauyu. Then the medium of Chidyamauyu says we have to wait for the medium of Nehanda. Nobody dares to say yes to the project. They are afraid that if they do so, and they will have problems [with rain] later, Nehanda will blame them for accepting the project and will order them to pay a fine for the violation of her sacred areas.

In June, rumours started circulating about gifts that the government had presented to the medium of Chidyamauyu as well as to the new medium of Nehanda, as a reward for their support during the struggle for independence. The project manager confirmed this, he told me that the gifts for Chidyamauyu were offered by senior government officials, and that he himself had nothing to do with it. In fact, he was annoyed about the rewards. He said that these should not have been handed over until the medium had accepted the project.

Nevertheless, many people made a connection between the gifts presented to the medium of Chidyamauyu and the approval of the project sought from him. It was a frequent topic of conversation at the many beer parties held to celebrate the abundant harvest of that year (the first after the severe drought of 1991 and 1992). The medium himself was often absent during this period. I tried to interview him, but was unable to meet him till the end of August. Several village elders complained about his many trips away from Dande. It was rumoured that he frequently travelled to Harare (capital of Zimbabwe) to solve the witchcraft problems of rich businessmen. The elders complained that the medium forgot all about the problems of Dande. They suggested that he was more interested in money than in attending to his duties towards the people in his spirit province. Several people feared that the Mhondoro might leave the medium if he continued to neglect their problems. As one headman put it: 'The Mhondoro do not like their mediums to be so interested in money. Look what happened to the medium of Chiodzomamera, his Mhondoro killed him for that.'[12] During this time many people told me the stories of two mediums who had allegedly been killed by their Mhondoro for pursuing their own interests rather than those of their adherents.

Perhaps the rewards were bothering the medium, or maybe he was confused by the sudden emergence of a group of avowed proponents of the Mid-Zambezi Project. The meetings organized by the project manager independently of the medium seemed to have had effect. Some people actually believed that services and infrastructure in the ward would only be improved if the Mid-Zambezi Project was accepted. Those who openly started to advocate the project were mainly young, reasonably well-educated men. The spokesman for this group was a young man who was a member of the Apostolic Church. He was to stand as candidate for the post of ward councillor.[13] When I asked him why some people in the ward had changed their mind about the project he said:

> It was us, the youngsters, who wanted the project. We have travelled to other areas and we saw the development there. There where the project was accepted we saw that ... the roads are better, there are boreholes, schools, clinics. We want that development here. The older people refused. But we still have to see a lot, they are almost there, at the end, where they have to go. We want the development and we will have to teach the others to see the light of the project. ... When we would go to the [District] council to ask for those things we were told that the council does not give us development, only DERUDE and the project [do so]. That is how we came to understand it was good to accept the project and development.

The issue of the project and its supposedly developmental aspects may have exacerbated an already existing opposition between elders and youth. The advocates of the project not only stressed their youth, but also their religious affiliation. Village headmen and elders persevered in their opposition to the project. For most of the time, they had obtained support from the medium of Chidyamauyu. They continued discussing the Mhondoro's dislike of the project and how that had been the major cause of the 1991 to 1992 drought. They wanted the medium of Chidyamauyu to pronounce again that the project was wrong. The proponents of the project, on the other hand, emphasized their affiliation with Christian (mainly independent) churches, rejecting 'the old people's backward traditions'. Nevertheless, when I asked their spokesman whether he agreed with plans to demarcate arable plots at Tsokoto, the most sacred area of the spirit province – perhaps even of Dande – he said: 'I would refuse that. There are only few people living there, they guard the place. Why peg there? It is the place of our history. When people go there they will feel the history there. They cannot peg there.'

In August 1993 I finally managed to see the medium of Chidyamauyu again. He confirmed that he had received gifts from government officials as a reward for his assistance during the war: seven head of cattle, an ox plough, black and white cloth, a spear, a dancing stick and an axe plus some money. DERUDE officials had promised him that they would construct a house for him. He also said that the new medium of Nehanda had been rewarded handsomely by the Ministry of Defence for solving a problem at the building site of new army barracks near Harare. According to the medium of Chidyamauyu the reward constituted Z$ 20,000 (about fl. 5000 or US$ 2700) and 9 head of cattle.[14] But he maintained that despite this government reward, she still opposed the resettlement project. Strangely, he also said that the official presenting him with the gifts had told chief Matsiwo and the project officer (whom he said were present when the gifts were presented) to listen to the medium of Chidyamauyu and stop the project. '[The project manager] was told to stop that pegging by Cde S. [government official presenting the gifts]. Mbuya Nehanda said: If you want to peg the Dande, it is up to you, but if problems arise then do not come to me for help. Matsiwo then said to [the project manager]: You do not have to do anything in that area, as you have heard it yourself.'

Later that month the medium of Chidyamauyu publicly issued several statements against the project. From then on, I noticed that the rumours about his reputation and Mhondoro killing or abandoning their greedy mediums receded again.

At the time the rumours about the medium of Chidyamauyu were circulating, many elders expressed the hope that the new medium of Nehanda would finally come to her spirit province and give her verdict on the project. This, however, did not happen. Perhaps she was not allowed to come by those who guarded her home in the Hurungwe District. I tried to visit the new medium of Nehanda, but did not succeed. Around her house and yard a new barbed wire fence had been built. At the gate I was stopped by two men whom I suspected of being CIO (Central Intelligence Office) officers.[15] I spent about an hour trying to convince them I was harmless, but they would not open the gate. They did not even want to ask her mutape if I could see the medium. What struck me was that her house stood out from the other structures in the neighbourhood. While most people lived in pole and dagga huts, Nehanda's new medium lived in a newly built brick house with a corrugated iron roof. A herdboy brought in cattle and I counted 26, which is quite a big herd.

This coincided with what the medium of Chidyamauyu told me later. According to him the government official who had presented him with his reward had told him that the medium of Nehanda was guarded by CIO officers. Through the medium of Chidyamauyu the news of the handsome rewards for the medium of Nehanda spread through the ward. Many people started to doubt the authenticity of her claims. As one person said: 'If she is the real medium, why does she not come down here and help her people? Have you heard of all the money they have given her? I think she just wants to sit down and enjoy her money. But what is she doing in Karoi [Hurungwe]? That is not her area. No, the real medium would look after her people.'

After the installation of the new pro-project ward councillor, the chief was asked both by the project management and the new councillor to approach the spirit medium once more. Despite his affiliation with a Christian church, the new councillor tried to obtain support from the medium of Chidyamauyu. He told the chief to tell the medium that most of his people now had come to accept the project. He also said he was convinced that the Mhondoro would understand the problems facing his people and that he would not want them to miss out on 'development'.

The chief returned highly upset from his meeting with the spirit medium. He claimed that he had suddenly felt sick during the meeting and had fallen unconscious. He was revived again by the spirit medium who warned the chief never again to bring up the issue of the Mid-Zambezi Project. He related his story to me during an interview and said that he would refuse to see the spirit medium again, as he feared for his life.

Whether the medium continued to condemn the project because he found it difficult to reverse his statements or because most of the village headmen also continued their opposition, I do not know. The story was recited with great delight by the opponents of the project. The ward councillor was greatly disappointed. He and other project proponents denounced the Mhondoro cult as fake and claimed that Christianity was the only true religion. He even tried to persuade the project management to go ahead with the project without the approval of the spirit medium. The project staff, however, were very reluctant to do so. By the time I left the field the Mid-Zambezi Project had not been implemented in Matsiwo A ward. As funds were running out again, the project activities in Dande were slowly coming to an end and the Department of Rural Development was withdrawing its personnel from Dande. Why the project management decided against introducing the project without the permission of the Mhondoro medium when they have enforced the project in many other areas of Dande, I do not know. Maybe the project management feels it cannot abandon the strategy once embarked upon of consulting 'traditional' leadership without losing face and credibility. Also, fear on the part of the project staff may play a role. After all, an important Mhondoro – the almost nationally acclaimed Nehanda – is involved. Some employees of the Department of Rural Development fear working in the ward, afraid they will be punished by the Mhondoro or become victims of witchcraft practised by avowed opponents of the project.

When I briefly returned to the field in 1995, I discovered that the medium of Chidyamauyu was suffering from a serious loss of popularity. The District Development Fund (DDF) had taken over the duties of DERUDE employees and attempts to have the land reforms introduced were renewed by DDF and Agritex. I was told by many people that the medium had refused to become involved and had not publicly denounced the project for a long time. Many people I spoke to connected his apparent withdrawal from the conflict with the fact that the house that was promised to him by DERUDE had been constructed and that the medium was actually living in it.

The people in Matsiwo A were divided in their opinions concerning the land reforms. In villages where plots had been demarcated (but still not allocated) resistance was more general, among elders and youth, as people could see that the new land distribution would cause tremendous problems. In areas where no land was demarcated yet, people disagreed amongst themselves. Most elders still opposed the land reforms while younger people continued to place their bets on the development which they were sure would follow the land reforms.

Opponents of the project said they feared that this time the Mhondoro Chidyamauyu had really left the medium. As one elder stated:

Yes, he deserved a reward for his work during the war. He could have accepted the house for his wife and children. But how can he live in that house himself? Mediums are not supposed to live in these modern buildings. Mhondoro do not like corrugated roofs. You have spoken to many Mhondoro mediums. Have you ever seen one living in such a house? Mediums have to live in pole and dagga [huts], not surrounded by bricks. I am sure Chidyamauyu has left the medium. He is not satisfied that his medium lives in a house, which is as good as accepting the project.

Proponents of the land reforms were more divided in their opinions concerning the medium. Some agreed that the spirit of Chidyamauyu had left the medium. Others used the medium's 'betrayal' as proof that Mhondoro mediums in general are impostors and that Christianity is the only true religion.

When I visited the medium I found him living in a three roomed brick house with glass windows and a corrugated roof. I arrived when it was already dark and the medium complained that there was still no electricity in the valley. He was content with his house and felt that he had earned it during the war. He said that the Mhondoro had no problems with the house. He also said that his Mhondoro still objected to the project but that his people were divided. When I asked him why the previous rainy season had been bad again, he said: 'The drought is caused by people who no longer respect the Mhondoro. They cut trees they are not allowed to cut, they bathe in sacred pools. Maybe it will rain this year if they show remorse. But they have been misbehaving for a long time.'

Conclusion

Above we saw how a very important issue like the Mid-Zambezi Development Project was dealt with 'through' the Mhondoro cult. The chief, who was very erratic in his publicly stated opinions on the project, referred the issue to the medium of Chidyamauyu. He never dared to give his permission for resettlement without the backing of the medium. The village headmen seemed more open in their objection of the project, but I noticed that they only openly challenged project management in the presence of the medium. In their daily interaction with project staff their resistance was more indirect; they would delay meetings with resettlement officers, for instance, or tamper with lists of applicants for twelve-acre plots.

In daily informal conversations the issue of the project was nearly always connected with the Mhondoro. There was a constant debate going on about whether the Mhondoro agreed with the project or not, and whether their mediums were truly letting the Mhondoro speak through them or not. People watched nature very closely for signs of the Mhondoro. Spells of drought and the movement of wild animals were all interpreted in connection with the project.

Most literature on the Mhondoro cult focuses on the mediums of the Mhondoro spirits, rather than on the role of the adherents (see for example the work of Garbett and Lan). Though perhaps unintended by the authors, this may nevertheless have led Janzen to believe that the mediums lead the cult's adherents. One author who explicitly contradicts this idea is Bourdillon. In an article on the succession of a chief he describes how Mhondoro mediums had to change their nominee three times as most subjects of the chiefdom showed their dissatisfaction with the choices made by the mediums (Bourdillon 1979). Bourdillon argues that although adherents maintain that Mhondoro mediums always speak 'the truth' and also say that people who pretend to be possessed by a Mhondoro will be killed by the spirit, there are many instances when adherents doubt that a medium is truly possessed and question whether the Mhondoro's true voice is being heard. Sometimes only certain pronouncements are questioned, as temporal flaws in the ability of a medium to let the voice of the spirit through. At other times people are suspicious of the medium as a person. Like Bourdillon, I also discovered that the reputation of Mhondoro mediums is very fluid. As the case above shows, even well-established mediums who have been popular for years can have their reputations seriously damaged.

Mhondoro mediums are confronted with difficult problems and are operating in complex situations. Their potential adherents form a heterogenous group which may prove difficult to satisfy. At times opinions concerning certain issues vary so greatly that it is difficult for mediums to issue pronouncements that will be accepted by the majority of their adherents. In such cases mediums can sometimes 'get away' with blaming climatological mishaps on individually committed offences by unspecified perpetrators. However, at other times mediums experience considerable pressure to deliver social commentary. In the case above, when public opinion polarized it proved very hard for the medium of Chidyamauyu to withdraw from the debate on the Mid-Zambezi Project. His long absences from the valley led to a spate of rumour about the authenticity of his possession which only ceased when he returned and assured people of his continuing opposition. Both sides in the debate tried to obtain his support. When in the end he refrained from openly objecting to the project, his popularity dwindled.

Several options are open to adherents seeking to influence a Mhondoro medium's statements. Sometimes groups of people negotiate with the Mhondoro spirit through the medium when they do not agree with a certain statement issued. They may send delegations to the medium asking permission from the Mhondoro for certain practices or decisions. Mediums themselves can also openly consult their adherents, as was shown above. But the most important 'tool' available to adherents seems to be the medium's reputation as a true vessel for the spirit. What Janzen describes as the core of ngoma is in fact part of a political power struggle. As already stated above, many mediums do not completely fulfil the ideal conditions of 'strangeness' and often require more than one testing ritual to convince people of their possession. The very aspects that can serve as legitimation of the mediums' position can also be used by adherents in their attempts to influence the mediums' pronouncements. A suspected medium is accused of abusing his or her position, of trying to accumulate money instead of working in the interest of the adherents. In such cases the illness preceding mediumship can be turned against the medium, by labelling it as mere madness instead of a sign of possession. When long-established mediums come under suspicion, as in the case of the medium of Chidyamauyu, it is often said that the Mhondoro spirit has left them as it became disappointed with the behaviour of the medium. The untimely death of a medium is also often interpreted as a sign of the spirit's disappointment .

Certain groups within the community of potential adherents have stronger positions *vis-à-vis* the Mhondoro mediums. As mentioned above, village headmen are closely linked to the mediums. Vatape often claim intimate knowledge of how the medium of a certain Mhondoro is supposed to behave on account of their families' longstanding association with the mediumship. In the case described above we saw that the medium of Chidyamauyu explicitly asked the village headmen for their opinions several times. When the community became polarized, at first he continued to support the village headmen and other elders opposing the project. People who do not have such a strong position in the cult may withdraw from the cult and join one of the mainstream churches or independent churches. This does not mean, however, that church members do not participate in the Mhondoro cult; many church members do.

When serious suspicions are harboured, adherents may decide to ignore the medium representing the Mhondoro of the spirit province in which they are living. When the medium of Chidyamauyu was still popular, many vatape and village elders residing outside his spirit province went to consult him rather than the mediums of their 'own' Mhondoro. Now that the reputation of the medium of Chidyamauyu is damaged, he does not receive as many visitors as he used to.

We have seen that the Mhondoro of Dande are related to each other and placed in genealogies of two main families, one autochthonous, one an invading lineage. The hierarchy among Mhondoro mediums is partly based on their place in the genealogies. However, the reputation of their mediums can also play a role (see Garbett 1992). The medium of Chidyamauyu represented a (great-)grandchild of one of the senior Mhondoro. Initially, this spirit only had a very small territory. When his popularity increased, he became influential in an area much larger than his initial spirit province. But the opposite can also happen. Mutota is the head of the invading lineage, a very senior Mhondoro. However, the present medium who claims to be possessed by Mutota is hardly ever consulted by people from Dande. The medium before him, George Kupara, was a very popular and influential medium in the 1960s.

Mediums as well as their potential adherents, are trying to find out what it is that the Mhondoro want, what they accept and what they disagree with. When people doubt the authenticity of a medium, they do not necessarily doubt the Mhondoro spirits or the Mhondoro cult. Sometimes adherents criticize the Mhondoro spirits for punishing them too hard by withholding rains on account of mistakes made by a few people. But in general they seem convinced that the Mhondoro want the best for their subjects on earth. The difficulty, however, can be that ideas about what is the best for the Mhondoro's adherents may vary greatly among those same adherents.

Janzen describes the Mhondoro cult as a cult 'defining primary values and social patterns for generations of adepts'. I hope to have showed convincingly that the Mhondoro cult more probably serves as a platform for discussion of social patterns as well as economic and political developments, in which lay adherents play a crucial role. It is this in which interests me: the way in which ngoma cults react to socio-political developments; the interplay between cult leaders and adherents while coming to grips with such developments; and these topics rather more than the search for essential characteristics of ngoma cults.

Notes

1 This article is based on fieldwork conducted for a PhD study of local perspectives towards natural resource management and the role of the Mhondoro cult in Dande, northern Zimbabwe. I wish to acknowledge the financial support of the Netherlands Foundation for the Advancement of Tropical Research (WOTRO). I would like to express my gratitude to the director and staff of the Centre for Applied Social Sciences, University of Zimbabwe, for granting me the status of Research Associate during my stay in Zimbabwe, as well as for their intellectual support.

I would like to thank Bonno Thoden van Velzen and Peter Geschiere for their useful comments on an earlier draft. I also thank the members of the Amsterdam School for Social Science Research 'anthropology club', especially Birgit Meyer and Remco Ensel, for their valuable comments.

This paper was presented at the '11th Colloquium on Ritual and Religion in Africa', held at Satterthwaite in April 1996. I received some very helpful comments from the other presenters at the Colloquium, especially from Richard Werbner, Terence Ranger and Jocelyn Alexander.

Lastly, I would like to thank Kingsley Garbett for his prompt and helpful reaction.

2 Lan (1985: 49–56) offers a detailed description of the process of becoming a Mhondoro medium in which Janzen's 'going through the white', the personal song etc. can be recognized. Interviews I had with fifteen Mhondoro mediums (all but three of the mediums living between the Musengezi and Manyame rivers) confirmed Lan's description.

3 But not all village headmen will serve as mutape.

4 The word 'mhondoro' means lion. When the spirit is not possessing the medium it is believed to wander around in the bush in the body of a lion.

5 This incident also strengthened my opinion, which I share with Bourdillon (1987b: 271), that the refusal of many mediums to get into contact with modern, western items was not so much a sign of resistance towards pre-independence white domination, as a means of showing that they really are possessed by a spirit that lived long ago.

6 A ward is an administrative unit. Every district is divided into several wards, every ward containing approximately 10 to 15 villages.

7 After independence in 1980, a new system of local government was introduced. All villages were to elect village committees. For each cluster of villages roughly containing 100 households a village development committee (VIDCO) is elected. Originally, these elected bodies were to substitute the offices of kraal and village headmen, but in practice the latter still continue to function.

8 I thank Bill Derman for kindly providing me with a transcript of the tape he recorded at the meeting.

9 This is a highly unusual remark. In all my interviews with Mhondoro mediums (whether they were possessed or not), I have never come across such a remark. Issues that in some way or another are related to the land are usually singled out as issues over which Mhondoro mediums should be consulted.

10 In the project proposal no new clinics were planned for Matsiwo A ward. The only new school planned for had already been constructed. However, DERUDE had not officially declared the school completed, so that no teachers could be employed. It is not unthinkable that DERUDE used the approval of the school as a means of pressure.

11 Without mentioning that the schedule of drilling for waterpoints has been very much delayed in other areas in Dande and that there are serious problems in maintaining and repairing already constructed boreholes.

12 The medium of Chiodzamamera had opened a store after independence. He frequently travelled to Harare, in civilian clothes, to buy goods for his store. A few years ago he was killed in a road accident on his way back from Harare.

13 He was eventually to replace the sitting ward councillor, who was a fierce opponent of the project. How he managed to, is worth further analysis. However, at this moment I am not able to shed any light on this issue.

14 Though I had seen the medium living in relative wealth, it is impossible for me to ascertain how she obtained her cattle and house.

15 At every Police Station in Zimbabwe's rural areas some CIO officers are stationed, patrolling the surrounding areas. After some time one learns to recognize them, as they usually have a certain way of dressing as well as addressing people. The presence of CIO officers at the new medium's place was later confirmed by a DERUDE employee

Literature

ADF, African Development Fund (1986) Appraisal Report for the Mid-Zambezi Valley Rural Development Project. Agricultural and Rural Development Department.

Beach, D. (1986) *War and Politics in Zimbabwe 1840–1900*. Gweru: Mambo Press.

Bhebe, N. and T. Ranger (1995) 'Volume Introduction: Society in Zimbabwe's Liberation War: Volume Two'. In Ngwabi Bhebe and Terence Ranger (eds) *Society in Zimbabwe's Liberation War*. Harare: University of Zimbabwe; London: James Currey; Portsmouth, Heinemann; pp. 6–34.

Bourdillon, M.F.C. (1979) 'Religion and Authority in a Korekore Community'. *Africa* 49: 172–181.

—— (1981) 'Suggestions of Bureaucracy in Korekore Religion: Putting the Ethnography Straight'. *Zambezia* IX: 119–36.

—— (1987a) *The Shona Peoples. An Ethnography of the Contemporary Shona, with Special Reference to their Religion*. Revised edition. Gweru: Mambo Press.

—— (1987b) 'Guns and Rain: Taking Structural Analysis too Far?' *Africa* 20: 263–74.

Burck, D.J. (1989) *Kuoma Rupandi (The Parts Are Dry), Ideas and Practices concerning Disability and Rehabilitation in a Shona Ward*. Leiden: Africa Studies Centre.

Daneel, M.L. (1977) 'The Growth and Significance of Shona Independent Churches'. In: M.F.C. Bourdillon (ed.) *Christianity South of the Zambezi*, vol. 2, pp. 77–129. Gwelo: Mambo Press.

Derman, W. (1993) *Recreating Common Property Management: Government Projects and Land Use Policy in the Mid-Zambezi Valley, Zimbabwe*. Harare: Centre for Applied Social Sciences.

Fry, P. (1976) *Spirits of Protest: Spirit Mediums and the Articulation of Consensus among the Zezuru of Southern Rhodesia*. Cambridge: Cambridge University Press.

Garbett, K. (1966a) 'Religious Aspects of Political Succession among the Valley Korekore (N. Shona)'. In E. Stokes and R. Brown (eds) *The Zambezian Past*. Manchester: Manchester University Press

—— (1966b) 'The Rhodesian Chief's Dilemma: Government Officer or Tribal Leader'. *Race* 8: 307–426.

—— (1967) 'Prestige, Status and Power in a Modern Valley Korekore Chiefdom, Rhodesia'. *Africa* 37: 307–25.

—— (1969) 'Spirit Mediums as Mediators in Valley Korekore Society'. In Beattie, J. and Middleton, J. (eds) *Spirit Mediumship and Society in Africa*. London: Routledge & Kegan Paul.

—— (1977) 'Disparate Regional Cults and a Unitary Field in Zimbabwe'. In R. Werbner (ed.) *Regional Cults*. London: Academic Press.

—— (1992) 'From Conquerors to Authochthons: Cultural Logic, Structural Transformation, and Korekore Regional Cults'. *Social Analysis, Journal of Cultural and Social Practice*, 31: 12–43.

Government of Zimbabwe (1985a) *Communal Lands Development Plan. A 15 Year Development Strategy*. First draft. Ministry of Land, Resettlement and Rural Development. Harare: Government Printer.

—— (1985b) *Resettlement and Rural Development. Intensive Resettlement Policies and Procedures*. Revised version. Ministry of Land, Resettlement and Rural Development. Harare: Government Printer.

Holleman, J.F. (1969) *Chief, Council and Commissioner: Some Problems of Government in Rhodesia*. Assen: Afrika Studiecentrum.

Janzen, J.M. (1992) *Ngoma. Discourses of Healing in Central and Southern Africa*. Berkeley, Los Angeles, Oxford: University of California Press.

Kriger, N. (1988) 'The Zimbabwean War of Liberation: Struggles within the Struggle'. *Journal of Southern African Studies* 14: 304–26.

—— (1992) *Zimbabwe's Guerrilla War. Peasant Voices*. Cambridge: Cambridge University Press.

Lan, D. (1985) *Guns and Rain. Guerrillas and Spirit Mediums in Zimbabwe*. Harare: Zimbabwe Publishing House.

Pels, P. (1993) *Critical Matters, Interactions Between Missionaries and Waluguru in Colonial Tanganyika, 1930–1961*. Amsterdam: Amsterdam School of Social Research (PhD thesis).

Ranger, T.O. (1967) *Revolt in Southern Rhodesia 1896–7*. London: Heinemann.

—— (1985) *Peasant Consciousness and Guerrilla War in Zimbabwe*. Harare: Zimbabwe Publishing House.

—— (1991) 'Religion and Witchcraft in Everyday Life in Contemporary Zimbabwe'. In Preben Kaarsholm (ed.) *Cultural Struggle and Development in Southern Africa*, 149–65. London: James Currey.

Schoffeleers, J.M. (1978) 'Introduction'. In J.M. Schoffeleers, (ed.) *Guardians of the Land*. Gwelo: Mambo Press.

Weinrich, A.K.H. (1971) *Chiefs and Councils in Rhodesia*. London: Heinemann.

Werbner, R.P. (1977) 'Introduction'. In R.P. Werbner (ed.) *Regional Cults*. A.S.A. Monograph 16. London: Academic Press.

6

The Story
of a Scapegoat King
In rural Malawi

Matthew Schoffeleers

If the community is to achieve anything it values – good fellowship, children, many cattle, victory, in short, prosperity – *it must have food*. … Regular provision of food requires peace and good order, and the observance of Law. Since the political structure guarantees this order and peace, which will allow food to be produced, *the political structure becomes associated with food for the community at large.*

(Gluckman 1963: 134–35; italics added)

Introduction

The term *ngoma* as understood in this chapter refers to a collectivity of rituals which accompany the continuous reproduction of a society *as a whole*. A common characteristic of these rituals is that at some stage they evoke the image of an ideal society, in which there is no place for want and suffering. The idea of such a society eventually emerging is predicated on the belief that negative experiences such as drought and famine may transform into their opposites through the intermediation of a transcendent order. The drum with its infinite range of associations deriving from its shape, material and sound is the encompassing metaphor of this complex whole.

There are numerous types of ngoma pertaining to a variety of professions and functions, but we shall limit ourselves, following Janzen (1992), to politics and healing. Although Janzen acknowledges the political alongside the therapeutic ngoma, he has paid relatively little attention to the former. This had for one of its consequences that he deprived himself of the chance to elucidate their interrelationships in any systematic way. One observation he makes in that connection concerns a negative correlation: in centralized state systems the therapeutic ngoma tends to become marginalized as the state itself takes responsibility for public health (Janzen 1992: 74–9). Apparently, the political elite views therapeutic ngoma as a potentially hostile factor.

This may be explained by the fact that marginalization of therapeutic ngoma helps curb the emergence of charismatic healers critical of the political establishment. Yet critical charismatic healers, however relevant, are exceptional. What we should be looking for to account for the suspicious attitude of the ruling class is a more general factor. The factor we have in mind are the earth cults, which function as healing cults for the community as a whole. There are many such cults in sub-Saharan Africa. One need but think of the Earth Cult of the Tallensi in Ghana (Fortes 1964), the Rain Queen of the Lovedu in South Africa (Krige and Krige 1943), and the Mwari (Daneel

1970, Ranger 1967, Schoffeleers 1979b), Chaminuka, Karuva and Dzivaguru cults in
Zimbabwe (Gelfand 1962, Abraham 1966, Garbett 1969, Bhebe 1979, Bourdillon 1979,
Lan 1985), the Rain Cults of southeastern Sudan (Simonse 1992). They have variously
been called earth cults, rain cults, or rain and fertility cults. From the political view-
point they are to be characterized as territorial cults, since they are centrally
concerned with the political life of a specific land area, and since their constituency is
a group identified by their common occupation of and rights in that land area
(Schoffeleers 1979a: 1). However, as we are here primarily interested in their life-
restoring functions we shall refer to them as 'earth cults'.

Victor Turner has made an important contribution to our understanding of earth
cults in sub-Saharan Africa by contrasting them with ancestral and political cults. He
summarizes the crucial difference between them as follows:

> Ancestral and political cults and their local embodiments tend to represent crucial power divisions
> and classificatory distinctions within and among politically discrete groups, while earth and
> fertility cults represent ritual bonds between those groups and even, as in the case of the Tallensi,
> tendencies toward still wider bonding. The first type stresses exclusiveness, the second inclu-
> siveness. The first emphasizes sectional interests and conflict over them; the second disinterest-
> edness and shared values. In studies of African cults of the first type, we find frequent reference to
> such topics as lineage segmentation, local history, factional conflict and witchcraft. In cults of the
> second type, the accent is laid on common ideals and values, and, where there has been
> misfortune, on the guilt and responsibility of all rather than the culpability of individuals and
> factions.
>
> (Turner 1974: 185)

Turner himself cautions his readers that the contrast between political cults and earth
cults, as sketched by him, is a simplification of what may be a more complex situation.
Thus functions that he associates with mutually exclusive cults may actually be exercised by one and the same cult complex, as we shall presently see. Nevertheless, even
in such cases the set of contrasts noted by him remains operative.

Earth cults operate on the basis of a philosophy which holds that serious abuses in
the life of a community invariably lead to natural disasters which in their turn
endanger the life of that community. Or from a different angle: control of the climatic
cycle depends on the correct management and control of society (Homans 1965: 28;
M.Wilson 1970: 38). In a similar vein Beidelman notes that Swazi see

> an order both in the sphere of natural objects and events and in human society. In most respects it
> would seem that a distinction between nature and society is not made by them; rather the two are
> manifestations of the same principles of order in the universe, interdependent and validating one
> another. Order in one effects order in the other, and disorder in either jeopardizes the order of
> both.
>
> (Beidelman 1966: 373–405)

This interpenetration of the two orders has for one of its consequences that earth cults,
apart from their therapeutic, fertility-promoting function, have an important political
dimension as well. They often actively intervene in the political process. When cult
mediums exhort the population to plant a particular crop or employ a particular agricultural technique to the exclusion of other crops and other techniques, such actions,
although essentially economic, may have political consequences. Much the same can
be said when earth cult organizations urge a population to return to the ways of its
ancestors. However, such actions may not be more than peripherally political. This
view changes when it is seen that cult organizations also take part in the election of
chiefs or in the decision-making process of a chiefdom, or when they organize, lead or

support resistance movements against invading forces. This kind of action is unequiv-ocally political, and it is by no means exceptional. One can go further and state that territorial cults are by nature political since they are the religious representation of what are basically territorial and political groups, and because the boundaries between religious and secular politics are notoriously difficult to demarcate. There always exist areas of overlap which constitute a structural basis of conflict. Weber called them 'cults of political associations' (Weber 1971: 16), but that characterization would be misleading if it were taken to mean that they are no more than a religious extension of the political establishment. They constitute a different source of authority which on occasion may be identifiable with secular political institutions but which remains in principle different from them. It is this relationship between earth cults and secular authority which provides the closest analogy to the church-state rela-tionship in literate cultures. It is, however, strictly an analogy, because there exist significant differences between these two situations. Earth cults, unlike churches, recognize no distinctions which set the community of believers apart from the rest of society, nor do they possess an explicit creed on which this could be argued. The analogy derives its validity rather from the fact that in earth cult organisations ritual and secular authority are thought of as distinguishable and separable. It has become clear from a number of case studies (Schoffeleers (ed.) 1979) that this concept of dual authority and the variety of modes by which it is realized constitute a major locus of conceptual and organizational change. Earth cults thus offer a privileged case to explore the interconnections between the two kinds of ngoma, which is what this chapter sets out to do.

The classification of earth cults with the therapeutic ngoma implies a distinction between therapeutic ngomas which are concerned with the healing of individuals, and those concerned with the healing of a community as a whole. By revealing the social wrongs which are thought to have caused a drought or other calamity, earth cults address the structural causes of illness, and their inclusivist character allows for direct participation of the public in the quest for those causes.

Earth cults often feature a ritualist of the type known since Frazer's days as 'divine king' or 'scapegoat king'. The scapegoat king referred to in the title of this chapter is Chief Tengani who occupies a central position in the Mbona cult of Malawi, cited by Janzen as one of 'the well-studied examples' of centralized shrine cults that have persisted over centuries and continue into the present (Janzen 1992: 76). Mbona's is a cult which has been documented from the middle of the nineteenth century but whose traceable history goes back to the second half of the sixteenth century (Schoffeleers 1992). Its ritual cycle consists of annual rain prayers, the rebuilding of the main shrine every five years on average, and the installation of a new 'spirit wife' once in every generation. Tengani is the main actor in the rebuilding of the shrine. On that occasion he is symbolically treated as a slave, and there is a firm belief that any Tengani taking part in the ritual of rebuilding will die soon after. Tengani thus conforms to Frazer's concept of divine kingship around which an important discussion has developed in Africanist anthropology (Gluckman 1954; Beidelman 1966; Norbeck 1967; Turner 1969, 1974; Girard 1977; Morris 1987; Simonse 1992).

We shall begin by providing some detail about the history and political position of the Tengani dynasty. This will be followed by an account of their role in the rebuilding of the shrine. Next, we are going to review the discussion about divine kingship to see what relevance it has to the Tengani case. We shall then be in position to draw conclusions about the nature of the relationship between political and therapeutic ngoma, which is our primary interest.

The Tenganis

The Tengani chiefdom forms part of the Lower Shire Valley in southern Malawi. Its origins in all probability predate the close of the sixteenth century, when the valley became the centre of the powerful Lundu kingdom (Schoffeleers 1992: 117–39). Like the Lundus, the Tenganis belong to the Mang'anja section of the Maravi peoples (Tew 1950: 30–50), Maravi being the ancient spelling of Malawi. The documented history of the Tenganis dates from the arrival of the Livingstone expedition, which was active in the region from January 1859 to the end of 1863 (Rowley 1866; Schoffeleers 1973). Tengani is described by the members of the expedition as the paramount chief of the area. The then incumbent had at his disposal a small but effective army with which to keep Portuguese slave hunters at bay. However, in 1863 the valley was hit by a catastrophic drought, which finally enabled the slave hunters to defeat Tengani and decimate the population. In later years, the Tenganis played a crucial role in bringing the valley under British control. The British in return officially recognized the Tengani family as part of the traditional establishment. This was confirmed with the official introduction of Indirect Rule in the first decades of the twentieth century.

The power of the dynasty reached its apogee with the accession to the throne of Molin Tengani, who with the help of the colonial government managed considerably to expand his territory (Mandala 1990: 231–7). He also made a number of unsuccessful attempts to be formally recognized as paramount chief of the entire valley on the ground that his forebears were already settled there before the Lundus (Schoffeleers 1992: 107). Molin Tengani was greatly feared by the population, which in the end turned to the nationalist Malawi Congress Party (MCP) for support. Following the general elections of 1961, which was overwhelmingly won by the MCP, Molin was deposed and replaced by a relative, Stonkin Tengani. Molin died in May 1967.

The Mbona shrine which the Tenganis are supposed to help rebuild every five years or so is situated some sixteen kilometres south of their court. The shrine which is made of highly perishable materials, is never to be repaired, but always fully rebuilt. This happens when the valley is hit by a drought or other natural calamity. Droughts are viewed as the deity's reaction to serious instances of social disorder. They thus generate a protracted discussion amongst the population about their possible cause or causes. When this has been going on for some time and tensions have risen sufficiently high, the deity's medium will be in a position to summon the political hierarchy to his hut and reveal to them why Mbona feels offended.

One of Mbona's standard complaints is that his shrine-hut has not been cared for, although, as stated above, it is forbidden to carry out any repairs. He demands therefore that it be rebuilt as soon as possible. However, this is not a simple matter, since it requires the cooperation of the chiefs, who may not always be willing to grant a request of that nature without demanding that their own grievances be attended to first. Those wanting to obstruct the rebuilding can always do so by insisting that the ritual be executed in every detail, real or imaginary. Thus the rebuilding of the shrine becomes a political contest in which those involved test each other's strength while trying to improve their political position. One of the consequences of this state of affairs is that the negotiations for the rebuilding can only be successfully initiated when there is considerable pressure on the part of the general public (Schoffeleers 1992: 65).

The Mbona medium becomes possessed rather infrequently, sometimes at intervals of several years. Possession may be provoked by three interrelated types of events, namely, environmental calamities, offences against the social order, and offences against the cult. In fact, it may be difficult in any particular case to decide which of the three is to be regarded as the activating factor, since – from the perspective of the actors – nature, society and cult form an indivisible triad. Environmental and climatic disturbances are routinely explained in terms of social disturbances and vice versa, while both again are connected with the cult as the censor of public mores and as the possessor of the means of expiation. Whatever the immediate cause of possession, it invariably involves a pronouncement on the social and moral condition of the community. Moreover, the message transmitted by the medium is always centrally concerned with the policies of the chiefs and with the relationships between the chiefs and the population. Characteristically, the chiefs have to bear the brunt of the medium's criticism, because they are accused either of siding with the central government against the population, or of failing to put an end to social abuses within their territories. While this may be said of any chief, Tengani, as the most senior chief, is especially vulnerable.

There is thus much antagonism between the medium and the chiefs, who also function as the senior cult officers. At the time of my fieldwork in the late 1960s the latter were continuously criticized by the medium for 'despising the cult' (*kunyoza Mbona*). The officers in their turn criticized the medium for trying to become independent of them by promoting a shrine he had built in his own backyard. It was striking, however, that despite these criticisms, they left him in peace. The main reason for that was that he enjoyed considerable renown among the people.

The chiefs may also express their disagreement with the medium by refusing to attend a possession seance. They themselves maintain that this depends on whether the man's possession is 'real' or 'feigned', which they claim they are able to judge by the medium's behaviour. More realistically, though, the criterion used by the chiefs to judge whether the medium's possession is to be considered genuine is the degree of political pressure by which a seance is generated.

The events which may cause Mbona's medium to become possessed also provoke spates of fantastic rumour. Many such rumours circulated in the late 1960s, a time when particularly vigorous efforts were made to rebuild the shrine and to revive certain other features of the organization. According to one of those rumours, paramount chief Lundu had shot a monkey, one of Mbona's messengers, which had been sent to Lundu's court. Because of this atrocious act, all monkeys were said to have left the shrine, a sign that Mbona himself had withdrawn and that some calamity was certain to follow. Another rumour had it that fishermen on the Shire River had dragged up a small iron box from which emerged a little man with a pronounced limp. When asked how he got his limp, he said he had broken his leg walking through gardens which had been ridged and that he was now on his way to the district commissioner to tell him that the practice should be discontinued. To understand that rumour it should be known that the inhabitants had been protesting for years against the obligatory ridging of their gardens as an entirely useless exercise (Mandala 1990: 226–37).

According to yet another rumour, the waters of the sacred pool had turned red in a kind of replay of Mbona's martyrdom. This was taken as an omen of worse things to follow. Finally, rumours circulated to the effect that the medium had already become possessed and that he had spoken out on issues concerning the cult and the region. These rumours, fantastic as they may sound to outsiders, actually represented a collective effort by the population to establish unanimity on issues of general concern. Furthermore, they appeared to provide much of the pressure which finally generated the possession seance, and they also helped determine the message which the medium was to communicate.

The first person to be advised of the outcome of the seance is Chief Tengani, who has to play the central role in the rebuilding ceremony. As to that role, four items are invariably mentioned: first, that on that occasion he has to wear a slave's outfit; second, that the roof of the shrine is to be built upon his head; third, that afterwards he is to commit incest with one of his 'sisters', and, fourth, that he will die 'within a year or so'. It is said that for that reason some of the incumbents in the past took to flight rather than participate.

I have never witnessed the rebuilding of the shrine myself, and I cannot therefore say how much of what actually happens today accords with any of these descriptions. One point on which we have certainty, however, is that from the mid-1930s onward the Tengani incumbents have refused to take part in the ritual. Molin Tengani, as far as we know the first openly to refuse, invoked the fact that he was a Christian and for that reason was not allowed to participate. Stonkin Tengani, who succeeded Molin in the early 1960s, at first promised that he would cooperate but later revoked this on the ground that the shrine officials neglected the cult. At any rate, it is clear that for quite some time the rebuilding has been performed in the absence of a Tengani.

But in the olden days, it is maintained, as soon as Tengani's consent had been obtained, people began to collect grass, reed, poles and everything else needed for the occasion. The rebuilding of the shrine ideally signalled the end of a period of contestation and the beginning of an era of unity and cooperation. The traditional accounts of the ritual lay particular stress on this aspect. Thus, no household was to give more than one cob of maize or head of millet, so that the gifts of all could be used to brew the libational beer. Similarly, nobody was allowed to carry more than one shaft of reed or bundle of grass thicker than one's own arm, so that the labours of all would be required to build the shrine. On the eve of the rebuilding Tengani travelled to the village of Chief Malemia, some four kilometres from the shrine, where he spent the night. Next morning at daybreak, all moved to the sacred thicket for the ceremony proper. The following is an account by the officials Chapirira and Kumbiwanyati:

> On the appointed day everybody comes, including of course Tengani. As soon as he arrives, work on the hut commences, starting with the circular roof, which is always made on the ground. As soon as the measurements have been taken, he positions himself in the middle and the entire roof is then built upon his head. In the meantime, others are busy putting up the circular walls on which the roof is to rest. One really has to work fast if the job is to be finished before sunset, but this is not too difficult with so many people around. Spurred on by the sound of the great drum, *Kamango*, they busily move to and fro. While we are building the hut, it is impossible to distinguish chief from commoner, for on that occasion we are all equals. All of us, including our little children, are Mbona's slaves. When the hut is finished and the place has been swept, we elders begin rolling about in the dust, first Ngabu [the chief ritualist], then Tengani, and finally the others. Meanwhile the great drum is beaten and all of us pray, 'We have now built a hut for you. Have mercy on us and do not carry out your threats, for it can no longer be said that we disobeyed you! Do not reject us, your slaves, for we have given you the honour you deserve!'

(Schoffeleers 1992: 66)

After finishing the roof, they spread a dark-blue cloth, symbol of the rain clouds, over the grass thatching. But before lifting it onto the walls, they invited the rains by swaying it in the direction of the four points of the compass, beginning with the east, in the direction of the place where Mbona had been murdered. The moment they had finished their work, peals of thunder would be heard, lightning would flash, and a storm would break accompanied by heavy downpours, so that on their way home people would be drenched to the bone.

Immediately after the ceremony, Tengani would set out on his return journey, spending the night on the way with one of his real or classificatory sisters. The following day he would be back in his village, waiting for his death to occur.

As stated, the rebuilding of the shrine is an emergency measure, which becomes operative only when the rains are failing. Well before it, at the end of the dry season, Tengani would have performed the rain rituals at his own court, starting at the graveyard of his predecessors. In Molin Tengani's words:

> In the middle of the night following the ceremonies at his predecessors' burial thicket, the chief and his wife rose from their sleeping mat. They left their hut, the chief by the larger front door, his wife by the smaller backdoor. In the open space in front of his hut, the chief drew a large cross with his long-bladed, two-edged ceremonial knife (*kandranga*). Standing on the centre of this cross, he pointed with his knife to the north, west, south and east, while reciting a rain prayer. At this point the clouds began to gather. He now drew a circle around the cross, again beginning and ending at its north end. After this, he and his wife entered the hut again in the same way as they had left it. They had intercourse while thunder roared and lightning flashed, and copious rains began to fall. When the chief rose again, lightning stopped but rain continued to fall in downpours perhaps for two or three days. The rain is the work of the chief and his headwife!
>
> (Schoffeleers 1968: 165)

Tengani's account testifies to the rich symbolism surrounding the relationship between the chief and his wife. She is the land; the chief is the sky and, symbolically, the only male. His sexual activity is associated with thunder and lightning, and his sexual fluids with the rains. His rain-providing power was also expressed in the funeral rituals of the Tenganis. According to Molin Tengani, the body of the deceased chief remained unburied for a considerable time due to the lengthy preparations needed for the burial. Meanwhile it was placed on a scaffold while the liquids dripped into pots placed underneath. At the burial the remains were wrapped in a mat, and together with the pots carried to the dynasty's sacred grove where they were placed in an open grave. If they were covered, no rain would fall and the crops would wither.

When Molin Tengani died in May, 1967, a grave of normal depth was dug. In it were placed most of his personal effects, such as clothes, crockery, cutlery, and personal papers. On top of this sat the coffin, which contained the body of the chief and his hunting rifle. The coffin was made of wood and, to allow his spirit to escape, a hole was bored in its lid near the head. One of the sons protested, since according to him the father had left instructions that a small window be made at that place.

Before his death, he had divided his large cattle herd among his wives and children, but three cows were left to be killed on three consecutive days after his transformation had taken place. At the moment of death a dog gave birth to a litter of puppies under his bed. When some of those present proposed to remove the dogs from the hut, others protested for they considered this the work of the chief's spirit, and the animals were left in peace. There was no wailing or any of the usual signs of mourning so that the villagers were quite unaware of what had happened. Wailing would have made the transformation impossible. The burial took place the day after his death. The grave was not filled in, but planks were laid over it leaving a narrow opening at one side. A thin layer of earth was then strewn over the planks to show the footprints of witches in case they would visit the grave.

Usually, transformation is said to take place in the early morning following the burial. The undertaker and some of the chief's closest kin go to inspect the grave where they find that the corpse has disappeared. They see either a full-grown lion among the trees nearby, or a lion cub sitting on the earth mound beside the grave, or just lion spoors leading to the bush. In Tengani's case, however, transformation was effected three days after his burial according to his own prediction. On the first two nights after his burial hyaenas visited the grave, attracted by the smell of the corpse. When the chief's undertaker and some of his close relatives went to inspect the grave on the third day no hyaenas had been there, and they also noticed that there was no longer any smell. From these signs it was concluded that the corpse had indeed disappeared. Word was sent to the village that Tengani had risen from the dead, and the grave was duly filled in.

What followed is an interesting example of instant myth creation. The undertaker himself, whom I first interviewed, still wavered in his opinion. He said he was sure that Tengani had come back to life, but he was not yet sure that he had changed into a lion. One of the former incumbents he had known had been seen in the form of a lion standing on top of an anthill, but in this case no such clear sign had been given. Therefore, he was not sure as to what exactly had happened. Other villagers, however, maintained that the coffin had been found empty by the graveside. Lion spoors leading to the cattle kraal had been seen. The same evening, one of Tengani's sons who had gone outside to relieve himself saw a light follow him. Terrified, he fled back to his father's hut, where everybody was of the opinion that the light he had seen were the eyes of a lion. Others claimed they had seen a light moving about the late chief's cattle kraal. One man had actually seen the lion on his way to the bathing place on the river bank, and finally there was a report of someone who had seen a lion with a human leg.

The village was now in a festive mood, and started a celebration lasting three days. On each of these a cow was slaughtered and meat distributed. The royal drum *Kamango* was beaten till deep into the night, but its sound was nearly drowned by the noise of gramo-phones and transistor radios. After the feast the lion was said to have crossed the river into Mozambique to visit the chief's private medicine man from whom he had obtained the transformation medicine (Schoffeleers 1968: 172–4). What this amounts to is that Tengani forms part of two different rain cults: that of his own dynasty, and Mbona's. The first is exclusivistic as the ritual legitimates his position at the top of the political ladder. The second is inclusivistic and egalitarian, emphasizing the equality of all. But the very fact that Mbona's shrine has to be rebuilt means that Tengani's dynastic rain rituals have failed this time around, and that his rule has therefore come under severe criticism. It is at this point that he enters irreversibly the tragic phase of divine kingship.

Divine kingship

Frazer begins his study of divine kingship with an evocation of Diana's priest at Nemi, whose task it was to defend a tree. Only a runaway slave was allowed to break off, if he could, one of its boughs. Success in the attempt entitled him to fight the priest in single combat, and if he killed him he reigned in his stead until he was himself slain by someone stronger. To Frazer, the death of the divine king of Nemi, as well as divine kings elsewhere, and their succession by a younger and more vigorous person, was thought to be symbolic of the renewal of nature (Frazer 1963: 13).

Frazer also discusses the related phenomenon of public scapegoats, including scapegoats in classical antiquity (Frazer 1963: 736–68). It appears for instance that the Athenians regularly maintained a number of 'degraded and useless beings' at public expense; and when any calamity, such as plague, drought or famine, befell the city, they sacrificed these outcasts as scapegoats. Divine kings and scapegoats thus functioned in similar contexts, the fertility of man, beast and land, but their conceptual affinity remains unclear in *The Golden Bough*.

Frazer has exercised considerable influence on students of comparative religion. Even the earlier social anthropologists lauded him as one of the founders of their discipline and one of their foremost representatives, but those of later generations were less enthusiastic. Mary Douglas for one, is of the opinion that Frazer's influence has been a baneful one. (Douglas 1966: 28). Nor was she the only one. Brian Morris cites I. Lewis to the effect that Frazer's *Golden Bough* is nowadays considered a 'monumental exercise in futility', while Morris himself considers Frazer's theoretical value limited as it lacks originality, most of its central themes being simply an elaboration of Tylor's theories (Morris 1987: 103–4).

What goes for Frazer's work in general, also goes for his ideas on divine kingship. Few anthropologists saw in them anything more than an ill-conceived theory of cultural evolution. A breakthrough occurred with Gluckman's Frazer lecture of 1953,'Rituals of Rebellion in South-East Africa', republished in *Order and Rebellion in Tribal Africa* (Gluckman 1963: 110–36). Although Gluckman considers Frazer's treatment of divine kingship as suffering from oversimplification, he nevertheless acknowledges the important fact that Frazer at the very outset had recognized the political dimension of the institution by raising the problem of the priest-king involved in a 'ritual of rebellion'. More specifically,

> he (Frazer) stressed that these agricultural ceremonies were *connected with the political process*, and that the dying god was often identified with secular kings. He drew attention also to the rebellious ceremonial, for he described the widespread installation of 'temporary kings' who were sacrificed or mocked and discharged after a few days of ostensible rule.
>
> (Gluckman 1963: 126; italics added)

However, as Gluckman continues, the modern anthropologist, basing his analysis on detailed observation in the field, is concerned in greater detail with the ceremonial roles of persons, categories of persons, and social groups, in relation to one another. Frazer could not have pursued these problems for he lacked the relevant evidence (Gluckman 1963: 111–12). To make his point, Gluckman describes ceremonies among the south-eastern Bantu of Zululand, Swaziland, and Mozambique, at the break of the rains, sowing, first-fruits and harvest.

> Whatever the ostensible purpose of these ceremonies, a most striking feature of their organisation is the way in which they openly express social tensions: women have to assert licence and dominance as against their formal subordination to men, princes behave to the king as if they covet the throne, and subjects openly state their resentment of authority.
>
> (Gluckman 1963: 112)

Hence his suggestion to define them as rituals of rebellion. Such rituals proceed within an established and sacred traditional system, in which there is dispute about particular distributions of power. This allows for instituted protest, and in complex ways renews the unity of the system.

In the Incwala, the first-fruits ceremony of the Swazi, described by Hilda Kuper (1944, 1963) and others, he perceives the acting out of the powerful tensions which make up national life. This ceremony should not be seen as a simple mass assertion of unity, but a stressing of conflict, a statement of rebellion and rivalry against the king, with periodical affirmations of unity with the king, and the drawing of power from the king. The political structure, as the source of prosperity and strength which safeguards the nation internally and externally, is made sacred in the person of the king. He is associated with his ancestors, for the political structure endures through the generations, though kings and people are born and die (Gluckman 1963: 125–6).

Again we see that the dramatic, symbolic acting of social relations in their ambivalence is believed to achieve unity and prosperity. This acting of conflict achieves a blessing – social unity. 'Clearly we are dealing with the general problem of *catharsis*... the purging of emotion through pity, fear and inspiration'(Gluckman 1963: 126). The rebellious ritual occurs within an established and unchallenged social order. It is not meant to alter the existing social and political order, for in traditional African political life men were rebels and never revolutionaries. In a 'repetitive social system' particular conflicts are settled, not by alterations in the order of offices, but by changes in the persons occupying those offices (Gluckman 1963: 127–8). People may hate the kingship in resenting its authority, but they do not aim to subvert it. For, it is the kingship and not the king who is divine. The rebellion is in fact waged to defend the kingship against the king: 'If this emphasis on potential rebellion in practice made the nation feel united, is it not possible that civil rebellion itself was a source of strength to these systems?' (Gluckman 1963: 130).

There have been critical reactions to Gluckman's interpretation of Incwala. Beidelman for one has stressed the cosmological aspects of the ceremony, stating that the main theme of the Incwala is not the expression of conflict but the separation of the king from the other groupings in the nation so that he is free to assume the mystical, cosmos-related powers associated with his kingship (Beidelman 1966). Another critic has been Norbeck, who argues that these rituals

> take the form of a ritual drama portraying the many dangers that the king must face in pursuit of his duties of office, especially the hatred and hostility of his rivals in the royal clan. The ceremony also expresses the sympathy of the people for their king, their loyalty to him, his seeming reluctance to serve in the royal role, and (it) unites the people under the king.
>
> (Norbeck 1967: 207)

The abusive songs refer to the hatred of the king's rivals rather than that of his subjects, and they are not to be viewed as rituals of rebellion. Institutionalized licence, role reversals and other social antagonisms should be 'interpreted, in line with the reasoning of van Gennep, as events that point up by contrast the social importance of the occasion' (Norbeck 1967: 218).

Turner, while agreeing with Gluckman's interpretation of the structural aspects of the Incwala which are clearly present in its rites of separation and aggregation, draws attention also to the interstructural parts (Turner 1967: 108–10). By this he refers more specifically to the liminal phase of the ritual, a day and a night of seclusion, when the king is divested of all the outward attributes, the 'accidents' of his kingship, and is reduced to its substance, the 'earth' and 'darkness' from which the normal, structured order of the Swazi kingdom will be regenerated 'in lightness' (Turner 1967:

109–10). Turner's comment, though not explicitly critical of Gluckman, is nevertheless relevant to the discussion at hand because he veers away from the structural-functionalist framework, so characteristic of Gluckman, to offer an alternative theory of ritual, which he later elaborated in *The Ritual Process* (Turner 1969).

I take it that these alternative interpretations, rather than undermining Gluckman's, only testify to the Incwala's ambiguity and poly-interpretability. Beidelman is right when emphasizing that the Incwala also effects the separation of the king from the other groupings in the nation so that he is free to assume the mystical, cosmos-related powers associated with his kingship. Norbeck may be right also when reinterpreting the abusive songs as a dramatization of the actions of the king's rivals, for not all those participating in the singing may actually harbour hatred against the king. Turner too is right when drawing attention to the liminal phase in the ritual, for, as he has never tired of repeating, it is these moments of 'liminality' and 'anti-structure' which revitalize the institutional order (Turner 1969). However, saying that a certain ritual allows for a variety of interpretations is not enough. It would be more satisfactory, if that variety of interpretations could be shown to be logically interconnected.

The French literary critic René Girard claims to have made a step in that direction by means of a reinterpretation of Frazer's scapegoat concept (Girard 1977). Girard sets off with the observation that our desires are to a large degree mimetic, even if we are not aware of it. What proves attractive to others may thereby become attractive to us. Although he would probably not go so far as to maintain that virtually all our desires are mimetic, the tenor of his theory is that our desires are mimetic to a much larger degree than we would care to admit. The next point is that where many people are after the same thing, scarcity may be one of the consequences, followed by open conflict and the outbreak of violence. Violence in its turn may escalate to the extent that it threatens the continued existence or viability of a community. In such a crisis people tend more and more to resemble each other. They make use of the same tactics and the same arguments, and in the end they may even forget what started the conflict. Increasingly, those involved may mentally become each other's doubles or twins (Schoffeleers 1991). The process of undifferentiation which causes that multitude of doubles to come into existence evokes the idea of a contagious disease, which is what the birth of twins in some societies is believed to bring about. If that process is not halted one way or another it will involve ever larger segments of society.

One way to solve such a crisis is to identify a scapegoat, who will then be lynched or expelled. However, once the killing or the expulsion is over, and peace is restored to everybody's relief, people begin to realize that their scapegoat was not only the cause of their discord but also of the unanimity and peace that followed. In his person, fascination combines with abhorrence. The scapegoat thereby acquires the traits of a sacred being (Otto 1917) whose salutary potential may be activated again by repeating the original event in ritualized form, first and foremost in the form of sacrifice. Persons destined to serve as scapegoats at some later stage were sometimes required to commit certain moral transgressions which prepared them for their future role. They might be forced to eat certain forbidden foods, or commit certain acts of violence.

Turning to Africa, Girard considers a group of sacred monarchies, situated between Egypt and Swaziland, in which the king is required to commit an act of incest, either real or symbolic, on certain solemn occasions – notably, at his enthronement or in the course of the periodic rites of renewal (Girard 1977: 104). In societies where the incestuous act is no longer actually consummated – if, indeed, it ever was – a symbolism of incest persists. As Luc de Heusch has pointed out, the important role played by the queen mother can only be understood in that context (de Heusch 1958). In Girard's view, committing incest prepares the king for his role as scapegoat and thereby as a sacrificial victim. He must be looked upon as a future sacrificial object (Girard 1977: 11–12).

Girard's ideas have been fruitfully used in a recent study of scapegoat kings in southeastern Sudan (Simonse 1992). Simonse sets off by noting the existence in recent studies of African political systems of two methodological a prioris. One is the dichotomy between the sacred and the political dimension of power as separate fields of investigation. The other is the dichotomy between systems with centralized authority or 'states', and acephalous segmentary political systems. His objective is a study of African political systems in which this double a priori is suspended, and which allows us to grasp the interrelatedness of power, consensus and the sacred in the institution of kingship (Simonse 1992: 1). The idea of the king as a scapegoat is not new as it is one of the leading themes in Frazer's *The Golden Bough*. The idea that social consensus and scapegoating are intimately linked is not new either. But the combination of the two ideas, in the form of a systematic theory of sacred kingship, is a novelty (Simonse 1992: 2).

To be able to see the connection between the victimary dimension of kingship and the generation of consensus, Simonse develops two processual models or 'scenarios' which generate contrasting forms of social organization: the enemy scenario in which the antagonists are groups of more or less equal strength, and the scapegoat scenario in which there is serious disproportion between the party of the victim and that of the victimizers. In the enemy model, the typical situation has two more or less equivalent antagonistic groups. In the scapegoat situation the typical situation is 'all against one' (Simonse 1992: 24). We are particularly concerned in this chapter with the scapegoat model, which is considered the main organizing principle in centrally organized societies.

Kingship and the cult of divinity are the two principal historical forms of organized centralism. They are two solutions to a single problem. Throughout history, divinity cults have unified large numbers of people, just as the subjection to a king or emperor has. In kingship the events preceding the elimination of the victim are emphasized. In the worship of divinity more weight is given to the aftermath of the elimination, the accomplished transcendence.

> Compared to the cult of divinity, which celebrates the absence of the violence expelled with the victim, the person of the King lends himself more readily to a direct enactment of the original scenario – which puts a live victim on the stage. The King is present, the divinity – apotheosis of something *absent* (the victim, the expelled violence) – must be *re-presented*. The power of the sacred is more immediately tangible in the 'divinity' of the King than in the 'personality' of the god. For this reason Girard qualifies kingship as an institution particularly revealing of the scapegoat mechanism.
> (Simonse 1992: 29)

In Girard's view, modern concepts narrow the conception of the divine down to the supernatural and the non-empirical. To us, the god-like qualities attributed to kings appear as something separate, as something added on at a later stage, in an attempt to increase their importance or legitimate their power:

Everyone repeats that the king is a kind of 'living god' but no one says that the divinity is a kind of dead king, which would be just as accurate. In the end there is a persistent preference for viewing the sacrifice and the sacredness of the king as a secondary and supplementary idea, for we must beware of rocking our little conceptual boat. Yet what guides our interpretation is only a conceptual system dominated by the idea of divinity, a *theology*. Scepticism about religion does not abolish this theological perspective. We are forced to reinterpret all religious schemata in terms of divinity because we are unaware of the surrogate victim [i.e. the scapegoat].

(Simonse 1992: 30, citing Girard)

Simonse makes the important remark that this conception of the separate existence of worldly and divine power in sacred kingship, denounced as 'theological' by Girard, is still characteristic for most of the work done on African kingship. Research remains focused on the establishment of correspondences between the 'religious level' and the 'politico-economic level', which are seen as existing external to one another. In the one tradition the king's political role is privileged over his divinity (i.e. Fortes and Evans-Pritchard 1940: 3, 17). In the other, the neo-Frazerian tradition, the opposite stance is taken, privileging the king's divinity over his political role. Representatives of this latter group are Luc de Heusch (1958), Alfred Adler (1982) and Jean-Claude Muller (1980) (Simonse 1992: 31). From his neo-Frazerian position de Heusch has criticized Girard, referring to African myths and rituals of kingship as evidence contradicting the alleged general applicability of Girard's victimary thesis (de Heusch 1985: 98–124). But de Heusch's assumption that the scapegoat mechanism is directly reflected in myth and ritual is wrong. In Girard's theory, the scapegoat mechanism is not present at the surface level of myth and ritual. It has the status of a 'structuring device', which is not 'represented' but 'misrepresented'. According to Girard, the way cultures represent victimary violence is of necessity always distorted, since no society can afford explicitly to admit its violent origins. Instead, each culture presents a misinterpretation of the process, throwing light on some aspects, but obscuring others (Simonse 1992: 31).

Although Kopytoff (1987) is only indirectly concerned with the institution of divine kingship, he proposes a sociogenesis of African kingship, which may shed further light on the role of the king as scapegoat. He uses Frederick Jackson Turner's famous frontier thesis (F.J.Turner 1893 [1961]) as a way of bringing a new perspective to the history and anthropology of sub-Saharan Africa, though with substantial adaptations. Where Turner referred to a tidal process of limited duration which in his view gave America its distinctive national political character, the perspective taken by Kopytoff is that of the local frontier, lying at the fringes of established polities. There, traditional African societies endlessly reproduced themselves out of the bits and pieces – human and cultural – of existing societies. Such a conception of political development is entirely opposite to those theories that see small polities as arising out of some hypothetical archaic bands roaming over a hypothetical prehistoric land-scape. It is also opposed to the view of the frontier as an area where alternative forms of social organization are being tried out. The frontiersmen came to the frontier not with a sociological and political *tabula rasa*, but with a mental model of a good society shaped after their experiences in their homeland. The frontier situation, endlessly repeated, thus functioned as a stabilizing, revitalizing and adaptive mechanism, preserving the basics of a broadly defined sub-Saharan cultural unity.

Kopytoff identifies eleven recurrent themes in the 'frontier process', such as the systemic production of frontiersmen, their movement in groups, the institutional vacuum in which they settled, the use made by them of pre-existing social models, the recruitment of adherents and dependents, and the beginnings of hierarchization by distinguishing between 'firstcomers' and 'latecomers'. The virtue of Kopytoff's treatment of these various themes is not so much that he comes up with startlingly new findings, but that he places familiar data in a refreshingly new context or scenario.

This comes to light especially in his discussion of patrimonialism and African sacred chiefship. Having noted that in the growing frontier polity the solidarity of a corporate kin group gradually gave way to the solidarity of contractual inter-dependence between rulers and ruled, he links this process of transition with a duality of perspectives on the polity. That duality manifests itself not only in the two paradigmatic stories about the foundation of the polity – that of the ruler and that of the subjects but also in a dual view of its constitutional legitimation, – the idea that the king has a right to rule and the opposite idea that he rules by the will of his subjects. One of Kopytoff's contentions therefore is that this often noted duality in the ideology of kingship did not arise within kingship itself but is a continuation of the duality that inheres in the far more modest embryonic polity shaped by the frontier. The standard myths of the subjects depict the founders as intruders. The myths of the rulers, for their part, see the subjects in the metaphor of the late-coming adherents to the polity the rulers had founded. This accomplished a crucial reversal of chronological primacy – the original inhabitants could be seen as 'immigrants' into the new society, for they were incorporated into it after its creation. 'Political chronology' thus came to dominate 'real chronology' (Kopytoff 1987: 65).

This difference in chronological perceptions corresponded to the difference in the conception of the essential character of the polity. In the ruling groups' view it was their private estate that had only grown larger. Hence the ruler's ideology of rulership was patrimonial: the polity was an extension of the ruler's household. Yet the perspective of the subjects lingered on, and in that perspective he remained a stranger who, followed by others, insinuated himself into power and legitimized his regime by appropriated local ritual symbols. This has for one of its consequences that the ruler may be blamed for a variety of ills, from drought to civil unrest. Particularly in the earlier phases, when the two perceptions of the ruler's office have not yet been integrated into a single ideology shared by both parties, this may make the ruler a readily available scapegoat. Kopytoff thereby proposes a sociogenesis of the African scapegoat king that invites comparison with René Girard's controversial theory on the same subject. In Girard's case kingship develops from the scapegoat mechanism originating from kingship. This need not be contradictory, as they seem to stand in a complementary relation to each other, for if the scapegoat becomes king, the king in his turn becomes scapegoat. The Tenganis may have established themselves as over-lords in the manner described by Kopytoff, but they thereby made themselves potential scapegoats in the manner described by Girard.

Conclusion

We began this chapter by taking up Janzen's remark that in centralized states the therapeutic ngomas tend to be marginalized as the state itself assumes responsibility for public health. Apparently, the political elite views the therapeutic ngoma as a potentially hostile factor. It was suggested that earth cults, of wide occurrence in sub-

Saharan Africa, may be part of the explanation. Earth cults function as healing cults for the community as a whole, and in that capacity they constitute an interface between the private healing cults and the political system. This means among other things that they operate as a forum where traditional rulers can be publicly and legitimately censored on issues pertaining to the wellbeing of the population in the broadest possible sense. This censorial function they are able to perform on the basis of two fundamental properties.

One of these is that the entire population is included in their membership. The other is their worldview which posits that the successful management of nature depends on the correct management and control of society. In other words, natural disasters are interpreted as a consequence of some serious malfunctioning of society. This in its turn leads to a generalized search for possible causes in the way the community is managed. The conclusion is invariably that those in power are to be held responsible or co-responsible because they were either actively involved themselves, or condoned wrongs committed by others. If everything goes well, the end of the affair is that the political elite promises to take corrective action, which promise is sealed by a ritual of penance and reconciliation.

The political elite are therefore viewed as influencing the health situation in two ways: directly, by the way they control people's access to the essential means of existence; and indirectly via the functioning of the seasonal cycle. State politics, rain and health thus constitute an indivisible triad. By providing a legitimate channel of protest against undesirable state policies earth cults are a major locus of rituals of rebellion.

In the second part we introduced the Tengani dynasty as being involved in rain rituals of its own as well as those of the Mbona cult. Whenever the dynastic rituals were successful, the ruling chief would be left in peace, but should the rains fail, he would be accused of political malfunctioning and summoned to take part in the rebuilding of the shrine. This, it is believed, would unfailingly produce rain, but the chief had to pay for this with his life. Upon his death he would join his predecessors and transform into a major rain-spirit himself. Special attention was paid to Molin Tengani, who made a name for himself not only as a shrewd politician but also as a Big Man. Although he was the most powerful Tengani since the one visited by Livingstone, the others were also regarded by the population as far superior to the other valley chiefs despite the fact that they were of equal rank. The Tenganis thus embody a real paradox. They are at one and the same time the most autocratic and the most dependent of the traditional chiefs, as well as the most respected and the most despised.

Having defined Tengani as belonging to the category of divine kings we next reviewed the discussion initiated by Frazer. The latter was seen to hover between two scenarios for the death of the divine king. One centres on the king's failing health, establishing a direct link between the king's health and the country's health. The other scenario centres on the king as a scapegoat being held responsible for the society's woes and being killed or driven out in return. This allowed for a political interpretation of the king's death. Gluckman has developed that line in a systematic fashion by his theory of ritual rebellion. The sentiments of hatred expressed in certain Incwala songs and ritual activities were considered genuine and directed against the king, but they were to be interpreted as part of a cathartic mechanism and expressed no revolutionary intent.

The crucial element added by Girard is that the Incwala and similar rituals are not sufficiently explained as a rite of rebellion against the king, a way of venting communal anger. It is also to be seen as a way of establishing, renewing or consolidating social consensus by the whole of the community turning against the king. This in its turn reinforces the king's sacrality as he is at one and the same time the paragon of evil and a source of blessing. Royal incest, which is such a conspicuous feature in sub-Saharan Africa, thereby receives an altogether different meaning. It is not just something 'good to think' as the structuralists would have it (Lévi-Strauss 1962), but also the summation and confirmation of the evil perpetrated by the scapegoat.

In the case of the Tenganis, the rebellious element is quite evident in the spates of rumour and the criticisms by the Mbona medium, ultimately forcing Tengani to perform the ritual of rebuilding. The rebuilding of the shrine might be interpreted in Durkheimian fashion as a celebration of unity finally restored. But in the light of Girard's scapegoat theory we are able to see that it is by no means the end, for Tengani has still to seal his fate by committing incest on his way home. It is only his death which is supposed to establish a more lasting unity. The rebuilding is rather to be seen as the liminal phase of a protracted ritual process, which culminates in Tengani's funeral and deification. One tell-tale sign of liminality is the fact that the participants, including Tengani, are in a state of near-nakedness, symbolizing their common humanity.

The Tengani story shows us that someone who is politically speaking a failure, transforms through that failure and the death sentence following it into a rain-dispensing deity. This suggests an altogether different aspect of the relationship between political and therapeutic ngoma. What politically-speaking is to be described as life-taking is cosmologically speaking to be described as life-giving. Political ngoma thus provides and grooms the scapegoats that therapeutic ngoma needs to replenish its stock of divinities. The scapegoat thereby emerges as a wounded healer of an altogether different type; not one who has been through an illness which predestined him to become a healer, but one whose supposed failure to function adequately in the social and political field transformed him into a provider of rain and fertility.

Acknowledgements

Fieldwork on the Tengani chieftaincy was carried out between September 1966 and December 1967 and for intermittent periods until January 1982. Some of the material has been written up in my doctoral thesis (Schoffeleers 1968) and in a study of the Mbona cult (Schoffeleers 1992). I am indebted to the Nuffield Foundation, London; the University of Malawi; and the Free University of Amsterdam for financing part of the research. I am particularly indebted to Stephen Tengani, son of the late Molin Tengani, for allowing me to make use of a manuscript containing a description by his father of the rain rituals at his court (Tengani 1967).

Literature

Abraham, D.P. (1966) 'The Roles of "Chaminuka" and the Mhondoro Cults in Shona Political History'. In E. Stokes and R. Brown (eds) *The Zambesian Past*. Manchester: Manchester University Press, 28–46.

Adler, A. (1982) *La mort est le masque du roi. La royauté sacrée des Moundang du Tchad*. Paris: Payot.

Beidelman, T.O. (1966) 'Swazi Royal Ritual'. *Africa* 36: 373–405.

Bhebe, N.M.B. (1979) 'The Ndebele and Mwari before 1893: a Religious Conquest of the Conquerors by the Vanquished'. In Schoffeleers (ed.) *Guardians of the Land. Essays on Central African Territorial Cults*. Gwelo: Mambo Press, 287–96.

Bourdillon, M.F.C. (1979) The Cults of Dzivaguru and Karuva amongst the North-Eastern Shona Peoples. In J.M.Schoffeleers (ed.) *Guardians of the Land. Essays on Central African Territorial Cults*. Gwelo: Mambo Press, 1–46.

Daneel, M.L. (1970) *The God of the Matopo Hills*. The Hague: Mouton.

de Heusch, Luc (1958) *Essai sur le symbolisme de l'inceste royal en Afrique*. Brussels.

—— (1985) *Sacrifice in Africa. A Structuralist Approach*. Manchester: Manchester University Press.

Douglas M. (1966) *Purity and Danger. An Analysis of Concepts of Pollution and Taboo*. London: Routledge and Kegan Paul.

Fortes, M. (1964) 'The Political System of the Tallensi of the Northern Territories of the Gold Coast'. In M. Fortes and E.E. Evans-Pritchard *African Political Systems*. London: Oxford University Press, 239–71.

Fortes, M. and E.E. Evans-Pritchard (1964) *African Political Systems*. London: Oxford University Press.

Frazer, J.G. (1963) *The Golden Bough. A Study in Magic and Religion* (abridged ed.); London: Macmillan and Co, 1963.

Garbett, K. (1969) 'Spirit Mediums as Mediators in Korekore Society'. In J. Beattie and J. Middleton (eds) *Spirit Mediumship and Society in Africa*. London: Routledge and Kegan Paul, 104–27.

Gelfand, M. (1962) *Shona Religion*. Cape Town: Juta.

Girard, R. (1977) *Violence and the Sacred*. Baltimore: Johns Hopkins University Press.

Gluckman, M. (1954) *Rituals of Rebellion in South-East Africa*. Manchester: Manchester University Press.

—— (1963) *Order and Rebellion in Tribal Africa*. New York: Free Press.

Homans, G.C. (1965) 'Anxiety and Ritual: The Theories of Malinowski and Radcliffe-Brown'. In W.A. Lessa and E.C.Vogt (eds) *Reader in Comparative Religion*. New York: Harper and Row

Janzen, J.M. (1992) *Ngoma. Discourses of Healing in Central and Southern Africa*. Berkeley: University of California Press.

Kopytoff. I. (1987) *The African Frontier*. Bloomington: Indiana University Press.

—— (1987) (ed.) *The African Frontier: The Reproduction of Traditional African Societies*. Bloomington and Indianapolis: Indiana University Press.

Krige, J.D. and E. Krige (1943) *The Realm of a Rain-Queen*. London: Oxford University Press.

Kuper, H. (1944) 'A Ritual Kingship among the Swazi', *Africa* 14: 230–56.

—— (1963) *The Swazi: a South African Kingdom*. New York: Holt Rinehart.

Lan, D. (1985) *Guns and Rain*. London: James Currey.

Lévi-Strauss, C. (1962) *Totemism*. Harmondsworth: Penguin Books.

Mandala, E.C. (1990) *Work and Control in a Peasant Economy. A History of the Lower Tchiri Valley in Malawi 1859–1960*. Madison: Wisconsin University Press.

Morris, B. (1987) *Anthropological Studies of Religion. An Introductory Text*. Cambridge: Cambridge University Press, 249–52.

Muller, J.C. (1980) *Le roi bouc-émissaire. Pouvoir et rituel chez les Rukuba du Nigéria Central*. Québec: Serge Fleury.

Norbeck, E. (1967) 'African Rituals of Conflict'. In John Middleton (ed.) *Gods and Rituals*. Garden City NY: The Natural History Press, 197–226 (Reprinted from *The American Anthropologist* 65 (6), 1963: 1254–79).

Otto, R. (1917) *The Idea of the Holy*. Harmondsworth: Penguin Books.

Ranger, T.O. (1967) *Revolt in Southern Rhodesia, 1896–97*. London: Heinemann.

Rowley, H. (1866) *The Story of the Universities' Mission to Central Africa*. London: Saunders, Otley and Co.

Schoffeleers, J.M. (1968) *Symbolic and Social Aspects of Spirit Worship Among the Mang'anja*. DPhil thesis, St.Catherine's College, Oxford.

—— (1973) 'Livingstone and the Mang'anja Chiefs'. In: B.Pachai (ed.) *Livingstone, Man of Africa*, 111–30.

—— (1979a) 'Introduction'. In J.M.Schoffeleers (ed.) *Guardians of the Land. Essays on Central African Territorial Cults*. Gwelo: Mambo Press, 1–46.

—— (1979b) 'An Organisational Model of the Mwari Shrines'. In J.M. Schoffeleers (ed.) *Guardians of the Land. Essays on Central African Territorial Cults*. Gwelo: Mambo Press, 297–315.

—— (1991) 'Twins and Unilateral Figures in Central and Southern Africa: Symmetry and Asymmetry in the Symbolisation of the Sacred'. *Journal of Religion in Africa* 21(4): 345–72.

—— (1992) *River of Blood. The Genesis of a Martyr Cult in Southern Malawi, c. A.D. 1600*. Madison: Wisconsin University Press.

Simonse, S. (1992) *Kings of Disaster. Dualism, Centralism and the Scapegoat King in Southeastern Sudan*. Leiden: E.J.Brill

Tengani, S.M. (1967) 'Ufumu wa Tengani'; MS, Tengani Village, Nsanje District, Malawi.

Tew, M. (1950) *Peoples of the Lake Nyasa Region*. London: Oxford University Press for the International African Institute.

Turner, F.J. (1893) 'The Significance of the Frontier in American History'. In Ray Allen Billington (ed.) *Frontier and Section: Selected Essays*. Englewood Cliffs, N.J.: Prentice Hall, 1961.

Turner, V.W. (1967) *The Forest of Symbols. Aspects of Ndembu Ritual*. Ithaca/London: Cornell University Press.

—— (1969) *The Ritual Process*. London: Routledge and Kegan Paul.

—— (1974) *Dramas, Fields and Metaphors. Symbolic Action in Human Society*. Ithaca: Cornell University Press.

Wallis, J.P.R. (ed.) (1952) *The Zambezi Expedition of David Livingstone, 1858–1863*. 2 vols. London: Chatto and Windus.

Weber, M. (1971) *The Sociology of Religion*. London: Methuen.

Wilson, M. (1970) *Communal Rituals of the Nyakyusa*. London: Oxford University Press.

7

The Politics
of Therapeutic Ngoma
The Zionist churches
in urban Zambia[1]

Cor Jonker

Introduction

In his book *Ngoma: Discourses of Healing in Central and Southern Africa*, Janzen (1992) proposes the use of the word *ngoma* instead of cult of affliction, possession cult, divination, rite of affliction or drum of affliction, because all these are analytical names, while ngoma has multiple meanings and is ambiguous. The use of the name ngoma has the advantage that 'we tie into the conscious level of awareness of it' and that it 'offsets certain scholarly excesses that have distorted the identity and definition of the institution in the literature' (ibid.: 175,176). Analytical terms would do injustice to the various ngoma institutions as they limit them to certain Western preoccupations, such as cult, trance, possession, spirit, etc. Instead, Janzen considers ngoma a 'classical institution of Central and Southern Africa' (ibid.: 178), visible in a number of activities, rituals and organizations that are involved in the 'doing ngoma process' in which various types of knowledge are handled. I welcome his attempt to conceptualize the institution of ngoma. Nevertheless, I consider his handling of ngoma (disregarding my unease with the actual choice of the word 'ngoma') as one-sided. Even though Janzen stresses that ngoma includes political processes, he focuses on healing. The fact that ngoma has political connotations requires more than just lip service because political activism is very often an important characteristic of ngoma organizations. By stressing the healing aspects of ngoma, one may produce the picture of an acquiescent medical system, whereas in ngoma this is not the case. In this contribution I wish to show how political activism and healing are coinciding forces. I will do this by presenting a case study of an ngoma-type movement: the *Mdzimu* churches in Zambia. This way I hope to contribute to Janzen's attempt to develop an understanding of the ngoma institution.

There have been many publications on independent churches in Southern and Central Africa. Most studies of these churches are of a political-historical or of a theological nature. Many independent churches in Southern African have made 'healing' (in the broadest possible meaning) the very centre of their activities and it is because of this that I, as a medical anthropologist, became interested in the study of an independent church. During earlier research in Lusaka, Zambia, I noticed that so-called healing churches drew many patients. A closer review showed that there were many types of healing churches. They appeared to attract more female patients than the government clinics. This I could partly explain by pointing at the extremely low quality of service rendered by these clinics and their constant lack of essential drugs. Hence these churches seemed to have a large impact on the available health services for the major part of the population and I made this the subject of my research.

I have studied one healing church, or rather one movement of healing churches, in Zambia. During this research project special attention was paid to one particular church branch active in a certain part of Lusaka. This research took place during the years 1990 to 1993. It became clear that even though the study of 'healing' was at the centre of my attention, this aspect could not be separated from other aspects such as the theology of the movement. This is also true for political aspects: politics and healing are interconnected and this is the theme of the present contribution.

There has been some dispute over the interpretation of the political nature of the Zionist churches in Southern Africa and in this article I will contribute to this discussion as well. In my opinion, it is possible to provide a more sophisticated interpretation of the political nature of these churches by placing them in a local context and by studying the differences between the churches as well as the variety of groupings within these churches.

The existence of this variety of groups within such healing movements leads me to my main critique of Janzen's work. Janzen (1992) did not distinguish between the various segments within ngoma and the way in which these maintain their own political and healing ideologies, as well as their own social dynamics. This differentiation in analysis provides a more nuanced view of how health and politics interact within ngoma and contributes to the development of our understanding of ngoma.

Independent churches

For a long time, anthropological, theological and other studies divided independent churches in Southern Africa into Ethiopian and Zionist churches (Sundkler 1961; Daneel 1971, 1974). The so-called Ethiopian churches usually originated from mission churches and often looked like carbon copies of their mother church. The schism that stood at their origin and which usually took place on political grounds (Sundkler 1961; Balandier 1965; Saunders 1978) often occurred as far back as the 1920s and 1930s (Daneel 1971). These churches, together with the more progressive sections of the mission churches, played an important role in the development of the African political elite and the liberation movements.

Because the origin of the Ethiopian churches was directly related to political activism and because these churches were closely connected to new nationalist leaders shortly after independence, many social scientists considered independent churches as movements of political activism, as organizations for political change. Times, however, changed quickly and dramatically. Liberal leaders of the independence movements became conservative dictators. After independence, as Ethiopian and often independent former mission churches became loyal allies of the national leadership, many Africans came to view them as conservative rather than progressive forces.

The second type of church, the Zionists, from their inception stressed inspiration by the Holy Spirit and are often of a prophetic nature. Their organizations are usually unstable and often they have been seen to participate in witch-finding and exorcizing of evil spirits (Daneel 1971). An important part of their services consists of prayer healing (Mitchell 1963). Theologically (Sundkler 1961; Becken 1971/2; Ojo 1988) and organization-wise (Welbourn 1969, Rounds 1982) they can be considered as syncretist: a mixture of Christian doctrines and ritual practices with indigenous elements.

Zionist churches can be divided into Apostolic churches on the one hand and healing churches on the other (cf. Schoffeleers 1991). Apostolic churches often develop an antagonist relationship with the state. They expect their members to refrain from consulting a government clinic or accepting a government job. They often attempt to form a closed group and try to separate themselves geographically from the remainder of the population or distinguish themselves through dress and style. In some cases this has led to confrontations with the government. An example is the Apostolic Church of Johane Masowe, which came into conflict with the South African, the Rhodesian/Zimbabwean and the Zambian governments (Dillon-Malone 1978). Another example is the Lumpa Church of Alice Lenshina, which clashed with the Zambian government (Van Binsbergen 1981: 266–316).

In most studies, Zionist churches are portrayed as forms of counter-culture (Buijtenhuijs 1976; Comaroff 1985), as forms of protest. Illness and healing are seen as metaphors of protest against living conditions. Even though it is clear that political concepts are part of the religious doctrine of the Apostolic churches, on the level of the nation-state they cannot be considered as activist movements vying for political change. On the level of the individual and his or her immediate social environment, Schoffeleers (1991) pointed out that Apostolic churches are antagonistic towards neighbours who are not inclined to become part of their secluded community (see also Chidester 1992). Their aim is to create their own closed communities, protected from society at large which is full of temptations, adultery, witchcraft and evil medicine. It is this objective of forming their own closed societies which is unacceptable to governments and which leads to confrontations with these churches.

Healing churches

In addition to Zionist Apostolic churches, there are also Zionist churches of the healing type. In this contribution I will specifically focus on these churches.

Zionist healing churches, which can be found all over Southern Africa, focus more on healing than their Apostolic counterparts. In many of these churches the healing of patients is an important, if not a crucial, part of the church service. Some Zionist healing churches limit themselves to prayer healing, but most of them also use herbal medication. An important characteristic of their ritual practice is that members of the church are either possessed by the Holy Spirit or by a representative of the Holy Spirit. Illness is seen as caused by evil spirits and exorcism is considered the most important, although not the only, form of therapy. The fact that these churches stress healing as the core of their activities, and that the healing rituals are available to everyone including non-members on request (provided they are willing to pay for them), makes them more open to society as compared with the Apostolic churches. The healing churches do not segregate themselves from society as the Apostolic churches do.

According to Comaroff the concepts of illness and healing that are so central to these churches are important symbols of the way these people experience their existence. As such they are symbols of protest. Reis (1992) pointed out that members of healing churches in Swaziland often consider illness to be caused by evil medicine and not by the behaviour of the patient. This means, in Reis's opinion, that not only the cause of, but also the responsibility for the illness is placed outside the patient, i.e. the cause and guilt emanate from the evil, sinful society. The health problem of the patient is not personalized, but conceptualized as a social problem. She concludes that symbols of protest are present in the rituals of diagnosis of these healing churches and therefore have a political significance.

Acknowledging this, I will show, in my case study of a Zambian healing church (below), that the responsibility for the health problem is assigned partly to society but also partly to the patient. Furthermore, I will point out that it is important to recognize which group in society is perceived to be the cause of the health problem.

The absence of a central doctrinarian authority, and the importance of the personality of the prophet for the local church and its organization, are characteristic features of Zionist healing churches. It is therefore very difficult to identify shared political attitudes among the members of these very heterogeneous churches.

Central and Southern Africa showed a major shift towards freedom of speech and multipartyism in the 1990s. Some countries had multiparty elections and the apartheid regime fell. This has had major implications for the intra-organizational discipline in many churches and other religious movements and organizations. Until the 1990s, internal differences of opinion were hidden or forbidden by the leadership of the various organizations. In Zambia, religious organizations were compelled not to offend the government, and copied the rigid discipline of the one-party-state. With the winds of freedom blowing at the national level, people at grassroots level also felt free to express their hitherto hidden differences. Former distinctions between types of churches, as discussed above, are gradually becoming blurred. Also, as a new development, Neo-Pentecostal and Born-Again movements are springing up, either independently or in various established and indigenous churches (Van Dijk 1992).

As a consequence of these developments the outsider is now in a position to get a much clearer view of the intra-dynamics of religious and political organizations. These dynamics show that the various segments of a single organization may very well have different ritualistic and organizational characteristics while retaining economic, motivational or ideological similarities.

In this chapter I would like to explore a case study of a healing church in Zambia. This study will not seek general conclusions on political aspects of healing in this particular church which can be extended to the understanding of healing churches in Zimbabwe or South Africa, or even in the whole of Zambia. Instead it will illustrate that if one studies the various organizational groupings and ritual aspects within a healing church, as well as their practical consequences, a more sophisticated perspective appears on the relationship between politics and healing.

The focus of the case study will be the *Mdzimu* churches of Zambia in which different groups can be distinguished, namely: (a) the leaders of these churches, (b) the members of these churches, and (c) their patients. For each of these groups I will discuss the relation between their socio-economic position in society, their political ideas, and their involvement in healing practices. I will comment on the variety of ideologies within these healing churches as compared with Neo-Pentecostalism.

After this I will engage with the debate on the characteristics of the ngoma institution presented in the introduction to this volume.

The leaders of the Mdzimu churches

The Zion Spirit Church and a number of break-away churches such as the Paradise Spiritual Church, the Jordan Holy Spiritual Church and the Central African Spirit Church are often referred to as the Mdzimu church (by outsiders and sometimes by church members as well). The movement started in the 1950s and 1960s among migrants in the east of Zambia. These migrants worked in South Africa and Zimbabwe, and came into contact with Zionism in those countries. After returning to Zambia, they were no longer part of village societies. Many settled in their native regions, though not in their native villages but instead in the smaller towns. There they opened up shops or were employed in the informal sector.

The movement lasted until 1974 before the first Zion Spirit Church was officially registered with the authorities. After this registration, a drive for institutionalization began and within a few years many church branches were registered under the name of Zion Spirit Church. Divisions became apparent right from the start, as branches broke away and registered under different names.

In 1992, 104 church branches registered with the Zambian government under the name of Zion Spirit Church; 26 under the name of Paradise Spiritual Church; 21 under the name of Jordan Holy Spiritual Church; and 151 under the names of other split-offs. A total of 302 churches were officially registered that could be considered part of the movement of Mdzimu church.

In addition to these registered churches, there are many unregistered churches and church branches. This is caused by the current prohibition against registering new churches and by the fact that in many church branches there are constant leadership conflicts which often prevent proper organization and formal registration. It is therefore likely that the number of 302 can be doubled or even tripled in order to get the correct estimate of the number of church congregations.

The membership of the Mdzimu churches is de facto limited to the ethnic groups of the east of Zambia, the so called Nyanja-speaking groups.[2] If we estimate the real number of Mdzimu churches to be 600, then this would mean that there is a ratio of one Mdzimu church congregation to every 2000 Nyanja-speakers.

The need for formal organization of the Mdzimu churches did not become apparent until the 1970s, after the declaration of the one-party-state in Zambia in 1972. This is no coincidence, as many people from the political opposition were forced to leave the political organizations and joined other, non-politically aligned organizations, such as churches and trade unions.

Mr Mazyopa is the Archbishop of the Zion Spirit Church. He was born in 1922, the son of a Ngoni chief, not far from what was then called Fort Jameson (now Chipata). He went to school until he reached Standard IV, which was considered quite a high level of education in those days. After he left school he joined his brother who was a carpenter and cabinet-maker in Fort Jameson and who taught him the craft. When he reached the age of twenty he was employed as a carpenter by the government and worked at various places in the country. At the age of 36 he joined the African National Congress (ANC), led by Harry Nkumbula, and was appointed as a youth leader. The ANC provided him with a house in one of the low-density areas of Lusaka and he worked at the ANC headquarters until the Choma declaration in 1972. This declaration made Zambia a one-party state under the leadership of Kenneth Kaunda and the United National Independence Party (UNIP). All members of the ANC were supposed to join UNIP. Mr Mazyopa refused and left the party organization. He was forced to vacate his house and settled in one of the high-density areas of Lusaka. Here he became a vegetable seller. What had started as a steady career in government employment, leading towards a promising political career, ended in a slum and a job in the informal sector.

Mr Mazyopa changed his ambitions from party politics to church politics and became active in the Reformed Church of Zambia, his home church. Even though he was given some work to do within the church organization, he discovered that he could not achieve his real ambition: a position with social status and influence; for this he did not have enough education and, most importantly, he did not have the right political colour.

Mrs Mazyopa, his wife, had gone through a period of psychic problems which were probably related to the sudden deprivation and loss of social status. Because of her mental problems she had become a member of what was to become the Zion Spirit Church. In 1975, three years after the Choma declaration, Mr Mazyopa also joined the Zion Spirit Church and soon became one of the leaders. Together with Jeremiah, a Chewa from Malawi, he brought prosperity to the church. Jeremiah, who would later become the leader of Paradise Spiritual Church, was the prophetic leader of the church, while Mazyopa was the organizer. The number of members was growing fast and financially the organization was sound. It even managed to build a church big enough for several hundreds of people, right opposite the Independence Stadium. This achievement encouraged Mr Mazyopa to challenge for the national leadership. After many manoeuvres he managed to become the national leader in 1982.

However, at the local level of the church, his struggle for leadership caused a falling out with the prophet Jeremiah. This attracted the attention of the government who had intervened in the internal affairs of the church on earlier occasions. This time the government decided to infiltrate the church organization. In 1983, a year after Mr Mazyopa became the national leader, with the aid of the Registrar of Societies, a member of the church who had close ties with the security forces took over the national leadership. Mr Mazyopa was expelled, but took the matter to court. Six years later he won the case and regained national leadership. The church however, had known many splits by that time because of the conflicts and it was disorganized and in a financially poor state. Membership had dropped and the church was no longer politically significant to the government, which by then was fighting the tide of multi-partyism.

Besides being Archbishop of the Zion Spirit Church, Mr Mazyopa is also a shopkeeper. He owns shops in two markets in Lusaka and he rents out a number of houses. Although he lives among the destitute, he is, because of his commercial activities, considered to be well-off by his neighbours.

The career of Archbishop Mazyopa is not exceptional for the leaders of these churches. They all have a number of characteristics in common: they are almost all men; they live among the destitute; they can read and write; they are migrants; they have been active in political or social organizations; when asked they often give politically motivated reasons for joining the Mdzimu church, such as white dominance in mission churches or the prohibition of the practice of African rituals. Without exception they are engaged in a continuous power struggle over local leadership; they all take a keen interest in national politics; and they are all part of the informal sector of the economy. Their political points of view are aired during church services. For instance, at the time of the campaigns for the multi-party elections it was common during church services for the leaders, while being possessed by the Holy Spirit, to call upon the congregation to register as voters or to vote for the opposition. Also during preaching it is common to refer regularly to 'hot items' in national politics.

It is obvious that the leadership of these churches show all the characteristics of political activism. The leaders of the Mdzimu churches oppose the UNIP government[3] and the mission churches, or the political and ecclesiastical establishments of Zambia. Traditionally UNIP and the mission churches had their electorate mostly among the farmers in the villages and among the civil servants and the working class in the cities; the Mdzimu church leaders belonged to none of these groups, but were part of the informal sector of the economy.

The members of the Mdzimu Churches

While the leaders of the Mdzimu churches are overwhelmingly male, the overall majority of the members are female. As in the leadership, so all ages are represented among the members. Like the men, the women are mostly migrants and belong to the very poor. They are uneducated and part of the informal sector. In contrast with the male leaders, the women are usually not politically interested and have not been active in political or social organizations.

For the members, the church provides a social network which replaces a number of the functions of the extended family they left behind when migrating. The church is also a source of income to them, because it gives them the opportunity to rise to the status of spiritual healer. The status as healer means that they attract patients whom they can treat privately, with the aid of their fellow church members, at their homes. This gives them a direct source of cash income as they, in flat contradiction of the official bylaws of the Zion Spirit Church, demand relatively large sums of money for their healing services.

Political activist involvement, as described for the male leaders, is absent among the female members. However, their participation in the Mdzimu church and their careers as healers show that they are independent of husbands and men in general (in contrast to the male leaders, the female members are typically not married). This corresponds with their position as self-employed in the informal sector. They are self-assured, self-reliant women who, even though they are uneducated and live among the destitute, try very hard to improve their social and economic position. These are political stances in male-dominated Zambian society and this image does not accord with the usual portrait of female adepts of cults of affliction. A tradition exists among Africanists to interpret possession cults as a way for women to obtain finances, material matters and personal attention from husbands or male relatives. This tradition was set in motion by the studies of I.M. Lewis and was transferred to possession cults in Central and Southern Africa. Examples are the studies of Van

Binsbergen (1981) and others. In this article I will not dwell on the role of female adepts of the many possession cults in Zambia, now and in the past, nor on the (still ongoing) discussions about the Lewisian role of these women. I would like to limit myself to two remarks.

First, it is custom that patients of non-Christian possession cults become full members of the cult. The spirit that has taken possession of the patient and that causes the illness, needs to be accommodated. Only through membership of the cult and regular participation in its rites can accommodation of the spirit take place. Because of this conviction there is no real distinction between adepts and patients except chronologically. Patients will ultimately become adepts. At the healing churches there is a difference between adepts and patients, because few patients will ultimately become members of the church. The rituals of the church do not, in contrast with the non-Christian possession cults, concentrate on accommodating the spirit, but on exorcism, a time-limited therapy. The Lewisian pattern of cult membership is therefore here not applicable. Moreover, I do not consider this pattern to be a characteristic for ngoma.

Second, the members of the healing churches are in general women who have attained a certain level of independence already, who have developed a degree of self-confidence and who are typically not married. This is not the image of a woman who joins a possession cult as part of her domestic war of the sexes (Lewis 1971; Van Binsbergen 1981) and consequently the discussion on Lewisian adept behaviour does not apply here. Instead, here, the adepts use their affliction (i.e. their possession by a Holy Spirit) and their subsequent membership as a means to become financially independent. Also, it should be concluded that there is a distinction between members of the Mdzimu churches and the patients.

The patients of the Mdzimu Churches

The last category of people within the Mdzimu churches that I wish to discuss are the patients. Elsewhere (Jonker 1992), I have given a description of the patients of the Mdzimu churches and of the treatment they must undergo. Patients are usually not members of the church and are not forced (though encouraged) to become church members. Usually they attend a number of church services during the course of the treatment (as patients of one of the healers of the church). The patients, most of whom are women, usually show symptoms that Westerners would label as forms of depression, and often suffer from childlessness as well.

There are socio-economic differences between the female patients and the female members of the Mdzimu churches. The members of the churches are typically unmarried and mostly self-employed in the informal sector, while most of the patients are housewives with a husband who is employed in the formal sector. Another characteristic of the patients is that most have recently – a few months to a few years ago – come from the village to town in order to join their husbands. This means that they have become dependent upon their husbands and can hardly rely upon their own relatives. Their husbands expect them to be subservient and to bear them children.

Female patients are usually taken to a church healer by the husband or by the relatives of the husband. Reason for the action is the illness of the woman, who feels unhappy, the tensions between husband and wife, and the aggravating condition of childlessness. Central in the diagnosis is the concept that the illness is caused by a demon, an evil spirit, and that exorcism will bring about deliverance. In the opinion of the healers of the Mdzimu churches, possession by evil spirits is only possible because of the sinful behaviour of the patient, while the evil spirit is often portrayed as the spirit of a deceased and sinful relative of the woman. The sins of the deceased relatives are often brought in connection with witchcraft, while the sins of the female patient are often considered to consist of adultery. Either way, the responsibility is placed with the woman and/or her relatives and the solution is obvious: besides admitting the accusations and acquiescing in a number of frightening and humiliating rituals of exorcism, the woman will have to promise to stop her sinful behaviour and cease contact with the outside world – cease contact, that is, with her sinful relatives and their ancestral spirits. As a consequence the woman will become more dependent upon her husband and is expected to behave likewise. She is forced to accept her new urban situation and is required to keep her relatives at a distance; away from her husband and his urban wealth.

The case study of the Zambian Mdzimu churches shows that here it is not the aim of the healing process to reintegrate the patient in the rural society, but to mould the patient into her new role of obedient housewife in an urban situation. The healing process aims at the transformation of the patient from her role as economically active member of a extended rural-based family into a dependent isolated urban housewife. Why do women endure the healing rituals of the Mdzimu churches? Foremost, the women have been put under pressure to undergo the treatment. But their participation is not fully enforced: the patients also show willingness to go for the treatment, they are acquiescent and show the expected symptoms at the right moments during the rites. Apparently, to them there are also positive aspects to the treatment and one could speculate on their nature. Here I would like to submit two possibilities.

Firstly, healing churches offer a medical treatment: they offer, within the concepts of indigenous etiology, a possible solution to a medical problem. Anita Spring, who did research among the Luvale in Zambia, points out that spirit possession is mostly a manner which women use to cope with a personal illness. In epidemiological terms fertility problems are widespread in Zambia and therefore it is not surprising that it is this particular illness which is especially connected to spirit possession and is being interpreted as caused by social tension (Spring 1978).

Secondly, it is possible that female patients appreciate the attention they receive, even though the treatment has negative consequences for them. The dependent position of these women which causes their feeling of unhappiness, the longing for their relatives and the feelings of guilt towards their relatives, may cause them to express the stress they are under, by exaggerating their negative position. They may be willing to take all the blame, to call all their relatives witches, to label all their ancestral spirits as demons, to endure humiliating exorcism rituals and to demonstrate their servility and dependence by seizures of spirit possession. This hypothesis would bring us close to the former anthropological practice of labelling the behaviour of women who are suffering from spirit possession as a form of protest against male dominance.

The political ideology of healing churches

Analysing the healing churches in Zambia, I would like to state that there is no single political role or function that can be ascribed to these churches as such. Rather, we will have to distinguish between the constituent groups that make up the Mdzimu churches: the leaders, the ordinary members, the patients and the in-laws of the patients. These groups have different intentions for participation in the healing rituals. No wonder these churches are so diverse and prone to schisms. The leaders are politically very active within the church organization and these activities are not limited to power play within the church, as they link their own activities to national political events. The female adepts, the ordinary members, are mostly involved in strengthening their own economic position. The men with jobs, however, use these churches as medical facilities, providing them with opportunities to deal with unhappy wives and to strengthen their nuclear family and their personal authority at the expense of the influence of the extended family of the wife.

There is no contradiction between the fact that the healers, that is the members of these churches, are independent self-assured women and the fact that the healing rituals which are being led by these same women, are aimed at submission of the female patients. This is because these female healers/members of the church still hold the ideal of housewife who is submissive to her husband, very high. Their choice to become economically independent and to become healers, is a second-best choice in their view. Failure to become such housewives and mothers was one of the reasons to opt for membership of the healing church.

There is one factor that all the constituent groups of the healing churches have in common: an ideology of the nuclear family as the core of the society, of stressing strict Christian moral standards, of submissiveness of wives to their husbands. In Western terminology, the political convictions could be called a 'middle-class' ideology, a conservative doctrine. In African terms this cannot be called conservative, as it proposes a quite radical change. The support of the nuclear family at the expense of the extended family, the labelling of ancestral spirits as demons, stressing the importance of the Holy Spirit as personal guidance, the idea of curing by exorcism instead of accommodation, the calling for the Holy Spirit to take possession of a cured patient in order to prevent further illnesses – all these are radical changes in both lifestyle and ideology in the African context. The treatment of the healing church is therefore mostly aimed at curing those who suffer personally in the process of social change: the rural women who join their urban husbands.

The leaders and the members of the healing churches, as described here, are more closely connected with the informal sector than with the middle class. In Zambia it is becoming more and more clear that the middle class – the business men, the petty industrialists, and all those who would like to belong to this class – join the so called Neo-Pentecostalist, the Born-Again groups. Some of the Born-Again groups are active within existing churches; others have organized themselves under their own names[4] (see Van Dijk (1992) for a more in-depth study of the Born-Agains). These movements and churches also gain support from the better-educated youngsters who live in the less poor areas of the Zambian cities. The television broadcasts of American preachers and their Zambian Neo-Pentecostalist imitations attract a lot of support among these groups. The Neo-Pentecostalists are also active in national politics, as the recent change of government in Zambia shows. The government which replaced the Kaunda regime was headed by Frederick Chiluba, former leader of the trade unions in Zambia and leader of the Movement for Multi-Party Democracy. Immediately after his election to the presidency he made it clear that he was a Born-Again Christian and that he would make this the dominant feature of his policies. He pronounced Zambia to be a 'Christian Nation', just like Iran and Sudan had pronounced themselves to be 'Muslim Nations'; this statement caused commotion.

The Neo-Pentecostalists stress, like the healing churches, the possession by the Holy Spirit and the exorcism of demons; however, they put less stress on healing and more stress on personal conversion. The stress on personal conversion, on being Born-Again, and the idea that sinful behaviour is the cause of personal suffering and low social position, marks this movement as politically conservative in Western terminology, even though they stand for changes in life style which are quite radical in the African context.

Among the adepts of the Mdzimu churches, many point out the similarities between their movement and the Neo-Pentecostalists. This does not happen among Neo-Pentecostalists, as they consider themselves a church of the educated and well-to-do and the Mdzimu churches as a movement of the poor.

Interestingly enough, there is a movement involving more highly educated people within the Mdzimu churches which is imitating the Neo-Pentecostalist way of preaching by the usage of English (with simultaneous translations into vernacular on TV), by putting more stress on personal conversion, and by condemnation of the more traditional medical therapies (like the use of herbal medicine) and the more traditional manifestations of spirit possession. So, even here, distinctions between various movements seem to become blurred. This shows, once again, that analysis of the various constituent segments of these movements is required in order to assess their significance and to understand the direction of change.

My conclusion is that a political analysis of healing churches should not use the church as an entity for analysis, but that the various segments that make up these churches should be taken into consideration. Various segments of the population may have diverse motives for joining such a religious movement, depending on social class, the political context of the moment and changing social relations in general. I am using the case of the Mdzimu churches in urban Zambia as an example to show how the various constituent groups of these churches have their own reasons for turning to this movement.

Qualities and socio-historical boundaries of ngoma

It was my hope that with the publication of Ngoma, Janzen would shed some light on the relationship between politics and healing. My hope was generated by Janzen's presentation of his endeavour. Janzen proposes the use of the word ngoma to describe a 'classical institution of Central and Southern Africa' (Janzen 1992: 178), visible in a number of activities, rituals and organizations that are involved in the 'doing ngoma process' in which various types of knowledge are handled. This is a refreshing approach as it shows the socio-cultural and historical homogeneity of various movements and rituals hitherto described variously as folkloric leisure, initiation, politics, healing, and so on. All of the various types and forms of ngoma, as they have been visible throughout the history of Africa, show these various aspects though often in a symbolic or contradictory way. In order to show the true magnitude of the institution of ngoma, the diverse movements and rituals should be described in such a way that all the aspects are properly encapsulated. It is commendable that Janzen has recognized this and has embarked on describing the ngoma institution is this manner. However, even though his intentions are to describe the whole institution in all its facets, Janzen does not complete this endeavour. Instead he is focusing on only one aspect. Despite the fact that in theory Janzen includes political processes and resolutions of societal problems in the 'doing ngoma', in practice he focuses on healing, on what is identified in this volume as 'therapeutic ngoma'. Not only does Janzen neglect what is identified in this volume as 'political ngoma', he also neglects the ideological core of various ngoma movements and their periodic political activism. As I have shown in the case study, political activities can be an important characteristic of therapeutic ngoma organizations and should be included in the exploration of ngoma as an institution. By emphasizing the healing aspects as he does, Janzen makes ngoma look like yet another cult of affliction, which it is not.

Healing and political activities are considered to be opposing social forces by some (see Parsons 1952). Healing is considered to be aimed at bringing the patient into harmony with his/her environment by concentrating on the treatment of the suffering of the individual and not by focusing on the social conditions that led to the suffering. Personal problems of the patients that are connected with social inequalities and social changes are being individualized and treated as such. Therefore, in this opinion, a healing movement cannot be a political movement. This, however, is true for every medical curative system. Nevertheless, this does not prevent the treatment, and the healers and their patients, being part of a radical social, economic and theological change.

Even Janzen, who includes political processes in his 'doing ngoma', subliminally employs this hypothesis of antagonism. The case study presented here of a contemporary therapeutic ngoma movement, the Mdzimu church in Zambia, supports this hypothesis by showing how the two ngoma modalities interrelate: this church is not only a healing movement but a political movement as well, and these two amplify each other. In my opinion, it is this characteristic which makes this church part of the ngoma tradition. The healing process of the Mdzimu church does play a role in social changes and contains politically sensitive messages: large numbers of women are 'healed' by being moulded into a new role in society, complete with a new ideology and new religious notions.

Janzen stresses that ngoma transforms according to political and social changes. Thus he writes:

> Ngoma appears to fade away where there is a strong central authority with a highly developed judicial tradition ... . It seems to proliferate on the social and geographical margins of large empires ... or as a mechanism for the consolidation of authority in the interstices of society where misfortune lurks ... . It proliferates where misfortune is rampant and where social chaos prevails ... . In the wake of the demise of centralized states, it may take on the functions of the state.
>
> (1992: 79).

This review shows how diverse the configurations of ngoma are in various societies and ages. Janzen (ibid.: 82, 83) points out, rightly so, that in describing a ngoma institution it is not possible to limit the description to either a religious organization, a therapeutic group or a trading organization, for example. In urbanized societies, it is easier to distinguish the 'big four institutions': kinship, the economy, politics and religion (see ibid. 81). Yet Janzen insists on using the label ngoma for all the various institutions that he describes for so many societies and historical periods. If ngoma is so much part and parcel of the other institutions of African societies, then why does ngoma continue to exhibit the same distinctive features?

Of course ngoma does not remain unchanged throughout history and across nations. What is of importance here is to define the socio-historical boundaries of this institutionalized tradition. Ngoma has developed into the described institution and has shown many faces; it may also alter its appearance completely – beyond recognition – or simply fade away. We may therefore deliberate on which institution can be called ngoma and when this label no longer applies. I would like to propose that the latter might be the case when therapeutic ngoma and political ngoma become ritually disengaged.

Ngoma, healing churches, and centralized religion

In this chapter I have concentrated on healing churches in Central and Southern Africa, as they have grown rapidly in the past decades and because they offer a type of health care which is much in demand. Janzen perceives these healing churches as an 'interpenetration between the cults and independent Christian churches' (1992: 77) as they seem to unite both Christian theology and healing rituals of cults of affliction. Yet they can very well be called ngoma, even if they often (though not always) lack the performance of the drum, but include singing, clapping and related effects. In the narrow meaning of the word, it is the drum which makes ngoma. Interestingly, in the Mdzimu churches the drum is replaced by the Bible: during healing rituals, the Bible is hit hard with the hand in a rhythmical way in order to support the singers/dancers. Healing churches are Christian, but this does not make them Western instead of African. They are indigenous movements based on African spiritology and symbolism. It is true that they stress exorcism of afflicting spirits, but it is also true that they focus on accommodating the Holy Spirit who can equally act as afflicting spirit. The healing churches thereby adopt a spirit which transcends the boundaries of the lineage, the microcosm. Many cults of affliction, however, have been described as having appropriated various types of spirits. The healing churches have adopted the Christian Holy Spirit as their spirit of affliction and salvation. This places them in the tradition of cults of affliction, but makes them special as they verbally cross the boundary between an indigenous cult and a cosmopolitan centralized religion. The healing churches can be seen as a unique type of cult of affliction which religiously, medically, and politically deals with the psychological, social and economic problems individuals endure during processes of rapid urbanization in a cosmopolitan context.

Healing churches can also be called ngoma, because they are indigenous cults of affliction, responding to health problems related to local social tension. Healing churches play a role in social and political changes as they respond through religious adaptations. Analysis of the political aspects of healing churches shows us how they stand in conjunction with ngoma in opposition to mission-based churches as representatives of centralized religion.

As we have seen, healing churches share many characteristics with cults of affliction, and it is specifically in their commonality that ngoma is found. In the descriptions by Turner, Van Binsbergen and others, it is clear that most adepts are women whose illness and cult membership are their way of responding to their deprivation. Furthermore, it is important that the ngoma institutions are responses to social changes and that they cannot be separated from these changes. They aim at healing the ills of the changes by trying to find certain forms of compensation for the deprivation.

In the urban healing churches a division between the predominantly male leaders and the predominantly female adepts is visible. The men are heavily involved in church politics and in national politics as well; the women are mostly occupied with healing and their own careers as healers. What is most important here is that both share an ideology which is based on strengthening the nuclear family and its self-reliance – an ideology typical of the urbanized informal sector. Their patients are women who suffer from mental problems caused by their sudden change of life style from a rural-based extended family to an isolated nuclear family, in many cases aggravated by childlessness. Like other ngoma institutions, the healing churches are responses to social changes and they cannot be separated from these changes. The changes are accepted and no compensation is sought, but the patient is forced to accept her new role in society.

The newly emerging Neo-Pentecostalist movements are closer to national political activist movements and they stress openly that they wish to change society through mass action. They hold crusades and talk of changes in the national laws. The Neo-Pentecostalists thus openly combine the symbolic fields between ritual healing and national politics without denying the significance of individual healing. Nevertheless, they consider conversion more important than healing. What distinguishes them from ngoma and the Mdzimu churches is their degree of boldness in political activism.

Schoffeleers (1985) once suggested that there is a historical movement from cults of affliction to spirit churches to central religions. In the first phase women are the organizers who aim at healing and not at political activism. The next phase is the phase of spirit churches, when men take over the leading position in the cults and introduce certain types of political activism, while the women confine themselves to healing. In the last phase, the phase of a central religion, men have taken over all positions and politics is at the centre of the institution. It may be possible to identify these phases in the history of certain African societies. However, as I have pointed out above, all three types of religion mentioned here show political activity and all three types of religion respond to social changes and are trying to deal with these changes at a personal level. Moreover, all three types of religion – ngoma, spirit church and central religion – can be found side by side in contemporary Africa. In view of Schoffeleer's argument, this seems a paradox. However, by analysing how the various types of religious organizations attract their support from different segments of the population a different perspective emerges. Even though the various segments may differ in their involvement in either healing or political activities, the two activities belong to the same institution.

Healing traditions and critical political movements both try to change an existing unwanted situation; they form a common ideological discourse, as the presented case study shows. Within the Mdzimu churches, however, there is a division of labour: women are mostly involved in healing, while most men are also, and some even fully, involved in political action. This division is also expressed in the ideology of the movement in which new gender relations – based on the nuclearization of the family – establish and promote the role of housewife.

Politics and healing not only coexist; they create each other's existential framework. Without the political commitment and organization, this type of ritual healing would not have come into existence and would not have its present impact on the health care system. Similarly, without this type of ritual healing and the popular demand for it, this type of political movement would not have been possible. Even the ritual healing has a political aspect (the transformation of the migrant woman into a submissive housewife), just as the political ideology has a healing aspect (social problems should be solved with individual healing). Even though ritual healing and politics refer to different symbolic fields and relations, each is also the other's prerequisite.

Notes

1 This research has been made possible through a grant by the Netherlands Foundation for the Advancement of Tropical Research (WOTRO).
2 There are also registered healing churches that attract their membership from other ethnic groups in Zambia. These churches are not taken into consideration here.
3 UNIP was defeated during the multiparty elections of 1991.
4 These new churches, organized under their own names, have questionable legitimacy, as a result of the official ban on new churches. The fact that these churches are allowed to operate without proper registration shows both the present ambiguity of the Zambian government and of those in power who favour the Born-Again ideology: local police and security forces are not in a position to act against Born-Again and Neo-Pentecostalist movements.

Literature

Balandier, G. (1965) 'Messianism and Nationalism in Black Africa'. In Pierre L. van den Berghe (ed.), *Africa: Social Problems of Change and Conflict*. San Francisco: Chandler Publishing Company.
Becken, H.J. (1971/2) 'A healing Church in Zululand: "The new church step to Jesus Christ Zion in South Africa"'. *Journal of Religion in Africa* 4: 213–222.
Buijtenhuijs, R. (1976) 'Messianisme et nationalisme en Afrique noire: une remise en question'. *African Perspectives* 2: 25–44.
Chidester, D. (1992) *Religions of South Africa*. London, New York: Routledge.
Comaroff, Jean (1985) *Body of Power, Spirit of Resistance: the Culture and History of a South African People*. Chicago: University of Chicago Press.
Daneel, M.L. (1971) *Old and New in Southern Shona Independent Churches. Volume I: Background and Rise of the Major Movements*. The Hague, Paris: Mouton.
——(1974) *Old and New in Southern Shona Independent Churches. Volume II: Church Growth. Causative Factors and Recruitment Techniques*. The Hague, Paris: Mouton.
Dillon-Malone, C. (1978) *The Korsten Basketmakers. A Study of the Masowe Apostles, an Indigenous African Religious Movement*. Manchester: Manchester University Press on behalf of the Institute for African Studies, University of Zambia.
Janzen, J.M. (1992) *Ngoma. Discourses of Healing in Central and Southern Africa*. Berkeley: University of California Press.
Jonker, C. (1992) 'Sleeping with the Devil. Christian Re-interpretation of Spirit Possession in Zambia'. *Etnofoor* 5(1/2): 213–33.
Lewis, I.M. (1971) *Ecstatic Religion*. Harmondsworth: Penguin Books.
Mitchell, R.C. (1963) 'Christian Healing'. In Victor E.W. Hayward (ed.), *African Independent Church Movements*. London: Edinburgh House Press.

Ojo, M.A. (1988) 'The Contextual Significance of the Charismatic Movements in Independent Nigeria'. *Africa* 58(2): 175–92.

Parsons, T. (1952) *The Social System*. London: Routledge & Kegan Paul.

Reis, R. (1992) 'Het ziektestempel in Swaziland. Parsons in Afrika'. *Antropologische Verkenningen* 11(3): 27–43.

Rounds, J.C. (1982) 'Curing What Ails Them: Individual Circumstances and Religious Choice among Zulu-speakers in Durban, South Africa'. *Africa* 52(2): 77–89.

Saunders, C. (1978) 'African Nationalism and Religious Independency in Cape Colony'. *Journal of Religion in Africa* 9(3).

Schoffeleers, J.M. (1985) *Pentecostalism and Neo-Traditionalism. The Religious Polarization of a Rural District in Southern Malawi*. Amsterdam: Free University Press, Anthropological Papers.

——(1991) 'Ritual Healing and Political Acquiescence: the Case of the Zionist Churches in Southern Africa'. *Africa* 60(1): 1–24.

Spring, A. (1978) 'Epidemiology of Spirit possession among the Luvale of Zambia'. In J. Hoch-Smith and A. Spring (eds), *Women in Ritual and Symbolic Roles*. New York, London: Plenum Press.

Sundkler, B.G.M. (1961) *Bantu Prophets in South Africa*. Oxford: Oxford University Press. (2nd ed.)

Turner, V. (1968) *The Drums of Affliction. A Study of Religious Processes among the Ndembu of Zambia*. London.: International African Institute in association with Hutchinson University Library for Africa.

——(1973) 'Symbols in African Ritual'. In: Arthur C. Lehmann and James E. Myers (eds), (1985) *Magic, Witchcraft, and Religion. An anthropological Study of the Supernatural*. Palo Alto: Mayfield, pp. 55–63. Reprint from: *Science*, 179 (1973): 1100–05.

——(1975) *Revelation and Divination in Ndembu ritual*. Ithaca and London: Cornell University Press.

Van Binsbergen, W.J. (1981) *Religious Change in Zambia. Exploratory Studies*. London, Boston: Kegan Paul International.

Van Dijk, R.A. (1992) *Young Malawian Puritans. Young Puritan Preachers in a Present-day African Urban Environment*. Utrecht: ISOR.

Welbourn, F.B. (1969) 'Spirit Initiation in Ankole and a Christian Spirit Movement in Western Kenya'. In John Beattie and John Middleton (eds), *Spirit Mediumship and Society in Africa*. London: Routledge and Kegan Paul.

8

Ngoma &
Born-Again Fundamentalism
Contesting representations
of time in urban Malawi

Rijk van Dijk

Anthropology will survive in a changing
world by allowing itself to perish in
order to be born again under a new guise.

(Lévi-Strauss, 1966: 126)

Introduction

Janzen's 1992 book on *ngoma* is an attempt to define, describe and analyse a particular socio-religious phenomenon of healing – one we could identify as a musical ecstatic cult – for a wide area in the Southern African region. This attempt at regionalization of a particular religious phenomenon falls squarely within an anthropological tradition that seeks to explore the possibilities of uniting roughly similar, but still quite diverse socio-religious expressions which exist within a wider geographical area, into one conceptual framework. Similar attempts can be found in the work done on Southern African divination systems (Devisch 1985, Van Binsbergen 1995), the role of diviner-healers (the nganga paradigm as formulated, for instance, by Schoffeleers 1989), the role of the so-called territorial, trans-national cults (Werbner 1977, 1989; Ranger 1973; Schoffeleers 1979) and the spread of spirit-healing movements and churches over the Southern African region (Ranger 1993).

Janzen also effectively pulls together in one conceptual framework roughly similar expressions of drumming and healing rituals from an area ranging from Zaire to the Cape and from there to Nairobi (Janzen 1992: 10–50). Basically, the ground for this regionalization is a format concept that is comparable to Devisch's praxeological approach (Devisch 1985). This format is determined by a set of 'formal properties' (Janzen 1992: 174) in which overcoming misfortune, affliction and misfortune through transformation of the sufferer into a healer and through dealing with the spirit world are essential elements. These formal properties in Janzen's interpretation operate as a 'calculus', as a form for which the contents are created during the process; something like an empty building in which the interior walls, infrastructure, ceilings and decoration are invented and put in place while occupying the space available. Ngoma is the calculus (see also Janzen's analysis of ngoma in these terms: 1992: 79, 1995: 159) and in 'doing ngoma' the participants fill the contents of the healing process and its related practices through a process of creativity, experiment and exchange with the outside world. The end-goal is what Janzen prefers to refer to as a state of self-realization in which the individual through the ngoma calculus has been able to sort out his or her idiosyncratic 'solution' to the problems of life. Because of being a 'shell', ngoma can be considered fluid, mouldable and therefore easily transferable to all sorts of places and circumstances; or in Janzen's terms: 'It is a process that may address any type of situation in which the form is servant to the content' (Janzen 1992: 176).

Janzen thus presents a number of distinguishable features that create the space in which all ngoma forms that are found in the region can be represented. They offer the ground and context for the regional coherent existence of a variety of ritual expressions in widely differing places, times and circumstances, of which, as Janzen states, local healers and clients are usually only vaguely aware.

In addition, the calculus format allows ngoma to be represented as an undisputed institute in each of the respective societies in which the phenomenon was analyzed. The high level of adaptability of ngoma as a calculus through time and in a variety of places and circumstances, as emphasized by Janzen, may easily lead to the conclusion that its existence remains undisputed, a reality taken for granted in Southern African society over which no ideological battles are fought. If it is supposed to exist as an empty form which individuals are allowed to fill with rituals, dances, songs and other practices to their own liking, conflicts are unlikely to arise.

This chapter, however, aims to show that an interpretation which emphasizes the unproblematic, uncontested existence of a healing format, because of its extreme adaptability, is hardly conceivable in reality. Rather, this contribution intends to show that the development over time of what in Foucauldian terms could be described as a specific 'discipline' comparable to that of Western psychology, is beset by contestation and conflict from alternative regimes of power and knowledge (Foucault 1988). The questions then become: how and in what terms is its existence as a 'discipline with a specific genealogy' being disputed; what are the limits of its discourse; and by what is it confronted. These problems may be clarified by comparing Janzen's notes on ngoma with other healing movements in the same area. The comparison this chapter proposes is with a religious-healing movement which is relatively new in the field, namely that of the American-inspired Christian fundamentalist and charismatic grouping, known as the 'Born-Agains' that have emerged in the wider Southern-African region. The reasons for a comparison with a healing movement of this particular type are manifold, but let me start by saying that I do not aspire to an analytical level whereby the full geographical scale of the so-called Born-Again phenomenon will be included. On the contrary, I will limit such a comparison to a number of thematic keynotes that have been derived from the study of a small Born-Again grouping in an urban centre in Malawi. The legitimation for this at first sight 'unequal' comparison is that when addressing thematic issues, such as for instance the meaning of healing or the notion of spirits etc., the geographical scale as such does not improve, per definition, our understanding of these conceptualizations.

What I therefore propose to do is to compare format with format, problems with problems. The basic terms of the comparison between the ngoma proposition and the Born-Again movement in Malawi include the extent to which ideas on (evil) spirits and witchcraft are involved, the significance of healing the individual, the meaning of singing and dancing, the authority structure of leadership and the effectiveness of both religious-moral programmes. At the centre of the comparison, however, are the temporal representations that are made in both religious expressions. Here, this chapter will argue, the most interesting differences between the two formats can be found; and it is on this ground that ngoma is disputed and contested at a profound level by the very same Born-Again movement. It is not ngoma's distinguishable features as proposed by Janzen (1992: 174), which lie at the basis of this contestation, but rather its specific invocation of time and the representations of time in its operation. Janzen did not pay attention to the central importance of evocations of past time in ngoma's embodiment of ritual and spiritual power. The new healing movement in Malawi, however, is essentially different in its temporal orientation and, as this contribution intends to show, constructs specific representations of time that purposefully contradict those of ngoma.

In order to be able to tell what the differences are in the temporal conceptualizations we need to have an independent reference system, in the same way that differences in length can be indicated only by referring to an external measure such as the metric system. The first section of this chapter deals with this issue of establishing such a guide. The second section will implement this guide in order to be able to deduce the differences between the ngoma format and the Born-Again format. It will show how the study and interpretation of ngoma falls within a tradition of religious anthropology in Southern Africa in which a mnemonic or nostalgic paradigm was emphasized. Such interpretations primarily showed how religious movements and cults of affliction were dealing with pasts, with memory, by evoking it in new (predominantly urban) contexts, recreating references to a past as a way of coping with misfortune and difficult social circumstances. The outcome of this comparison is then used to shed some further light not only on temporal orientations in ngoma, but also on the anthropological study of these healing movements in the context of the development of an anthropology of time (see Pocock (1967) for some of the early remarks on this issue in anthropology).

Representing time

The first question to be tackled before one can start comparing two regionally expanded forms of healing, is by asking what exactly the basis of comparison will be. Apples and pears cannot be compared unless there is an independent standard, such as for instance a measurement of nutritional value, that allows a comparison to take place. Furthermore, the comparison which is proposed here is meant to highlight basic structures, concepts and principles on which, in this case, the formation of healing forms appear to rest. This may shed light on the question why these 'disciplines' prove to have a prolonged existence in different societies and seem to have a salient appeal to substantial numbers of people.

In Janzen's work on ngoma three key-words are underscored: transformation, representation and self-realization (see Janzen: 1995). Difficult experiences in life are presented to an audience in a ritualized form. Surrounded by a group of drumming, dancing and singing people the person to be 'appeased' by ngoma presents his or her problem to persons who may be called either 'investigators' or 'interpreters'. A verbal trial and error play subsequently develops whereby an investigator probes into a person's life and circumstances while an interpreter unravels the links this play indicates with the spirit world. What thereby occurs is a process of reformulation of the difficult experiences into an idiom that leaves room for the manipulation of spiritual power. The problem – say unemployment – is idiomatically transformed into a problem that concerns the relationship of that person with a specific spirit or a number of spirits. This boils down to an awareness that coping with day-to-day circumstances is related to coping with (at first) unidentified spirits. The ngoma thereupon develops into something that could be called a seminar, a workshop, on how the coping and appeasement directed at the spirit world should be dealt with. It creates a very comforting situation in which the initiand to ngoma may take many years to develop a deep-seated, affective-emotional bond with a spirit or spirits on a strictly personal basis. Janzen writes:

> The ngoma text [the interpretation and articulation of the person's 'difficult experience'] is created over the course of many months and years and finally is presented formally at the time of the sufferer-novice's emergence as a fully ready healer.
>
> (Janzen 1992: 110)

In the process of overcoming harsh daily experiences the initiand is gradually taught how to use the spirit(s) as a vehicle for reaching a state in which a sense of control over one's circumstances is regained. The spirits are a royal route to self-realization and self-control.

Janzen uses the image of a crab moving from land to water to exemplify this process (1991: 297; 1995: 147). This image is well-chosen as the land may be seen as the place of woe and lamentation, whereas the water is usually seen as the place where spirits reside. The crab stands for the initiand-within-the-ngoma-shelter who is taken from the land into the water and resumes his position on the land again after having been replenished by the water. At the same time it is a movement from inertia to fluidity, from harshness to softness, from a 'dry' state to a 'wet' state. As Pels (1993) has indicated for a specific area in Tanzania, the word ngoma indicates an essential change in the rhythm of life. To use the metaphor of the crab again, ngoma guides and accompanies the process of changing from the rhythm of the 'land' to the rhythm of the 'water'. In this sense all the ritual elements that accompany the change of rhythm are indicated with the term *ngoma*, and these elements may range from initiation rites of various sorts to various dances, but also to Christianity and even sports events for that matter. At the same time Pels clearly indicates that funerals and births certainly are not accompanied by the term ngoma as they do not signify a change in the rhythm of life.

In all these representations, described by both Janzen and Pels, that annotate ngoma it is rather clear that there is no vested, established control of form and content at stake. Rather, the calculus called *ngoma* deals or attempts to cope with, at some times more successfully than at others, the basic problem of control of time in periods of change that affect both the individual and/or society. While being such a calculus of form and content, ngoma offers a sacred, meaning 'ritually separate', invocation of time to empower and transform the person. Crucial here is that ngoma not only operates with the flow of time 'as it is' but also creates its own temporality in which the past is represented as a source of empowerment. A conceptual frame is established in which it is crucial for the process of transformation and healing of the individual and the community to perceive and to represent a past in such notions as ancestral spirits, former kings and important strangers, previous experiences, incantations, songs and rhythms.

Moving one step further in this line of reasoning we need to recognize and appreciate the fact that the evocation of the past in specific mnemonic or nostalgic forms makes up one temporal orientation and representation. As I have noted elsewhere (see Van Dijk 1998) present theorizing about such temporal representations in society proposes analytical differences in types of nostalgia. Strathern distinguishes two modes of nostalgia, each of which can be recognized in the way societies, or groups within societies, foreground specific evocations of the past (Strathern 1995: 110). She distinguishes synthetic nostalgia from what she calls substantive, but I would prefer to call syncretic, nostalgia. The former mode of nostalgia betrays a yearning for a past which is found lacking in the present. The past is closed and has no further bearing on the present, but at the same time a process of estrangement from the present state of affairs can be recognized in expressions of nostalgia. The second form of nostalgia is of more importance to the purpose of this contribution as it actively seeks to create a sense of tradition and social memory which has a bearing on the present. In this form of nostalgia, mnemonics are involved in how societies or groups deal with their present predicament, how certain claims of power and interests are substantiated, and how certain subjective identities are realized (see also Battaglia 1995: 93). As can be argued for religious syncretism as well, syncretic nostalgia, the blending of older and later representations, signs and images, may be viewed as opening up trajectories of personal and social empowerment. Syncretically blending the evocation of the past, of its memory and its experience, with present social reality creates a specific route of empowerment (see for instance the work of Werbner (1991, 1995, 1998). Such syncretism may, for one thing, counterpoise movements which instead emphasize the utopian or the millenarian. On the other hand, and elaborating on Strathern's notions, future ideals, the utopian and the millenarian, can be seen to inform present social action. Future ideals may blend syncretically with present ideas and images as a route of empowerment counterpoising8 nostalgic projects.

Therefore, in this 'politics' of time, I would like to propose to distinguish two perceptions and representations of time: a mnemonic moment by which the past is stressed and a prognostic moment in which the future is represented. This being a matter of emphasis, rather than a distinction in kind, the question becomes how, in religious discourses and practices, a politics of time is played out. In dealing with and accompanying changes in the rhythm of life ngoma offers sacred time to deal with representational moments of time. For instance, Pels (1996) describes how prior to the Second World War the involvement of Waluguru boys and young men in urban life, trade and traffic led to a feeling of urgency among Waluguru elders to create and promote a ngoma in which the nostalgic and the prognostic were present in order to constitue the Waluguru representation of the modern world. The various ritual forms of initiation, such as *Jando*, that entailed an attunement to the 'outside' world, in a sense prepared Waluguru boys for what they might enter on leaving the closed Waluguru society. Jando, so to speak, provided the time to tune in to representations of the outside world and within this 'empty' time frame allowed the Waluguru to 'play' with representational moments. By this playfulness I mean to say that the specific Jando that arose at a particular moment in Waluguru history was the result of a creative but nonetheless specific 'mixture' of represented elements from the past and a likely future.

In order to understand the importance of temporalities in 'disciplines' of healing and transformation one has to see that representation is also, equates to, alienation and is therefore prone to power relations. When the past is represented in mnemonic ritual, specific perceptions ('things' of the past) are uttered or produced in text, in physical performance (dance, song), through objects (pictorial presentations) and in other expressive ways. The individual is no longer owner of his or her mnemonics, nor of prognostics for that matter. They are placed at the mercy of the outer social world and its power relations. Sacred time on the other hand provides the opportunity for escape, together with a 'safer' environment for the production of representations; it may thus safeguard and protect the process of alienation that goes along with it. In other words although within sacred time the alienating effect of the production of mnemonics and prognostics cannot be reduced, the working of power relations on these representations can be controlled. Among the Waluguru the elderly clearly controlled the shuffle of temporal orientations that Jando entailed. This sacred time was intentionally used by the elderly to reinforce mnemonic representations to repress a more forward-looking one. That is to say, a process of mnemonicization took place whereby particularly the prognostic representations of the outer world by the younger generation were gradually incorporated in perceptions of the past by the elderly and were referred to the sacred time of initiation. In other words representations of experiences by the young men concerning styles of behaviour, dress and so on were represented again in mnemonicized form, as if they belong and belonged to the rhythm of Waluguru society.

In the healing phenomena for which Janzen tends to reserve the term ngoma, the importance of temporality is clearly detectable. In the ngoma usually the sick patient in the end comes out of the process of self-realization (again the notion of sacred time!) as a ngoma-healer. Self-realization in these cases rests heavily upon the process of mnemonicization; that is such as the individual or the group realizes itself in a difficult situation by fostering mnemonic representations, 'then and then I became ill, became an initiand to the ngoma (mnemonics) and now I am a healer like many others'.

At the same time the question that needs to be answered is whether in all cases in which people seek individual or collective realization in going through difficult periods mnemonicization plays such a crucial role. The relative positioning of mnemonic versus prognostic representations in sacred time, as matters of 'political' emphasis, probably varies according to circumstances, power relations and ideological strongholds in society. First of all, the fact that Jando vanished completely to be replaced by Christianity among the Waluguru suggests that this relative positioning indeed may change over time. Second, within the healing spectrum itself it is rather clear that the variety of 'healing programmes' carried out by the various institutions in the field (such as independent churches, prophetic movements, herbalist organizations, etc.) suggests that the emphasis on mnemonicization may differ substantially.

What is therefore proposed in this section is to use the relative positioning of representational moments, of the construction of temporalities (nostalgic versus prognostic) as the key to a standard of comparison. Independently of any of the healing institutions in the area, including ngoma, the question can be asked how does each relate to the relative 'strength' of each of the representational moments.

Mnemonical comfort

Now that we have established a rough guide for comparing healing movements on the basis of their representational power and the power relations involved, we may proceed by turning to the social and ideological implications of represented time.

In order to be able to explore this question from the African perspective we need to analyze the conception of time in African society and how this is reflected in anthropological literature in the first place. It was not until the ground-breaking study of Evans-Pritchard on the 'Nuer Time Reckoning' (1939) that Western notions of 'primitive time' as analysed by Levy-Bruhl (1923) were seriously contested. Whereas in such and similar early sociological studies the African was considered deficient in conceptualizing time, Evans-Pritchard showed that in Nuer social life a number of temporal structures and 'planes of rhythm' were recognized that influenced the daily, seasonal and ecological activities of ordinary people profoundly. In subsequent studies by Bohannan (1953), Beidelman (1963), Bourdieu (1963) and for other areas Lévi-Strauss (1966) the anthropological insight gained importance that temporalities were to be considered products of culture and environment rather than products of intellectual capacities. It was not until the work of John Mbiti (1969), however, that a theory which situated time as central to African cosmology was developed. Mbiti expounded the notion, very central to the argument that is developed in this contribution, that African time, contrary to Western time, was non-linear and was basically constructed on the basis of events in the past. As African time and its cosmological representation is event-time there is no sense of future and an explicit orientation on the past is omnipresent. Mbiti explains:

> The linear concept of time in Western thought, with an indefinite past, present and infinite future is practically foreign to African thinking. The future is virtually absent because events which lie in it have not taken place, they have not been realized, and cannot, therefore, constitute time.
>
> (Mbiti 1969: 21–11)

Representations of the past, such as the ancestors being considered the living dead in the present, reflect therefore a profound orientation towards the past as potential time for the now. In other words the future is moving 'backward' and does not allow for linear progression.

In a number of more recent anthropological studies the insight has gained momentum that the lack of prognostic orientation has to be linked with specific socio-economic power-structures 'on the ground' (Comaroff and Comaroff for Botswana (1991: 146, 234–6), Mazrui and Mphande for Kenya and Malawi (1994), Mudimbe (1988) for Africa in general), and with the specific rhetoric of academia in which time perceptions were used as an instrument in the 'othering' of the anthropological object (Fabian 1983, 1991). In the first series of studies the presence or absence of prognostic orientations is linked with the pre-capitalist or capitalist modes of production and social organization. In the pre-capitalist, largely agrarian societies, due to the cyclical nature of the ecological rhythms, the sense of time was organic and the construction of temporalities was therefore set within the framework of human activity that responded to such cycles (Adjaye 1994: 3–4, Van Binsbergen 1996).

In the advent of the capitalist and colonial modes of production a commoditization of time for the exploitation of human labour took place. Labour time was no longer conceived in a response to nature, the agrarian cycle, but became computed by the hour on the basis of a process of alienation of labour from the human body. The central challenge that faced colonial capitalism in its early phases in many African societies was the establishment of a work relation based on the 'voluntary' sale of one's labour power, a commodity that would be prized by the hour (Mazrui and

Mphande 1994: 103; see also Cooper 1992). This process required the conquest of the social body and its reorientation from a pre-capitalist to a capitalist time frame. In this time frame a sense of future was inscribed on the body, usually through harsh methods of labour discipline. Punctuality, strict organization of time, planning ahead for the optimal use of available time and planning ahead for making ends meet between what could be gained by selling one's labour power and labour time and what one was obliged to spend within the new colonial order on taxes, school-fees and the like, became imperative. Mazrui and Mphande show in great detail the extent of violence that was used by the colonial rulers to mould the African body into a time frame that would prevent the African from lapsing to 'primitive idleness' which was considered rife in village life by colonial officials. Only through time discipline would Africans be able to uplift themselves from their primitive state. Male labour was preferred to female labour as it was considered less subject to the unruly rhythms of nature.

What this type of analysis, including that of Mbiti seems to emphasize, however, is that a prognostic orientation within African societies and their cosmologies was only established at and through the inception of capitalist socio-economic relations. In other words 'from within' the African society such prognostic orientation could never emerge unless capitalist relations were introduced. This proposition can and should be seriously questioned and it opens the road to any research that would be able to refute this thought by exploring prognostic orientations that were in existence in pre-capitalist times. Although the reconstruction of prognostic views and representations in African pre-capitalist cosmologies is beyond the scope of this contribution, I would certainly like to register the view that absence of prognostic orientations must be considered a specific, cultural, spatio-temporal construction. In specific times, at specific places and in specific social, political and economic circumstances prognostic orientations seem to be absent while in others they are strongly present (see Worsley 1957, on the Melanesian cargo-cults). Only through detailed cultural analysis can we begin to understand the construction of such temporalities and their representations in signs, images, bodily discipline and the like.

Furthermore, differing discourses in society may reflect differing constructions of temporalities in which the body social is constituted. Discourses on healing seem particularly to reflect specific constructions of temporalities, as Dossey has shown for Western culture (Dossey 1982). In twentieth-century Africa a wide variety of healing discourses have emerged of which – as Vaughan has been able to show, for instance – the colonial medical discourse became very influential *vis-à-vis* existing and more indigenous healing systems (Vaughan 1991 see for a critique Van Dijk 1994). The point I want to make here is that healing regimes do not, obviously, only differ in their practices but in how these practices relate to specific constructions and representations of time (Antze and Lambek make a similar point in relation to the linkage between memory and therapy in different societies, see Antze and Lambek 1996). The adage 'time heals', therefore, is not an element of pan-human wisdom but rather a culture-specific, spatio-temporal construction.

Regarding ngoma I have tried to indicate in the previous paragraph that this calculus predominantly leads to a mnemonicization of represented time. The invoking of representations, carried out idiosyncratically for each and every single initiand, leads to a mnemonicization of experiences. As Janzen indicates, a period of eight years or more for a full initiation process into ngoma's secrets is no exception. Spierenburg (Chapter 5, this volume) highlights the significance of the recitation of long genealogical lines that are to be carried out by the initiand-medium and the relating Mhondoro spirit in Zimbabwe before an acknowledgement of the new status of the initiand can take place. A second result of the ngoma calculus – particularly for those ngomas and initiands confronted with the predominantly modern contexts of life – is that it provides new variations of perceived old themes that are intended to provide a mitigating, emotional gratifying, comforting environment.

This process of creating a comforting mnemonic model has already been well-described for urban healing churches in particular (see most recently the work of Devisch 1996) and not so much for ngoma (the question arises whether Janzen has familiarized himself sufficiently with the urban context). The explosive growth of all sorts of urban healing movements and churches that has been witnessed in Southern Africa, of which ngoma according to Janzen has been part and parcel, is generally associated with the increased rate of urbanization over the last decades (Sundkler 1961: 80–85; Daneel 1974: 55; West 1975: 4; Kiernan 1981: 142; Comaroff 1985: 185, 186). In general terms the healing churches/movements are seen and interpreted by these authors as adequate and apt vehicles for the adaptation and adjustment of the rural-to-urban migrant confronted with a confusing, anarchic and fragmented social reality. Basically the healing churches/movements provide in this view for a comforting rural-to-urban transference of a stock of religious symbols and conceptualizations, authority structures and, of course, of ways of coping with illness and misfortune. Daneel even goes as far as to say:

> It would be a valid conclusion that the urban Zionist and Apostle Churches are in the first place extensions of the rural congregations and act as a spiritual harbour for those members who occasionally live in town.

> [Their] sermons deal with rural problems or with urban problems from a rural point of view.
> (Daneel 1974: 23, 24)

What Daneel in fact observed was a mnemonicization of urban ritual which, as Dillon-Malone stressed for the Masowe communities he studied, provides a secure setting for the preservation and continuation of traditional styles of life and religious beliefs (Dillon-Malone 1978: 129–30). West notes how this process is linked largely with gerontocratic relations, as he indicates that the success of this process depends on the possibilities the healing churches/movements offer to the elderly to resume their influential position in the new, urban environment. It is rather unusual for a man under fifty years of age to hold any position of authority within these healing churches (West 1975: 55).

Comaroff in her 1985 publication takes one step further along this path as she indicates that the process of mnemonicization first of all pertains not only to symbols, beliefs, authority structures and the like but also, and most significantly, to the spatial organization of the rhythms of life. Second, she argues that the mnemonic model that has been developed by urban Tshidi Zionist groups serves the purpose of political protest as well. In the border town of Botswana and Bophutatswana, Mafikeng, a large number and variety of Zionist churches are found. In her view these churches, wherein healing plays a major role, were engaged in a highly coded form of resistance against the apartheid system by applying and resorting to age-old Tshidi elements, symbols and practices (Comaroff 1985: 169, 194–99). The churches do not strive for a direct return of the traditional concepts per se to a modern, urban setting, but opt for a transformation of these concepts in order to mediate between the one (Tshidi tradition, perceived past) and the other (apartheid, perceived present). The question is how this transformation occurs and how is it maintained.

Comaroff's answer is that we should focus on the exploration of the placing of the individual in a specific spatio-temporal organization (ibid.: 220, 213–17). In this analysis the importance of spatial organization – in the sense of buildings and areas, and the positioning of everyday practices therein – needs to be stressed. Symbols, signs and images thereby act as a social memory, a mnemonic scheme that is inscribed in the body personal, for instance through rituals of initiation, in order to place the individual in his or her rightful location and position in life. Tshidi indigenous culture had a tripartite locational structure that was of paramount importance to the position the individual occupied in social life (ibid.: 55–7). The tripartite structure, which consisted of the chiefly court, the house and the wild areas/fields, focused on the house as the elemental unit in symbolic space. The front of the house faced the chiefly court and the middle ground in between the house and the court was the male domain of ritual and political action, the domain strictly closed to women. The back of the house faced the wild areas and fields and was primarily the domain of women, where cultivation and other productive activity took place. The house, therefore, mediated between the two areas, but in itself held paramount reproductive importance as all sexual activity and food consumption would take place there. At initiation boys would be taken from the house to spend some time in the wild before entering the public domain at the site of the chiefly court, by which again the mediating position of the house was made clear.

In Comaroff's view, the position of the Zionist churches in the present-day South African context are serving a very similar specific mnemonic scheme:

> Zionists are what Zionists do: and their primary mnemonic is lodged not in Scripture but in the physical body and its immediate spatio-temporal location. (Comaroff 1985: 200)

In other words, Zionist churches under modern conditions reflect and resemble the 'house' and its important symbolical and structural functions for the individual in traditional society. The secluded Zionist meeting places and symbolical repertoire have the same mediating position that the house has with regard to the spatio-temporal arrangements between the chiefly court and uterine wild areas and fields. Signs, colours, dress and style are taken over from the traditional into the urban setting; they simultaneously retain their earlier significance and acquire new meanings within the Zionist Church (ibid.: 219–26). Comaroff warns us not to view this process of what I would like to call mnemonicization as a retreat into 'romantic nativism' (ibid.: 227). Rather it is a dynamic, wilful reconstruction meant to express distance both from the subordinated traditional world and from the predicament of apartheid which so deformed everyday experience. Therefore, the individual in modern oppressive capitalist labour relations who becomes a member of a Zionist healing church does not find himself re-integrated into a 'precolonial Eden' which would no longer suit his needs; the churches, like the urban migrant, have been irreversibly transformed by experiences outside the traditional setting. The Zionist church offers newly constructed, though mnemonicized, initiation and healing rites, meant to re-integrate the individual into the collectivity of Zion. Healing rites, baptisms, special attire, rituals, dances and songs are aimed at withdrawing participants into a collectivity, away from both the oppressed traditional scene of existence and the modern, afflicting conditions of life.

The mnemonics in this situation, as provided by these healing churches, serve a clear purpose of adaptation to stressful circumstances. In response to these circumstances ngoma also lays out a programme that attunes the behaviour of the initiand to a 'premeditated' world of spiritual forces. For Janzen this spirit world is both the intervening and intermediary party in accommodating the social circumstances. Ngoma is in this sense very similar to the Zion churches that like the Tshidi house intervene and mediate between the everyday social-political circumstances and the wilderness where the spiritual forces reside. Ngoma also relates both to modern (urban) conditions and to the history of contact with spirits and the practices of approaching them. Pels's statement that ngoma is the sort of programme that allows people to tune into modern conditions in such a way that a discussion, comment and response become possible is only partially true. Neither ngoma, nor a number of the healing churches for that matter, 'plan ahead', that is they do not provide a weather forecast on what future adaptations require from adepts in the present. There is no social programme for 'tuning ahead', so to speak, that would enable those involved in the sort of retrospective practices that are outlined by ngoma to be in the forefront of what society demands of their members under modern conditions. There are no future-oriented role models, no prognostic scenarios of what the society of tomorrow will look like, no ideology receptive to those global trends in practices and ideas that inform people of social states of mind in tomorrow's world.

The clearest examples that anthropology has offered of the prognostic ideologies that I discuss can be found in the so-called millenarian cults of native American Indians and the 'cargo cults' of Melanesia. Both entailed 'social programmes' not only for the individual lives of adherents concerning the aspirational future but also state of society. Although dealing with both types of movement is beyond the scope of the present chapter, it is safe to say that the 'programmes' of these cults have never been analyzed on the level of the existence of their politics of time, expressed in a prognostic healing ideology. It is therefore very difficult to relate the construction of temporalities by these movements to that of ngoma and similar healing institutions. Some may argue that the fundamental conservative impetus in healing practices as such prohibits the development of a prognostic programme in ngoma and its institutions, and that, the other way round, the absence of healing practices in other movements may definitely contribute to their prognostic capacities.

Instead, I would like to argue that the absence of prognostic thought needs to be problematized and not taken for granted on two levels simultaneously. First, the absence of prognosticism needs to be problematized on the level of anthropological theory, in the sense that anthropology seems to have failed to develop a paradigm, a method of analysis for exploring the field of prognosticism, the writing of scenarios and other future-oriented constructs.

Second, on a more basic level and remaining within the limited field of religiously inspired healing practices, it can be pointed out that there are movements that combine healing with a prognostic appeal. By their very existence these movements seem to problematize the absence of prognosticism within ngoma.

Comparable to ngoma groups and a number of Zionist churches is the Born-Again movement, the *abadwa mwatsopano* as they call themselves, of Malawi. It operates mainly in an urban context but, unlike ngoma groups and Zionist churches, does not thrive on mnemonicization. They have been studied by Van Dijk (1992a, 1992b,

1993a, 1993b, 1995) largely within the context of Malawi's largest city, Blantyre. The intricate relationship between healing and prognostic power as it is maintained in this religious movement is explored in the following section.

Prognostic power

A starting point in the analysis of modern African healing practices which do not rely on mnemonical relations, but instead seem to represent more prognostic notions, can be found in the work of Bauman (1993). He reaches the conclusion that in modern relations of time-space compression temporalities are linear and vertical rather than horizontal and cyclical (as opposed to Mbiti's conclusions, see page 139). Modernity, he argues, creates specific time-space conceptualizations, through processes such as conversion to Christianity, whereby 'before' means 'lower' and 'inferior' while the future is represented as 'superior'. A battleground thus emerges between the superior future and the inferior past whereby in this arena superiority is tested and proved in victory; inferiority in defeat (Bauman 1993: 226). Influenced by modernity, therefore, superior power in present-day society usually has a strong future orientation.

In this section I intend to show how Christian fundamentalists, Born-Agains as they are usually called, claim superior healing power by rejecting the past. By renouncing the experiences of one's 'inferior' past the road is opened to attaining Born-Again status and to obtaining 'superior' healing powers. These healing powers 'stretch out' into the imminent future as they are perceived to constitute the individual independently from an identity that relates to the family and its immediate cosmological relations. They are meant to 'seal off' (*kutsirika*) the individual Born-Again from those evil powers and influences that may 'erupt' from a person's former social environment and experiences. In this sense Born-Againism, as will be explained below, strongly presents a dichotomous view of past versus future, inferior versus superior, low versus uplifted. The social formulaic of these dichotomies, interestingly, is one in which the young position themselves *vis-à-vis* the old. The Born-Again movement in Malawi is very much a movement of the young; those who presently experience the social contradictions entailed in modernity.

Since the early 1970s Malawi's urban centres have seen the rise of a number of Christian fundamentalist groups and organizations led by young itinerant preachers, varying in age between nine and thirty (see also Van Dijk 1992a, 1992b, 1993a). These young people began to attract crowds by conducting large revival meetings at which, in fire and brimstone sermons, they strongly denounced the sinfulness and evils of everyday urban life. The preachers (*alaliki*, 'sayers', as they call themselves) who were the first to take up their 'call' to preach, belonged to an urban class of rather well-educated college and university students. The high level of education allowed them to take up higher-ranking jobs in urban society. These preachers can be called the 'part-timers' as they were and still are involved in preaching activities only in their spare time. Later on in the early and mid-1980s a second group of preachers stepped in who generally had been able to receive only a few years of primary schooling and certainly did not belong to a young urban elite. These preachers usually started to conduct their activities on a full-time basis: one way or another, their preaching activities were and are supposed to provide them with a livelihood.

These itinerant young preachers can still be found promulgating a doctrine characterized by strict morality. In strong terms the use of alcoholic beverages, cigarettes and drugs is denounced and they fulminate against adultery, promiscuity, violence and theft. Furthermore, the satanic habit of frequenting bars, hotels and discos is condemned, as these are understood to be places of utmost moral depravity.

In addition to these negative injunctions, clear demands for a rejuvenated morality are put forward in an atmosphere of religious excitement and emotionalism. While the audience is urged to sing and dance, sinners are commanded to kneel in front of the young people, who then insist that evil objects such as knives, tobacco, stolen goods and above all magical, esoteric objects be handed in. Those present are urged to step forward at the altar call in order to receive the 'infilling' of the Holy Spirit, which is stressed as the single most important way to become cleansed of worldly, defiling forces. Only after living through a mystical rebirth by experiencing this 'infilling' is a person considered to be born again (*kubadwa mwatsopano*).

Speaking in tongues (*malilime*) is the central element of worship, ritual and symbolic practice within the Born-Again movement. No meeting can be held without a session of religious ecstasy that accompanies speaking in tongues. This is usually displayed with great energy and force: people are found grovelling on the ground, sweating profusely while shouting all kinds of incomprehensible sounds. Going through such an ecstatic born-again experience is compulsory before one can be considered born again. Thereafter malilime functions as a check on the level of purity maintained by the individual believer. The general view is that by becoming born again a line is established with benevolent, heavenly powers. In this process malilime becomes the absolute assurance that one has succeeded in tapping into a superior power which purifies, protects one's day-to-day existence, and heals any sort of more or less mystical affliction which may even include witchcraft (*ufiti*). Malilime offers the true believer the possibility and power to withstand evil forces of witchcraft and various malign spirits. As one preacher told his audience, the Born-Again who feels attacked by witches which during sleep try to take people away to nocturnal orgies where human flesh is consumed, may counter them by malilime which holds witches trapped and paralysed at the door of the house. Some Born-Again preachers even feel empowered to detect witchcraft and related harmful objects, and are convinced that nothing will harm them if and when they lay their hands on such devilish objects and related practices.

Besides combating these threats from a nocturnal world, malilime also addresses the predicaments of modern urban society where it is difficult to obtain or complete education, to find paid employment and to pay for health services; and where because of overcrowding in the townships, social tensions easily arise. 'Counselling' provided by Born-Again preachers is meant to overcome these problems, and at such sessions both preacher and 'client' are invariably expected to begin speaking in tongues together.

In this sense the network that has arisen out of the many, weekly Born-Again meetings and the small organizations set up by cooperating preachers should be seen as a 'security circle', a safe environment, that is guaranteed by malilime. Through malilime, in a concerted effort of all participants at the Born-Again meetings, a defensive 'wall' against outside evil forces is erected. Within the niche malilime is a clear identity marker. This is unlike other puritan movements in that an encirclement as such does not exist in a materialized form in the sense of a closed community, compound or anything else of that sort. The Born-Agains do not need such encirclement; on the contrary, in an urban setting – with its mobility and its continuously changing sets of social relationships – it is only in abstract terms that an encirclement serves a clear purpose. Every 'true' Born-Again is the carrier of the spiritual, defensive circle, irrespective of the many sets the individual might get engaged in. A real breach of the circle occurs when the channel of inspirational power from the heavenly forces is either not maintained, or denied, or exchanged for a different and/or contesting line of power.

It is in this context that power is related to prognosticism, and not to mnemonics as we have seen in the case of other healing and purification movements. Two discursive practices within the Born-Again ideology and its ramifications indicate this emphasis on prognosticism rather strongly. First there is the emphasis placed on the 'instant', the immediate experience, in the entire ritual sphere which serves as a starting point for further development and 'growth', without an invocation of a person's past and its cosmological notions of ancestors and the like. Second, there is a discourse on the rejection of a person's past and all that relates to the construction of social position and authority within a perceived past.

To start with this last mentioned element of emphasizing prognosticism, one has to note that a most important aspect of malilime is that the rigid puritan order which is impressed on the individual and his/her social environment also entails a rejection of the way the elderly are generally believed to become 'ripened'. A person is considered to be *kukhwima* (ripened, empowered) if he has been able to build up a position of considerable influence in almost every sector of daily life. He is supposed to be wealthy and prosperous thanks to successful business schemes, he is expected to have an influential position in one of the bigger mission churches, as well as in his home village in kinship affairs, and even in political affairs a 'big man' should have been able to secure a powerful position. In being kukhwima every person, not least Born-Again preachers, is prone to the suspicion that he sought support from malicious, dark forces. In fact kukhwima here has the primary connotation of having been able to master the forces that lie in witchcraft and its related objects which can be applied, strategically, to one's own ends. The Born-Again preachers, however, stress the experience and empowerment of malilime instead of kukhwima. Success in the daily world, freedom and protection from any kind of affliction and misfortune, can only be reached and acquired through malilime, which in its turn requires maintaining a purified and unsullied status for the individual. On the other hand, being kukhwima almost by definition entails impurity and involvement in practices not meant for public scrutiny. Malilime thereby opposes the authority of the elderly as no allowance is made for the generally respected source of their powers.

In this sense the elderly are excluded from the niche as they represent the involvement in other lines of power such as witchcraft and politics; the two are comparable in the level of evil involved. The exclusion of the elderly, however, extends in a cultural sense beyond the boundary of age but refers also to a range of symbolic repertoires, styles and rituals that equally fall within a perception of 'the past'. It is this perception of a past in which the elderly of today have played their roles which contributes specifically to the outright rejection of important parts of

Malawian traditions. The Born-Again ideology includes the perception that those symbolic repertoires in which the elderly still play a dominant part, in fact belong to a 'past' that has to be both repudiated and forgotten.

In the Born-Agains' model of conversion there is no room for a conversation with a perceived past that would involve a recollection of a person's engagement in traditional rituals of any sort, or his or her engagement in activities considered sinful. The Born-Again experience presupposes a total rejection of a person's past life as a new and above all purified individual is expected to arise out of the experience of the 'infilling' with the *Mzimu Woyera* (the White Spirit, that is the Holy Spirit). In healing through 'infilling' no drums are used, while the very moment of possession by the Holy Spirit is not accompanied by rhythm, but by speaking in tongues (malilime) alone. This then serves as a clear boundary marker between the past and the present, as drums and rhythm no longer play the role of invoking the past in its mnemonical representation, as is common with ngoma.

The mnemonics in the form of objects, inscriptions on the body and ritual experiences that relate to the past are viewed as being controlled by and large by the older generation, who are suspected of having been able to put all sorts of bonding magical powers in place. They are, for instance, accused by the preachers of being responsible for keeping magical, esoteric objects which are capable of extending their powers from the past into the present. These objects therefore may haunt certain people long after their initial owners have died. Long, binding threads have been woven by the older generation through their dealings with evil powers that affect the activities of relatives in the present. The iconoclasm as presented by the preachers certainly includes the confiscation and subsequent destruction of objects of this type.[1] It thereby enables both the Born-Again preacher and the aspirant Born-Again member to cut off these long and binding harmful relationships laid down by the fabrication and usage of esoteric objects. To become Born-Again and thereby to become purified means to get rid of a past wherein all sorts of harmful influences may have been concocted.

In order to do so the young preachers present an ideology that is highly de-mnemonicized, that is to say an ideology in which the past is made 'powerless' but the future is presented as the main source of inspiration. Contrary to almost all of the independent churches in Blantyre and elsewhere in Malawi, the elderly have a minor role to play within the Born-Again groupings. They do not preach, they do not organize meetings, they do not enter into speaking of tongues. Neither are members of the older generation, not even those who lead the Pentecostal type of independent churches, the ones that come the closest to the Born-Again ideology, considered role models for the way in which a preacher is supposed to act. The ridicule which the older generation meets at Born-Again meetings provides a hostile environment to any notion of copying certain styles of behaviour from the older generation as far as religious conduct is concerned. In this way the process of de-mnemonicization also entails a full rejection of those experiences, primarily related to initiation or dealings with the traditional healers (*asing'anga*), that led an individual into the realm of the older generation. Secrets that relate to the relatively 'hidden' process of initiation (*chinamwhali*) are therefore easily and mockingly disclosed, restrictions and obligations related to funerals are openly neglected and mocked, the Nyau secret society to which initiated men belong in the Central and Southern regions of Malawi branded as devilish, and so on. Thus cutting the threads with the past certainly entails a wide variety of possible points of conflict and tension between relatives, and usually involves an escape from the immediate circle of family members by the new Born-Again.

This cutting of threads with the past and tradition becomes salient in another aspect of the Born-Again ideology. This is to do with the emphasis put on the 'instant' experiences of a number of key-note elements in becoming a Born-Again. First is the notion that one is instantly 'saved' in becoming a Born-Again by an on-the-spot transformation of one's life, one's social, religious and moral attitudes, and the like. In other words, unlike other religious groups such as the missionary and some of the independent churches, Born-Again groups require no period of catechumenate, neither is a period of training and initiation presupposed, as happens in some of the non-Christian possession groups. By rejecting their past a person can be turned instantly into a full member of the Born-Again circle. Once entered into the circle every affliction and misfortune that affects the Born-Again can be coped with by instant healing. Again this notion of instant healing deviates in very clear lines from the diagnostics, aetiology and patient histories that are the centrepieces of the healing practices of both the traditional *nanga* system as well as those of the majority of spirit-healing churches. The Zionist Churches in Blantyre, for instance, are known for members acting as 'X-rays' capable of penetrating an afflicted person's soul and history in order to 'see' what the main causes of the troubles are. Within the abadwa mwatsopano's healing practices, however, there is no diagnosis, no probing into a person's life history, no examination of one's social environment. There is only the instant experience of the healing powers of the Mzimu Woyera through the laying on of hands by one of the preachers, and no questions asked.

Again, there is also the notion of the instant sealing off (kutsirika) of a house or any other place from all sorts of outside evil, devilish powers. Once the preacher, or any other Born-Again for that matter, has entered the phase of speaking in tongues and the walls are touched, nothing evil enters the place anymore or will be cast out. The long preparations by a sing'anga that are required to seal off a house in the traditional way are no longer needed and are even ridiculed.

This process of de-mnemonicization, which puts the entire Born-Again movement in a different perspective from a large number of other urban religious movements, seems to be balanced by a strong future-oriented impetus in the religious ideology. The preaching and sessions of speaking in tongues seem to be geared at a future, ideal end-state of society. Beyond the salient eschatological notions on the imminent return of Jesus Christ and the final Day of Judgement that will see the wrath of God extend to every sinner, there is a noticeable striving towards the advance reordering of society. This aspect of the Born-Again ideology is comparable to certain elements found in the cargo cults. Preparing for the cargo to come, the cult members created a future-oriented ideology by which social relations, role models, leadership structures and even the physical outlines of entire villages were reshaped according to what the expected wealth would require (Worsley 1957). Instead of a diagnostic line of thinking (what is wrong with our society?) this religion set out a prognostic line of thought and practice which focused on the expected incoming wealth from another society (as evolved out of their contacts with the American war economy).

Likewise the young preacher's role models and authority styles, as well as their end-goal of an entirely purified Malawian society, are profoundly based on what they see as coming to Malawi in the context of increasing globalized contacts. Important role models to the young preachers are the world-famous Pentecostal/revival preachers such as Billy Graham, Jimmy Swaggart and Reinhard Bonnke – mainly in the ways they operate, their dress and style, their effective ways of getting their groups organized, the identity they assume, the success and prosperity they seem to represent. The influx of this type of Anglo-American Pentecostalism (Reinhard Bonnke visited Malawi in 1986, bringing with him truckloads of equipment for his gigantic revival meetings) provided the preachers with an extraneous source for new religious ideas, modes of organization, dress, style and general identity (see Gifford 1987, 1991, 1993 on the spread of Pentecostalism in the Southern African region). These were, and still are, omens of a society wherein the gerontocratic control, manifest in all sorts of 'daily' and 'nocturnal' manipulations, does not maintain any relationship to the level of success, prestige and socio-economic standing that one can attain by relying on inspirational power. The end-state of society perceived by the preachers is one in which the real source of power and authority lies beyond its own perimeters and therefore beyond the clutches of tradition and its gerontocracy.

As the inspirational power of the Holy Spirit is perceived to reside outside society, those who are able to bring in this source, as the famous Pentecostal preachers did in Malawi, are welcomed with great awe and respect. The young preachers themselves on many occasions, brought, this line of power that provides instant healing from the urban areas into the villages. The focus on the creation of a religious Utopia, purified of all sorts of contaminating evil influences, implies assuming an 'outsider' identity and gratifies the idea that being a Born-Again in fact means to become a stranger to one's immediate relatives, friends and peers. As this is accentuated by dress and style (some preachers only speak English at their meetings, which is then translated into Chichewa by an interpreter) their meetings are considered safe havens in which the new puritan order is already effective. Men and women, freely intermixing, all claim that powers from the past world, mainly in the form of witchcraft and politics, are here on the spot abhorred and discarded. So in the rural places islands of the 'righteous' are created by the young preachers that reflect and pre-empt what they have perceived on a much wider scale of puritan efforts directed at the nation, or even at the wider world for that matter.

Once the individual has stepped into such a circle a programme unfolds that entails a 'training' in establishing the link with the outside residing purifying force provided by the Mzimu Woyera. The programme includes the mastering of speaking in tongues as this is the most clear and expressive sign that the purifying force has been 'contacted' and has set about doing its work on the individual and the social environment. In other words, the more people are involved in speaking in tongues, the purer society becomes. The end-goal for the programme is thus set, while the training itself – joining the Born-Agains, engaging in their healing and sessions of speaking in tongues – turns every member into a preacher. The programme is aggressive and assertive in the sense that every Born-Again is expected to share vicariously in the task of preaching in increasingly bigger social circles (one of the Born-Again groups in Blantyre, tellingly, was called The Aggressive Christianity Mission Training Corps). The religious agenda is thus set for reaching ever higher levels of purity; an agenda heavily influenced by incoming doctrinal material in the form of Jimmy Swaggart's videos, Billy Graham's booklets and Reinhard Bonnke's taped speeches.

The future-oriented programme, to conclude, has led to a strong impetus in the Born-Again movement to ridicule important aspects of the symbolic repertoire as well as those who are considered the guarantors of ritual practice and power; the elderly, the local traditional healers (asing'anga) and the local traditional authorities. On many occasions this process of de-mnemonicization resulted in hilarity and laughter as preachers proved to be artists in mimicking such local authorities and their ritual behaviour while conducting their meetings. The process of de-mnemoni-cization therefore can be understood as an assertive and vivid form of protest against gerontocratic authority; contrary to Comaroff (1985), it is not a mnemonic scheme that has fuelled this form of protest in an urban setting.

Conclusion

Although 'make a complete break with your past' is an oft-heard cry among many Pentecostal, Born-Again groupings throughout various parts in Africa (see Meyer 1998 for Ghana, Van Dijk 1998), each of these Pentecostal movements requires in terms of scrutiny the future-oriented programme it presents. Pentecostalism in coun-tries such as Ghana and Malawi speaks a language of modernity in which the past represents the bondage of a person to 'evil' life styles, to the ways of the ancestors and the worship of the elders, which are to be denounced and regarded as inferior. It would, however, be a mistake to think that Pentecostalism is becoming popular in Africa only because it is able to reject an individual's past and declare it inferior to a superior present. Severing the ties with the past, thus turning the person from a 'dividual' locked eternally within the bonds of the (ancestral) family into an indi-vidual, is cast within a wider social programme. It is this social programme, focusing on an immanent future moral reordering of society, which puts the entire movement of Born-Agains, with its notions of superior individuality, in a very different perspective as compared with earlier religious movements. Modernity prompted young people not to long for a 'pre-colonial Eden' but to seek a type of healing that engages in prognostic activities, foreseeing a near future and delivering 'weather forecasts' on the society to come. The force of ideology, certainly a fundamentalist one, is important – but the cultural exploration of the temporal orientations that come into play when religion is creating a rupture with the past, and a rapture into the future, certainly contributes to anthropology's understanding of what modernity's impact is on African societies today.

The next question to be answered is what are the social limitations of the production of 'futures' and ideological scenarios? In his seminal paper of 1981 Appadurai states that every society in creating and discussing 'pasts' can only do so by referring to a set of 'parameters' that set the contours or framework within which the creative process finds its limitations. He identifies four basic parameters or minimal dimensions – *authority, continuity, depth and interdependence* – concerning which, he claims, all cultures must make some substantive provision. For each of these four dimensions some sort of consensus has to be reached, without limiting or predetermining the substantive outcome of the 'content' of the constructed past, as to what is credible and permissible in creating a past. On each of these the dimen-sions some consensus has to be reached on what, respectively, can be considered credible sources, acceptable linkages in time, perceivable time-depth, and genuine relationship with other constructed pasts (Appadurai 1981: 203). As Appadurai shows for the writing of pasts at a Hindu temple in Madras City, once consensus is reached along these dimensions pasts are not produced in infinite variety by the various groups that visit the temple.

The question that needs to be answered in, view of a process of de-mnemoni-cization, is whether such or similar parameters can be identified that guide the creation of 'futures'. In other words, does the future-oriented programme arise out of a context of unbounded variety by which futures can be constructed, or are there clear demarcations as to what should be answered, discussed or allowed for?

As has become increasingly clear in recent anthropological studies (among others Wallman *et. al.* 1992) much still has to be unravelled as to how futures are constructed in societies under the weight of (specific religiously charged) ideologies (see also Boissevain 1992). In a rough sense certainly the future-oriented programme laid down by the Born-Again movement seems to fulfil the requirement of discussing the indicated parameters. If, for the sake of brevity, we limit ourselves to the question of the credibility of *authority* it is clear that the future is linked to a type of religious authority that still falls within the consensus of what power actually is, by what sort of extraneous sources a person may become empowered and to what extent this commands both 'daily' and 'nocturnal' forces. There is consensus on what the credible source of authority is that sets the agenda for the future, as becomes evident in the importance of malilime. As such the content, or substance in Appadurai's words, of the parameter of authority that produces statements on the future is being discussed (malilime instead of kukhwima, purification instead of power-strongholds in the nocturnal world) and not the parameter itself. It is the substance of the notion of purity that links up, for instance, with the dimension of *depth*. As to this dimension, the future is probed in the context of a clear eschatology which leaves no doubt as to at what point in time the purified level of society will be fully attained. Again, the notion of depth in Malawian society – what, for instance, religious/magical acts might mean over a longer period in time (magical objects produced in the past still being considered active in the present) – is not contested, but given substance according to the preacher's religious ideology. The future constructed by the young preachers on these dimensions still seems to fall within what the society's framework for the representations of time allow for – although more research is needed within the context of an anthropology of the future. Despite its programme of breaking with the past, the constructed future is not the result of an unlimited, unbounded social experiment.

Appadurai's remarks on the construction of pasts certainly inspires an agenda for an anthropology that is capable of deciphering both the basics and the conditions of the relationship between modernity and prognosticism in society.

Notes

Portions of this article, specifically the last two sections, draw on Van Dijk 1998.

1   Of particular significance here, as I have shown elsewhere (Van Dijk 1995) were the nation-wide actions of Linley Mbeta, a preacher in her mid-twenties, who after a mystical recovery from death, claimed to be able to see a hand coming down from heaven pointing out to her the 'sinners' among her audiences who could be suspected of possessing such 'devilish' objects.

Literature

Adjaye, J.K. (1994) 'Time in Africa and Its Diaspora. An Introduction'. In J.K. Adjaye (ed.) *Time in the Black Experience*. London: Greenwood.

Antze, P. and M. Lambek (1996) 'Introduction: Forecasting Memory'. In P. Antze and M. Lambek (eds) *Tense Past. Cultural Essays in Trauma and Memory*. London: Routledge.

Appadurai, A. (1981) 'History as a Scarce Resource'. *Man* 16: 201–219.

Battaglia, D. (1995) 'On Practical Nostalgia: Self-Prospecting among Urban Trobrianders'. In D. Battaglia (ed.) *Rhetorics of Self-Making*. Berkeley: University of California Press.

Bauman, Z. (1993) *Postmodern Ethics*. Oxford: Blackwell.

Beidelman, T. (1963) 'Kaguru Time Reckoning: An Aspect of the Cosmology of an East African People'. *Southwestern Journal of Anthropology* 19: 9–20.

Bohannan, P. (1953) 'Concepts of Time among the Tiv of Nigeria'. *Southwestern Journal of Anthropology* 9: 251–62.

Boissevain, J. (1992) 'On Predicting the Future: Parish Rituals and Patronage in Malta'. In S. Wallman (ed.) *Contemporary Futures. Perspectives from Social Anthropology*. London: Routledge, ASA-Monograph 30.

Bourdieu, P. (1963) 'The Attitude of the Algerian Peasant toward Time'. In J. Pitt-Rivers (ed.) *Mediterranean Countrymen: Essays in the Social Anthropology of the Mediterranean*. Paris: Mouton.

Comaroff, Jean (1985) *Body of Power, Spirit of Resistance. The Culture and History of a South African People*. Chicago: University of Chicago Press.

Comaroff, J. and J. Comaroff. (1991) *Of Revelation and Revolution. Christianity, Colonialism and Consciousness in South Africa*. Chicago: Chicago University Press.

Cooper, F. (1992) 'Colonizing Time: Work Rhythms and Labor Conflict in Colonial Mombasa'. In N. Dirks (ed.) *Colonialism and Culture*. Ann Arbor: University of Michigan Press.

Daneel, M.L. (1974) *Old and New in Southern Shona Independent Churches. Vol.II, Church Growth; Causative Factors and Recruitment Techniques*. The Hague: Mouton.

Devisch, R. (1985) 'Perspectives on Divination in Contemporary Sub-Saharan Africa'. In W. van Binsbergen and M. Schoffeleers (eds) *Theoretical Explorations in African Religion*. London: Routledge & Kegan Paul.

——(1996) '"Pillaging Jesus": Healing Churches and the "Villagisation" of Kinshasa'. *Africa* 66(4), pp. 555–87.

Dillon-Malone, C.M. (1978) *The Korsten Basketmakers. A Study of the Masowe Apostles; an Indigenous African Religious Movement*. Manchester: Manchester University Press.

Dossey, L. (1982) *Space, Time and Medicine*. London: Shambala.

Evans-Pritchard, E.E. (1939) 'Nuer Time Reckoning'. *Africa* 12: 189–216.

Fabian, J. (1983) *Time and the Other. How Anthropology Makes its Object*. New York: Columbia University Press.

——(1991) *Time and the Work of Anthropology: Critical Essays, 1971–1991*. Reading: Harwood Academic Publishers.

Foucault, M. (1988) 'Technologies of the Self'. In L.H. Martin (ed.) *Technologies of the Self. A Seminar with Michel Foucault*. London: Tavistock.

Gifford, P. (1987) ' "Africa Shall Be Saved": An Appraisal of Reinhard Bonnke's Pan-African Crusade'. *Journal of Religion in Africa* 17: 63–92.

——(1991) *The New Crusaders: Christianity and the New Right in Southern Africa*. London: Pluto Press.

——(1993) 'Reinhard Bonnke's Mission to Africa, and his 1991 Nairobi Crusade'. In P. Gifford (ed.), *New Dimensions in African Christianity*. Ibadan: (AACC) Sefer Books.

Janzen, J.M. (1991) 'Doing Ngoma: A Dominant Trope in African Religion and Healing'. *Journal of Religion in Africa* 21(4): 290–308.

——(1992) *Ngoma: Discourses of Healing in Central and Southern Africa*. Berkeley: University of California Press.

——(1995) 'Self-representation and Common Cultural Structures in Ngoma Rituals of Southern Africa'. *Journal of Religion in Africa* 25(2): 141–63.

Kiernan, J.P. (1981) 'African Religious Research; Themes and Trends in the Study of Black Religion in Southern Africa'. *Journal of Religion in Africa* 12(2): 136–47.

Lévi-Strauss, C. (1966) 'Anthropology; Its Achievements and its Future'. *Current Anthropology* 7(2).

Levy-Bruhl, L. (1923) *Primitive Mentality*. Boston (Mass.): Beacon.

Mazrui, A. and L. Mphande, (1994) 'Time and Labor in Colonial Africa: The Case of Kenya and Malawi'. In J.K. Adjaye (ed.) *Time in the Black Experience*. London: Greenwood.

Mbiti, J. (1969) *African Religions and Philosophy*. Portsmouth: Heinemann.

Meyer, B. (1998) '"Make a Complete Break with the Past.": Memory and Postcolonial Modernity in Ghanaian Pentecostal Discourse.' In R.P. Werbner (ed.) *Memory and the Postcolony. African Anthropology and the Critique of Power*. London: Zed Books, Postcolonial Identities Series.

Mudimbe, V.Y. (1988) *The Invention of Africa: Gnosis, Philosophy and the Order of Knowledge*. Bloomington: Indiana University Press.

Pels, P. (1993) *Critical Matters. Interactions between Missionaries and Waluguru in Colonial Tanganyika, 1930–1961*. Ph.D. thesis, University of Amsterdam.

——(1996) 'Kizingu Rhythms: Luguru Christianity as Ngoma'. *Journal of Religion in Africa* 26(2): 163–201.

Pocock, D.F. (1967) 'The Anthropology of Time-reckoning'. In J. Middleton (ed.) *Myth and Cosmos*. Garden City (NY): Natural History Press.

Ranger, T.O. (1973) 'Territorial Cults in the History of Central Africa'. *Journal of African History* 14: 581–597.

——(1993) 'The Local and the Global in Southern African Religious History'. In: R.W. Hefner (ed.) *Conversion to Christianity; Historical and Anthropological Perspectives on a Great Transformation*. Berkeley: University of California Press.

Schoffeleers, J.M. (1985) *Pentecostalism and Neo-Traditionalism. The Religious Polarization of a Rural District in Southern Malawi*. Amsterdam: Free University Press.

——(1989) 'Folk Christology in Africa: the Dialectics of the Nganga Paradigm'. *Journal of Religion in Africa* 19(2): 157–83.

——(1979) (ed.) *Guardians of the Land: Essays on Central African Territorial Cults*. Gwelo: Mambo Press.

Strathern, M. (1995) Nostalgia and the New Genetics. In D. Battaglia (ed.) *Rhetorics of Self-Making*. Berkeley: University of California Press.

Sundkler, B.G.M. (1961) *Bantu Prophets in South Africa*. London: Oxford University Press.

Taussig, M. (1993) *Mimesis and Alterity: a Particular History of the Senses*. New York: Routledge.

Van Binsbergen, W. (1995) 'Four-tablet Divination as Trans-regional Medical Technology in Southern Africa'. *Journal of Religion in Africa* 25(2): 114–41.

——(1996) 'Time, Space and History in African Divination and Board-games'. In: D. Tiemersma (ed.) *Time and Temporality in Intercultural Perspective: Studies presented to Heinz Kimmerle*. Amsterdam: Rodopi.

Van Dijk, R.A. (1992a) *Young Malawian Puritans. Young Puritan Preachers in a Present-day African Urban Environment*. PhD thesis, ISOR, Utrecht University.

——(1992b) 'Young Puritan Preachers in Post-Independence Malawi'. *Africa* 62(2): 159-81.

——(1993a) 'Young Born-Again Preachers in Malawi; the Significance of an Extraneous Identity'. In P. Gifford (ed.) *New Dimensions in African Christianity*, Ibadan: (AACC) Sefer Books.

——(1993b) 'La guérisseuse du docteur Banda au Malawi'. *Politique Africaine* 52: 145-50.

——(1994) 'Foucault and the Anti-Witchcraft Movement'. *Critique of Anthropology* 14(4): 429–35.

——(1995) 'Fundamentalism and its Moral Geography in Malawi. The Representation of the Diasporic and the Diabolical'. *Critique of Anthropology* 15(2): 171-91.

——(1998) 'Pentecostalism, Cultural Memory and the State: Contested Representations of Time in Postcolonial Malawi'. In R.P. Werbner (ed.) *Memory and the Postcolony. African Anthropology and the Critique of Power*. London: Zed Books, Postcolonial Identities Series.

Vaughan, M. (1991) *Curing their Ills: Colonial Power and African Illness*. Cambridge: Polity.

Wallman, S. (1992) 'Introduction: Contemporary Futures'. In S. Wallman (ed.) *Contemporary Futures. Perspectives from Social Anthropology*. London: Routledge, ASA-Monograph 30.

Werbner, R.P. (1977) *Regional Cults*. New York: Academic Press.

——(1989) *Ritual Passage, Sacred Journey: the Process and Organization of Religious Movement*. Washington: Smithsonian.

——(1991) *Tears of the Dead. The Social Biography of an African Family*. London: AI, Edinburgh University Press.

——(1995) 'Human Rights and Moral Knowledge. Arguments of Accountability in Zimbabwe'. In M. Strathern (ed.) *Shifting Contexts. Transformations in Anthropological Knowledge*. London: Routledge.

——(1998) 'Smoke from the Barrel of a Gun: Postwars of the Dead, Memory and Reinscription in

Zimbabwe'. In R.P. Werbner (ed.) *Memory and the Postcolony. African Anthropology and the Critique of Power*. London, Zed Books, Postcolonial Identities Series

West, M. (1975) *Bishops and Prophets in a Black City. African Independent Churches in Soweto, Johannesburg*. Cape Town: David Philip.

9

Afterword
John M. Janzen

'Doing scholarly ngoma'

Kofi Agawu wrote recently about John Blacking that 'given the range of subjects that interested him, it would have been a miracle if he had managed to avoid taking contradictory positions' (1997: 491). This is the position I find myself in after reading the excellent chapters of *The Quest for Fruition*. Many aspects of my 1992 book *Ngoma* are carefully scrutinized, their tendencies toward contradiction illuminated, in this careful work backed up with rich ethnographies and histories based on extensive fieldwork on particular aspects of ngoma by a range of authors.

Yet, what a pleasure it is to have one's work gone over so thoroughly! Seven critical scholars actually read and studied my book! They held a seminar on it. How gratifying! I had hoped that my work on *Ngoma* would serve as a catalyst. *The Quest for Fruition* has done this most successfully. I recall discussions with Professor Schoffeleers in Provo, Utah and in Satterthwaite about the political dimension of ngoma and healing. I should have known his queries would not simply dissipate. The direction of his curiosity is now evident. I welcome this critical effort. I sincerely thank all the participants. *The Quest for Fruition* is the ultimate review. It is also a monument to the excellence of Dutch anthropological training and adequate fieldwork budgets for students and senior scholars.

This volume has a lot in common with the critical process that is used by the journal *Current Anthropology*. Comments are solicited from a variety of authors on the article that has been submitted. Once these comments are in hand, the original author then has the opportunity to reply to his critics. Both comments and rebuttal are published along with the original article. An important difference between the *CA* format and the present project is that here the critics met to hold a seminar on the work to be discussed, and then they wrote entire chapters that include a presentation of their own extensive work. This of course invites the original author not only to respond to the critiques of his work, but also to offer review and critique of the mirror studies that the chapters represent.

Now that I am in the midst of writing both commentary of the collected critiques of my book *Ngoma* as well as offering critiques of the substantive essays, the thought has come to me that I am going through an exercise similar to that to which we subject PhD students. In the 'comprehensive written examination' the student not only reviews the work that has been studied, but must answer new questions that challenge him or her to synthesize these readings around salient themes in the field of study. Professor Schoffeleers and his students or former students must feel ironic enjoyment in the realization that I am doing this 'written comprehensive' on *Ngoma*.

Yet there is another obvious exercise to which this scholarly procedure might be compared right at the heart of the subject matter to which it is addressed. In a sense we are 'doing ngoma' around *Ngoma*. On several occasions during my 1982–83 researches on ngoma I experienced becoming the subject and object of ngoma attention. In a Swazi divination in which my wife and I introduced a family concern, we became the focus of the '*ukuvumisa*' call-and-response routine. But the third party helper, a novice diviner who was responding to the diviner's diagnostic assertions, did not understand our case well enough to know when to agree or disagree. So the presiding diviner interrupted her bone throwing to simply listen to us and to offer her advice. In the end we received a quite good insight into our concern. On another occasion, in a ngoma 'dispensary' in Dar es Salaam, the gathered group of *waganga* proposed to offer me a 'greeting of the visitor'. This took the form the assembled group dancing toward me to offer me sets of three 'traditional' handshakes while drumming and singing. I felt a sudden onrush of energy and a palpable presence of ngoma-ness. The experience was also humbling. In these settings, and elsewhere, the 'ngoma' – whether that is song, dance, or song-dance rhythm led by drumming – is passed around from one performer to another within a constantly performing group. Although at the time I did not 'take up' this ngoma, it became clear that just as one 'has ngoma done for one' so 'one does ngoma' with and for others. This is the meaning, in southern Nguni society, of '*i-sa-ngoma*', those who do ngoma. In our present very Western rational manner of doing ngoma, strung out across time and distance, our ngoma is about Ngoma itself, and perhaps our academic careers.

I begin this Afterword by taking up the individual chapters and some of the issues the authors raise about my work in *Ngoma* in the context of their own scholarship. Then I present the background and reasons why I came to emphasize the therapeutic in *Ngoma*, and how I see the relationship of the therapeutic to the political now. I offer my own ideas on this central theme, partly in response to the emphasis of *Fruition*, partly independently of it as a result of my own further thinking and study of the salient variable of power in ngoma. Finally, I close with impressions and sketches on what is happening in the postcolonial, postmodern, post-Cold War world of ngoma, and directions being taken in its study.

Comparing and critiquing ngoma in Southeastern Africa

The setting of the dialogue with *Ngoma* in these chapters is a focus on ngoma and ngoma-like procedures from Tanzania southward to Swaziland, by way of Zambia, Malawi, and Zimbabwe. The chapters are presented and argued in the best ethno graphic and ethnological manner. That is, vivid local action over time is described, and from it generalizations are drawn.

Editors Van Dijk, Reis and Spierenburg set the course of the volume toward answering several questions. What are the subject and its object of the discourse of ngoma? And within that context, what are the outer limits of that discourse? The wider intent of the volume is to broaden the exploration of ngoma beyond the ther-apeutic by looking particularly at the political dimension of ngoma-type institutions. As the editors suggest, they wish to go beyond the 'therapeutic' to understand all types of ngoma. For this they follow especially the political dimension, the variable of power.

The order of the chapters appears to be an intentional one. They move from more or less 'classical' ngoma in the first four chapters to settings and institutions that define the limits of the discourse of ngoma. The first four chapters deal with contrasting ngomas in single settings around marriage (Blokland), gender tensions within women's initiatory ngomas (Drews), clients and healers in one national tradition of ngoma (Reis), and clients or members, shrine leaders, and government officials in the negotiations around land reform in a peasantry (Spierenburg). The final three chapters are about sharply hierarchical shrine and royal manifestations of 'ngoma' (Schoffeleers), and ngoma in relation to Christian churches, one of which upon examination bears the signature of ngoma (Jonker), the other of which, by its negation, rejects the values of ngoma to adopt modernizing ideology (Van Dijk).

This sequence of authors, and pattern of presentations, happens to coincide with gender patterning which has been called 'ladies first'. I do not know whether this is intentional, but it suggests gendered realms of scholarship such that women do 'inside' work, and men do 'outside' work on the boundaries.

In any event, the rich ethnographies offer a vivid picture of the full universe and range of ngoma rituals and institutions. They trace the power relations of the ritual contexts; they identify the background of the 'difficult issues' (Janzen 1992) that spawn and perpetuate ngoma rites and structures.

Henny Blokland makes her case for an inclusive understanding of ngoma among the Sukuma-Nyamwezi in her chapter 'Kings, Spirits & Brides in Tanzania' by describing contrasting ngoma rites that are performed in the context of marriage. These are: the Kota, which is a sacral rite alluding to kingship, and the Puba/Gika competitive dance ngomas. I need not review Blokland's rich ethnography here to glean the lessons she makes by the force and eloquence of her in-depth ethnography, resulting from several years in this field setting and a deep knowledge of the Sukuma-Nyamwezi language. That lessons are first, that ngomas are in the service of contrasting social principles, and that the ethnographer cannot know what these are without looking at the full context of particular performances. Who can take issue with this?

Blokland also demonstrates that rich contextual ethnography helps us clarify distinctive meanings of so polysemous a construct as ngoma (p. 19–20). Firstly, there is the very widespread name of the drum, the instrument or object, whose wide-spread distribution is made apparent by the proto-Bantu construct *-goma, 'drum'. Secondly, there is the widely used term 'ngoma' to refer to the music, singing and dancing accompanied by the beats of the drums, the drums in action, the performance. Thirdly, in a more limited number of Bantu languages the term is used to refer to the group of performers, members of an organization, or the organization itself. For this level she uses the capitalized Ngoma, to refer to the proper name that always appears with this usage- (e.g., Kota), and all the rest of the some 107 historical and contemporary Ngomas she documented among the Sukumaland in Western Tanzania. Thus, we have 'drum', 'performance', and 'organization', in a sliding and often tiered construction. This could easily, and should, become a convention for scholarship.

It is thus not suprising that Blokland should be offended by my suggestion, in parts of my book *Ngoma* dealing with East Africa, that only some of these Ngoma, those that have to do with healing, represent the 'core', and that others pertaining to dance competitions and folklore represent a less genuine periphery. Yet Blokland's greatest criticism of my book, arising from this privileging of some ngomas as healing ngomas, is reserved for the way in which I depart from my own theoretical reasoning of inclusivity of definition of the ngoma phenomenon as first articulated in *Lemba* (1982), and enunciated at places in *Ngoma*. The hallmarks of this more inclusive theoretical strategy included regarding the range of movements, cults, states, and institutions in a given region or society within one rubric around 'ngoma' as process; and, related to this, as I do in *Ngoma*, suggesting that the healing that goes on may be understood as a kind of 'social reproduction' of society and search for holistic well-being. Blokland agrees more or less with this definitional strategy. There are other nuances to Blokland's argument and critique which I take up later. I shall also explain the emphasis on the therapeutic in *Ngoma* in a later section.

Annette Drews in her chapter 'Gender & ngoma: the Power of Drums', offers an insightful picture of ngoma discourse in girls' initiations in Kunda society of Eastern Zambia. Drews shows why a particular area of social life – in this case the definition of women's place – may come to be articulated in ngoma discourse. Because I am not aware of any term in an African language that describes this process, I have alluded to it in most general terms as a 'difficult issue' or 'difficult experience' (see Chapter 11, 'What Were the Questions?' in *Lemba* (Janzen 1982: 323ff.), and 'From Spirit to Song-dance: Articulating Metaphors of Difficult Experiences', in *Ngoma* (Janzen 1992: 145ff.)). Drews suggests that gender relations are structured by two conflicting types of discourse: equality with men on the one hand in traditional matrilineal social definitions, yet subservience to men on the other in Christianized versions of initiation, and in relation to male-dominated formal household and political society (p. 40). Drews captures precisely the process by which the 'difficult issue' – the conflicting discourses – transform into the 'power of the drums'. This is a critical transformation that scholars of ngoma may well assume to exist within or beneath each and every Ngoma, at least at its inception and its vital continuation. Thus, the unresolved contestation over young women's entrance into adult society and the public arena generates both the acting out of the tension as well as the cathartic energy of the ngoma.

Ria Reis, in her chapter entitled 'The "Wounded Healer" as Ideology: the work of ngoma in Swaziland' addresses two primary issues. The first of these, the 'wounded healer', is a code for the transformation of the sufferer into the healer, the premise that every healer must have gone through the ordeal of suffering. Her second issue is over the significance of ministering to the sick in the role of the healer, and to the relative emphasis placed on this 'work of ngoma', as she calls this emphasis by contrast to 'doing ngoma', the rites of transformation.

Of course, the two sides of ngoma are not altogether separate. Divination ngoma in Swaziland, which constitutes 'doing ngoma', at all levels, may be performed for clients, as the 'work of ngoma'. The lengthy femba divination of a sick child that I describe (Janzen 1992: 45–8) is an example of this combined 'doing' and 'work' of ngoma. I also describe the clientele – on average ten per day – of sangoma Ida Mabuza whose centre was my main source of information on Swazi ngoma (Janzen 1992, 40–41). I am not sure why she asserts that I am not at all interested in the 'work of ngoma'.

Nevertheless, her distinction between 'work' and 'doing' of ngoma is useful because it allows one to see, if nothing else, the relative numbers of suffering clientele who are treated versus the life-transforming experience of a small percentage of the 'wounded' who go on to become healers. Reis indicates that four per cent of the cases she interviewed in her epilepsy study (p. 64) led to a '*twasa*' diagnosis that made them eligible to become sangoma. This is in keeping with the percentage of the clientele Swahili waganga told me moved on to become full-scale healers (Janzen 1992: 171). Perhaps it is a guide in the understanding more widely of the relative ratios of mere sufferer to sufferer/novice in ngoma.

Some of the concerns Reis raises with regard to my depiction of ngoma in Swaziland are due to the fact that I concentrated in the southern suburban area between Manzini and Mbabane, and worked with Zulu anthropologist Harriet Sibisi (Ngubane), whereas Reis worked mainly in the northern region. Sibisi saw Swazi divining with foreign Manzawe spirits as a recent development in the south, and still unknown in Zulu South Africa. I of course could not determine whether this was the case. Sibisi's perception at least was that the rise of 'alien', or 'enemy' spirits, as Reis calls them, was a relatively recent development, and very uncommon in southern Nguni (Zulu, Xhosa) society.

This perception of the recent rise of dramatic trance-driven alien spirit divination, as represented in the Manzawe (as opposed to the ancestor spirits) led me to situate this in a kind of dichotomy between the traditional bone-throwing *pengula* mode of divination, and the mediumistic mode. I apparently underplayed the *ukuvumisa* dialogue between diviner and client, but I did not altogether miss it. I describe this procedure (Janzen 1992: 42) as I witnessed it, in conjunction with the pengula 'bone throwing'. The diviner, seated face-to-face with the client, spells out the interpretation, as a third person who is sometimes a diviner trainee and who has spoken with the client before the divination, responds to each phrase by the diviner with a counter phrase of 'I agree' (*si ya vuma*) or 'I disagree' (see Plate 9 which shows the hand clapping that accompanies this). According to Reis, this dimension of '*vumisa*' divining occurs on its own.

Reis would reject my distinction between 'mechanistic' and 'mediumistic' divining, the first being epistemologically separate from the latter. In fact she emphasizes that ukuvumisa is ancestor-inspired and thus is an example of possession divining. Reis offers additional important clarifications on the modes and hierarchic courses of healing and divination in Swaziland. First she stresses that one must always include the *inyanga* specialists – herbalists – in any presentation of Swazi healers. This is important because in practice the different techniques of healing and divination are more continuous than the labels designating types of healers would suggest. Thus she speaks of a 'Swazi discourse of illness and healing' rather than a discourse limited to one type of healer or another (p. 63). For her, this Swazi discourse includes, centrally, the spirit world in the work and the doing of ngoma, as well as herbalism, and the moral order of the entire nation as it is manifested in Swazi kingship.

This picture of a unified continuous fabric emanating from, at least including, the ancestors, leads both Reis and Blokland to object to my handling of the role of the spirits in ngoma, a process I have labelled as 'spirit hypothesis'. Blokland suggests that I, like Sukuma and Nyamwezi men, 'have a problem' with spirit-filled song-dance, and with drumming. She further notes that I have prioritized song over drum in ngoma. If that is true, it is subconscious.

However, the issue I am addressing in the spirit hypothesis is the same one noted by Lambek, as cited by the editors in their introduction (p. 2). Like Lambek (1989: 38–9), I stressed the distinction between 'possession' and 'trance' first made, years ago I believe, by Bourguignon (1967). Possession belief is the individual or societal premise that spirits may visit and influence individual fates. Possession trance is the actual demonstrative behaviour of that visitation. Whereas Lambek seems to have spoken of 'possession' as an indigenous hypothesis or ideology to explain trance behaviour, I introduced the 'spirit hypothesis' to account for those many ngoma settings in which there is reference to spirits by diviners and client groups in the absence of demonstrative trance. Scholars of African ngoma will surely recognize and appreciate the distinction. A diviner's imputation of ancestors or other spirits in a case would suggest possession belief. Demonstrative dancing or other behaviour suggestive of spirit visitation would indicate possession trance. By 'spirit hypothesis' I was therefore offering an analytical device to account for those many situations in ngoma where one has possession belief without trance. I was also trying to account for the pattern of trance in the cycle of a particular Ngoma, or amongst multiple Ngomas in a given society, where some exhibit trance and others not (Janzen 1992: 140–3; 1998).

The next two chapters bridge the ngoma world of predominantly, or historically, segmentary societies with those of more centralized societies and the land cults which are prevalent in Southeast Africa. Marja Spierenburg's 'Social Commentaries & the Influence of the Clientele: the Mhondoro Cult in Dande, Zimbabwe' is a richly reasoned ethnography about the role of Mhondoro priests, government officials, and residents over the negotiation of postcolonial land reform in Zimbabwe. Matthew Schoffeleers' 'The Story of a Scapegoat King in Rural Malawi' brings fascinating ethnographic details to bear on the subject of ngoma in centralized shrines and cults such as Mbona in Malawi

Spierenburg shows that the Mhondoro priest does not really take an independent stand on land redistribution so long as the local community remains unsure, suspicious of government's motives, or is simply divided. Spierenburg uses her deep understanding of the Mhondoro cult of Dande to take issue with my reference that centralized cults 'define primary values and social patterns for generations of adepts' (1992: 76). I do not wish to, indeed cannot, take issue with her on the particulars of this case. Her account is a very important study of the politics of land in modern Africa. But I do wonder whether her understanding of the cautious, basically reactionary, stance of the Mhondoro priests means that all land cults and centralized shrine priesthoods are cautiously traditionalist, content to play the role of stage managers of the public forums in which issues are debated. Would the resolution of this question not be a matter of the power differential of these cult hierarchies, their publics, and the state, in each case?

Schoffeleers' chapter is an essay that I believe he has anticipated writing for a while; it is definitely an essay that I have been eager to read, for it lays out the transformational character and the hidden links between different kinds of ngoma manifestations. The opening paragraph of this essay (p. 98) captures exactly the full extent and the dynamics of ngoma as I understand it, the key phrases being: 'a collectivity of rituals [for] "continuous reproduction of a society as a whole" [based on] "a transcendent order" [represented by the] "drum with its infinite range of associations deriving from its shape, material and sound is the encompassing metaphor of this complex whole" '.

Schoffeleers uses this backdrop to describe the earth cult in relation, or rather as manifested in, therapeutics on the one hand and politics on the other. Just how this happens is of prime importance to the linkage of some rather different manifestations within ngoma. Schoffeleers's analysis is a kind of test of the proposition that the political and the therapeutic may indeed be related within the ngoma universe. This linkage or transformative connection is found the case of Mbona within a particular history. But this particular history may be compared with many other historical examples to which Schoffeleers alludes.

Just what kind of transformative relationship is this that converts a single institution from therapeutic to political? It is not just a typological separation between therapeutic ngoma and political ngoma. Nor can we say that these are two 'functions' of one and the same institution, although this is perhaps closer to what actually occurs. I think the transformation is more that of a cyclic process peculiar to each earth cult's particular history. At one point the earth cult and its officials serve as king maker and king legitimator; but at another point over issues of rain, conflict, and other issues these same officials serve as healer of the collective nation. Schoffeleers's account of the Tengani is a moment – a particularly crucial and interesting moment – within Mbona. Taking on the apparel of the slave, receiving the vision, committing incest with his sister, and dying within a year are the signals that propel the office holder into a liminal stance and perhaps represent the shift from the therapeutic to the political mode – or is it the other way around? Schoffeleers's lifelong study of Mbona has certainly taught us a lot about this rich history; with this chapter we continue to learn more about it as we seek to situate it alongside other forms of ngoma.

Schoffeleers's rich historical ethnography of Mbona challenges anthropological and theoretical comprehension. In his search for appropriate analytical models he has cited the comparative studies from across Africa. Turner's suggestion that we are dealing with 'inclusive' and 'exclusive' cults is also offered as a helpful perspective. Even Frazer's interpretation of the death of the priest of Nemi as presented in *The Golden Bough* is put forward as insightful. However, I remain uncomfortable with the suggestion that there are separable 'therapeutic' and 'political' ngomas. This reduces the analysis into a typological approach based on our differentiation of politics from healing. Whose definition will we use? I think we must rather acknowledge the power dimension of all ngoma-type institutions, at whatever phase of a cycle they may be in, whether or not they have to do with healing. I will return to this question below.

The final two chapters show the interpenetration of Christianity and ngoma. I discuss these together because they both deal with African Christianity, and with the boundary of ngoma discourse. Cor Jonker in his 'The Politics of Therapeutic Ngoma: the Zionist Churches in Urban Zambia' demonstrates that despite their Christian identity, these *mdzimu* (spirit, ancestor) churches reveal many of the attributes of ngoma. In particular, Jonker examines the manner in which politics are played out alongside healing. By contrast, Rijk van Dijk, in his 'Ngoma & Born-Again Fundamentalism: Contesting Representations of Time in Urban Malawi' studies another variant of African Christianity to show the character of a radical turn away from ngoma-like attributes. His case is built around an analysis of the sense of time in ngoma and in these modernizing young African Christians. The handling of power and time are used to assess the boundaries of what is, and what is not, ngoma.

Jonkers usefully situates ngoma-like attributes within the received scholarly typologies of independent African churches (pp. 118–19). He concentrates his attention on a 'Zionist healing' church that, unlike the separatist 'Zionist Apolistic' church, engages in contestation with its parent bodies and within the national political sphere. The hallmark of ngoma elements within the independent churches lies in their being able to integrate the political and the therapeutic in one and the same space: 'healing traditions and critical political movements both try to change an existing unwanted situation; they form a common ideological discourse' (Jonkers: 130).

For Van Dijk, one of the distinctive features of the ngoma approach lies in its very functional fluidity: it can address any kind of issue. But the way it goes about dealing with issues is marked by a unique temporal orientation. The invocation of the ancestors as the source of legitimation is by definition a backward-looking, as well as a communal orientation. This is characteristic of all ngoma, regardless of the problem or issue being addressed. And it is on this point that the Born-Again churches of Malawi and elsewhere differ radically from ngoma-type organization and problem solving. They reject the ancestors to individualize the focus of transformation. Rather than seeking ancestral – that is past-oriented – legitimation of personal change, they adopt a prognostic – future-oriented – sense of time. Thus while both ngoma and fundamentalist Christianity seek personal transformation of the adept, the outcome and the construction of time is very different in the two cases.

I find both the Jonkers and Van Dijk analyses very convincing and helpful. The compelling power of ngoma, whether it is in a classical form with ancestors, or in the independent church mould devoted to the Holy Spirit, still lies in the way misfortune and adversity – 'difficult issues' – are dealt with. Such issues are brought into the realm of the spirit through the drum and are transformed into a source of strength. The spirit churches thus reach people where they hurt, although they also represent power. Born Again fundamentalism may well appeal to young adults wishing to create a new Africa, but will this individualist ideology attract the sick, isolated, poor? There is a merger zone between the Christian message of redemption to the poor in spirit and the suffering, and the attraction which the ancestors still hold for the suffering. How this energy of the margins is controlled, and the time-orientation it is given, whether it will be 'this worldly' or 'other worldly', will shape the overall outcome, and whether or not it looks like ngoma, or North American entrepreneurial individualist Protestantism.

Politics and therapeutics in ngoma

The central issue in this volume has been how power is manifested in, and theorized around, ngoma. My announced strategy of considering a range of institutional types within a field as an interrelated set has been generally praised. I have been criticized for not taking this approach seriously, for not following through on it. Rather, it is suggested that I have slipped into the rut of equating ngoma manifestations with therapeutic drums of affliction, regardless of what their apparent role has been, even when it has been patently political.

How could this apparent contradiction in my work have come about? Or is it really a contradiction? In the past twenty years, it has become fashionable in some social science and humanities circles to bash medicine because of the way it 'medicalizes' life. In the African context, a 'therapeutic' preoccupation of a movement, group, or organization often connotes the absence of political will – as Jonkers points out with regard to the Apostolic Zionist independent churches. Therapeutics has come to be identified with the anti-revolutionary. This is implicit in some of the chapters of the present work. More disturbing, and misleading, is the consequent assumption that 'the therapeutic' is mutually exclusive with 'the political', and, in the present context, that some ngoma may be 'therapeutic' whereas others are 'political'. I have consistently refused such a dichotomy. All movements and organizations are political, including – especially – those that capture and embody a particular articulation of suffering.

In order to reason out my stance on the political and the therapeutic in ngoma, I need to briefly review the course of my scholarship on this subject. It is pertinent that my research and writing began in the Lower Congo and the Southern Savanna regions of Africa, in the broad cultural and linguistic traditions known as Western Bantu. The picture of healing traditions presented in *The Quest for Therapy* and *Lemba* is that of specialists commonly known as *banganga* doctors (more recently also *bangunza*, mediumistic prophets) practising a range of arts, including divination, diverse applications of floral, faunal, and other materia medica, bone setting, and ritual treatments. Common verbs that refer to healing are *buka* and *nyakisa*, and other terms of ritual invocation. The most widespread historic terms for materia medica and types of therapeutic practices would include (but not be limited to) *ti*, *bilongo*, *nkisi*, and *ngoma*. *Minti* (sing. *muti*) are the raw ingredients from plants. *Bilongo* are the compound ingredients that make up a more complex, finished medicine, including all of biomedicine. *Nkisi* (pl. *minkisi*) is a specially consecrated constellation of materials, techniques, and their pedigree of discovery from the original creator's vision. Some minkisi are activated by the individual nganga or owner of the technique. Others originated in ngoma-like, drummed, public performances (Janzen 1979: 1981).

It was in the Lemba study in the Lower Congo north bank region that I first saw the importance of establishing a larger framework that included shifting healing cults, earth shrines, and kingdoms. The range of Kongo minkisi was broad, as the following example shows (Janzen 1982: 16). Nsemi Isaak's turn-of-the-century inventory (in Janzen and MacGaffey 1974) listed a range of individual and societal minkisi. The individualized or domestic minkisi pertained to 'personal growth', 'a child's upbringing', 'spirit children and how to deal with them', 'twinship and the parenting of twins', 'headache', 'purification with the cupping horn', approaches to divination, 'origin, residence, identity', and a variety of those dealing with women's reproductive issues. Then there were those minkisi which were characterized by being 'drummed up (*sika*) with ngoma'. Those pertaining to chiefship (Matinu, MaBunzi) and to clan leadership (Kinkita) were exclusive, in Turner's sense, whereas those pertaining to water spirits (*mbola*), judicial affairs (N'kondi) and orders in markets and public places (Lemba) were inclusive. Those which were exclusive were of course the more centralized, whereas those which were inclusive were the more segmentary or network-like.

The analytical challenge here was to establish the range and the scope of 'the therapeutic'. A great deal hinged on how one translated the term *nkisi*. MacGaffey suggested (1991: 4) that there simply was no translation for nkisi. Yet he entitled his book on the subject *Art and Healing of the BaKongo*. Elsewhere MacGaffey has defined nkisi as a mediating instrument of the 'dead and the living' around private and public domains (1993: 39). I have tended to translate nkisi as 'consecrated medicine', a tactic which creates a very broad therapeutic domain covering phenomena of misfortune ranging from headache and reproductive issues all the way to judicial affairs and public order. This seemed justified in that even the public minkisi drummed up with ngoma were spoken of as having symptoms and signs, causes, and a prescribed procedures for treatment. N'kisi are 'composed' or 'created', as implied in the verb *kuhanda* (alt., *kuvanda*). To call them medicine was thus not far-fetched, especially since their application was to heal (*kubuka, kunyakisa*), or simply kuhanda, to compose or to initiate. In recent years however scholars have used the demedicalized definitions such as 'charm', or 'power object', which seem imprecise. Had one drawn the definitional net more tightly around 'the therapeutic', it would still have been arbitrary, and based on the imposition of outside criteria.

In any event, by labelling minkisi as medicine, I claimed a very broad domain of the therapeutic in Kongo and neighbouring societies. This certainly influenced me when I shifted my regard to Eastern and Southern Africa, where there appeared to be no equivalent term to nkisi.

Given that the therapeutic domain was so broad in Kongo society, it was clearly not possible to assign as 'political' all non-therapeutic movements, rites, and institutions. Even chiefship and kingship, where these occurred, were consecrated by minkisi, often with therapeutic overtones. Should one then have described Kongo society as apolitical? Hardly. A requisite reading of the political in this context needed to be based on other criteria than the non-therapeutic. As readers of *Quest* and *Lemba* will realize, I applied the criteria of charisma, authority, and corporation theory from Weber and Maine (via Smith and MacGaffey) to the global institutional picture of Kongo society. I closed my extensive discussion of these matters in my introduction to *Lemba* with these words. 'It is apparent that the waxing and waning of kingdoms, centralized shrines, diffuse cults, drums of affliction, ephemeral movements, and consecrated medicines can best be accounted for in terms of a unified theory of differential corporateness' (Janzen 1982: 23). The point was that one could not dichotomize the political and the therapeutic into mutually exclusive spheres. The therapeutic does not negate the political. Nor is it right to speak oppositionally of 'political' and 'therapeutic' ngoma.

No doubt, the criterion of corporate status is not sufficient in describing the political dimension of the therapeutic, nor is the language of authority, charisma, and legitimation entirely adequate for an understanding of power in something like ngoma. Medicine, healing resources, mediation, common consciousness of suffering, the powerful embodiment of suffering that ngoma represents, are perhaps theorized more adequately in the language of Foucault (Comaroff 1985; Kleinman 1995: 274–5). The resistance that is implied in the ngoma-centred awareness of suffering, or any other kind of 'difficult experience', brings us closer to the ways in which power and healing are intertwined.

These were, at any rate, the lines of understanding with which I set out, from a western Congo base, to explore the broader outlines of healing in Central and Southern Africa. Ngoma – along with the other Proto-Bantu cognates *-ganga*, *-ti*, *-dog-* – was the intriguing thread I followed because it seemed, from my preliminary research and experience on the southern savanna and lower Congo, as well as reading on South Africa and East Africa, to be the most inclusive framework of sub-Saharan African medicine. Throughout this entire region I saw practitioners working with the ngoma phenomenon, transcending the local, via specific issues and challenges, to come to terms with 'difficult issues'.

There was another formative influence shaping my inquiry into the therapeutic in sub-Saharan Africa. After *The Quest for Therapy* was published, I was invited to the Joint Committee for African Studies of the Social Science Research Council and the American Council of Learned Societies, to co-direct, with Steven Feierman, a research planning project called 'Medicine and Society in Africa'. We conducted several conferences, the papers from which were published (Janzen and Feierman 1979; Janzen and Prins 1981; Feierman and Janzen 1992). One of the gaps that we perceived in the current research on African health and healing was in the study of trans-local traditions. Sub-Saharan African medicine was represented almost entirely by local or 'tribal' studies. To remedy this distorted colonial view we commissioned regional essays on sub-Saharan African medical traditions to demonstrate trans-local comparability with Galenic medicine, Islamic medicine, medicine of the Prophet, and colonial and postcolonial biomedicine. As it turned out, my 1982 to 1983 research on ngoma was the only project on trans-regional health and healing that reached publication. To add to the medicalized focus of ngoma, the resulting volume was published in a series entitled 'Comparative Studies in Health Systems and Medical Care'. The thrust of all these frameworks and expectations predetermined a largely therapeutic orientation to the work, without necessarily theoretically negating the broader social and political background that had appeared in earlier writing.

Looking back with all the benefit that hindsight offers, I could now say that a fateful step in my work on ngoma was the way I projected into the East and Southern African setting my understanding of nkisi, the widespread Western Bantu cultural and linguistic cognate. In Western Bantu, ngoma serves as a vehicle to stage and publicly empower minkisi, which may be said to usually be therapeutic. In Eastern Bantu regions, this explicit stage is either filled in on a piecemeal basis, or it is subsumed under ngoma, as in the work of Nguni diviners, the *isangoma*. But clearly not all that is ngoma or done with ngoma in Eastern Bantu is therapeutic.

Now, with this volume, *The Quest for Fruition*, we have begun a conversation between scholars of western and eastern ngoma, from which a new convergence of insight emerges. Towards this end, I hazard a characterization of power in ngoma without reducing it here to an academic theory. I do not believe that a theory or rubric has yet been found that can adequately model the power that is found both in segmentary and in centralized settings, whose 'calculus' plays itself out in a continuum or a cycle. At one end – or at one point – one finds the power that emerges from the common experience of misfortune and suffering. Ngoma gives this experience sacred legitimation through the ancestors or other spirits. The representation of such suffering in embodied forces becomes a power that rulers seek to capture or repress. The diffuse bonds of common suffering provide ample authority for social control, of the kind that Blokland describes in Sukumaland, Spierenburg attributes to Mhondoro of Zimbabwe, and Jonkers discusses in the *mdzimu* church. In some settings this basis of ritual authority evolves into an ideology of the wounded healer and the martyred king. Social and spatial concentrations of symbols, especially in agrarian societies, lead to earth cults and royal dynasties of the kind so well described by Schoffeleers. At the extreme end of the continuum one finds the power of sharply centralized ngoma, embodied in the state drums that are usually crusted over with the blood of sacrificial victims or enemies slaughtered in battle. Here the martyr king motif may be no more than a distant echo, as in the story of Ryangombe the martyr of the Kubandwa rite of Rwanda. But this sketch is the subject of another lifetime project, a conference, or a full book.

Ngoma redux

The authors of this volume are to be congratulated for their effort to reduce ngoma to its varied and fundamental characteristics, thus 'ngoma redux', from the Latin *reducere*, to lead back, bring back to its essentials. The editors summarize key phrases from my book *Ngoma* (p. 4). The editors also set the stage for the project of the volume's essays, to identify the outer limits of the ngoma discourse. Blokland's simple articulation of a set of three distinctive elements in the composite whole of ngoma should become a convention for scholarship. She distinguishes *ngoma* the drum (or any other instrument); next, *ngoma* as the performance; then, *Ngoma* as the particular set of performers, or the organization that may be identified in social time and space.

Propositions are enunciated regarding ngoma, such as this one propounded by the editors:

1 ngoma is a way of articulating and commenting on processes of transition or transformation;
2 it produces a certain type of power and authority which is based on claims to specific association and communication with the spirit world;
3 this power is embodied, expressed and effected in rhythm (drumming, singing, dancing) (p. 7).

Other authors offer more descriptive definitions, such as the one already quoted by Schoffeleers (pp. 99, 160–1).

Lest ngoma still remain a vague foreign concept, this work will set in the minds of all readers that the appropriate English term for that to which *ngoma* aspires is not health, but *fruition*, 'the pleasurable use or possession; the state of bearing fruit; realization, accomplishment'. Fruition appears in various idioms throughout the book. It is used to suggest a wider state of wellbeing than health, or healing, which also includes procreation and the growing of crops. It is also supposed to connote the enjoyment of performance, of art. It is identified as social reproduction. These are the hallmarks of a clarifying, defining work that helps us understand a classical institution of great flexibility. I also catch the shift that is proposed in the substitution of my earlier title *Quest for Therapy* to the revisionist *Quest for Fruition*.

The power of ngoma as classical institution, as reality, as metaphor, as medium, is such that, as a cultural universe akin to the physical universe after the big bang, it continues to expand in all directions. Scholars continue to discover new ngoma fronts including its interpenetration with not just Christianity, as presented in this volume, but with Islam. Scholars trace the rise of Maulidi within the mosque congregations on Lamu, in which fundamentalist reformers seek to resist this incursion of the African, the rhymthic. In the shambles of dynastic Rwanda and Burundi, a few captured war drums of old survive to stand in museums encrusted with blood; the exiled king is said to 'have given his drums to Jesus', and the girls play church drums while the men kill each other on the hillsides.

The therapeutic front of ngoma continues to be researched. As Reis suggests in this volume, epilepsy cases are brought to ngoma but only a minority of its sufferers become initiated. On Zanzibar, Juli Magruder studies the diagnosis of schizophrenia by psychiatrists and their families, and the extent to which these cases reach ngoma healers, and with what result. In Bulawayo, Sue Schuessler studied the interaction of ngoma practitioners within the national organization of healers with the earth cults and with their clientele. Stan Moore studied the entire gamut of healers in Dar es Salaam, and the pressure of modern economic necessity upon the ritual and spiritual prerequisites of those waganga who do ngoma (Moore 1997). Studies such as these, to be published in more volumes such as the present one, or in specialized journals, will lead to a recognition of the ritual and therapeutic value of ngoma. Indeed, in a recent graduate paper on the incorporation of non-Western techniques in academic medicine, Li Jian wrote that ngoma had reached the first stage of such incorporation, namely to have research done on it (Jian 1997). The use of ngoma to further the ends of state-supported biomedicine may well be farther along than Jian appreciates. In Natal province of South Africa, a serious effort is under way to employ the assistance of *sangoma* diviners and *inyanga* healers in health education and health promotion, particularly in an AIDS awareness campaign (Villion Films 1997).

But the universe of ngoma is shifting in other directions. Increasing numbers of ngoma practitioners are themselves scholars in the academy, holding advanced degrees in sociology, anthropology, psychotherapy, history. They are not just African, but European and American, persons who bridge the divide of practitioner and scholar.

Ngoma has attracted the attention of performers worldwide who borrow not only the musical style, but the name. A cursory check on the Internet reveals at least one touring East African group that calls itself '*Ngoma*', and the Rap Group nGOMa of Denver, Colorado, USA, identifies itself with this 'Swahili word that means drum and rhythm', on its first CD called 'Collage Mindset'.

We are witnessing the globalization of ngoma.

Literature

Agawu, K. (1997) 'John Blacking and the Study of African Music'. *Africa* 67(3): 491–9.

Bourguignon, E. (1967) *Possession*. San Francisco: Chandler and Sharp.

Comaroff, Jean (1985) *Body of Power, Spirit of Resistance. The Culture and History of a South African People*. Chicago: University of Chicago Press.

Janzen, J. M. (1978) *The Quest for Therapy in Lower Zaire*. Berkeley, Los Angeles, London: University of California Press.

——(1979) 'Ideologies and Institutions in the Precolonial History of Equatorial African Therapeutic Systems'. *Social Science and Medicine*, 13B, 3: 317–26.

——(1981) 'The Need for a Taxonomy of Health in the Study of African Therapeutics'. *Social Science and Medicine*, 15B, 3: 185–94.

——(1982) *Lemba, 1650–1930. A Drum of Affliction in Africa and the New World*. New York: Garland.

——(1992) *Ngoma. Discourses of Healing in Central and Southern Africa*. Berkeley, Los Angeles, London: University of California Press.

——(1998) '*Ngoma*'. *Encyclopedia of African Philosophy and Religion*. Stanford: Stanford University Press.

Janzen, J.M. and S. Feierman (1979) 'The Social History of Disease and Medicine in Africa'. Special Issue, *Social Science and Medicine*, 13B, 4 (December).

Janzen, J.M. and W. MacGaffey (1974) *Anthology of Kongo Religion: Primary Texts from Lower Zaire*. Lawrence, KS: University of Kansas Publications in Anthropology, No. 5.

Janzen, J.M. and G. Prins (1981) 'Causality and Classification in African Medicine and Health'. Special Issue, *Social Science and Medicine*, 15B, 3 (July).

Feierman, S. and J.M. Janzen, (eds) (1992) *The Social Basis of Health and Healing in Africa*. Berkeley, Los Angeles, London: University of California Press.

Jian, Li (1997) 'The Study of Non-Western Medicine (1870–1990): Exploration, Recognition, Incorporation and Medical Pluralism'. MS, PhD Program in Anthropology, University of Kansas.

Kleinman, A. (1995) *Writing at the Margin: Discourse Between Anthropology and Medicine*. Berkeley, Los Angeles, London: University of California Press.

Lambek, M. (1981) *Human Spirits: A Cultural Account of Trance in Mayotte*. Cambridge: Cambridge University Press.

——(1989) 'From Disease to Discourse: Remarks on the Conceptualization of Trance and Spirit Possession'. In Colleen A. Ward (ed.) *Altered States of Consciousness and Mental Health. A Cross-Cultural Perspective*. Newbury Park: Sage.

——(1993) *Knowledge and Practice in Mayotte: Local Discourses of Islam, Sorcery, and Spirit Possession*. Toronto: University of Toronto Press.

MacGaffey, W. (1991) *Art and Healing of the Bakongo: Commented on by Themselves*. Stockholm: Folkens Museum Ethnografiska.

——(1993) *Astonishment and Power: The Eyes of Understanding – Kongo Minkisi*. Washington DC: National Museum of African Art, Smithsonian Institution.

Moore, S. (1997) *Indigenous Practice and Knowledge in the Medical Culture of Dar es Salaam*. PhD Dissertation, University of Kansas Department of Anthropology.

Villon Films (1997) *Sangoma: Traditional Healers in Modern Society*. Vancouver.

Index